Ka, Olivier, 1967–
Why I killed Peter /
2008.
WITHDRAWN
ca   05/11/09

P9-AFV-013

Why I Killed Peter

STORY:
OLIVIER KA

ADAPTATION & ART:
ALFRED

COLOR:
HENRI MEUNIER

ComicsLit

Also available from ComicsLit:
Ordinary Victories, vols. 1, 2, $15.95 each
The Castaways, $11.95

Add $4 P&H first item
$1 each additional.

We have over 200 titles, write for
our complete catalog:
NBM
40 Exchange Pl., Suite 1308
New York, NY 10005
www.nbmpublishing.com

ISBN 10: 1-56163-543-X
ISBN 13: 978-1-56163-543-6
© 2006 Guy Delcourt Productions
© 2008 NBM for the English translation
Translation by Joe Johnson
Lettering by Ortho

Comicslit is an imprint
and trademark of

NANTIER · BEALL · MINOUSTCHINE
Publishing inc.
new york

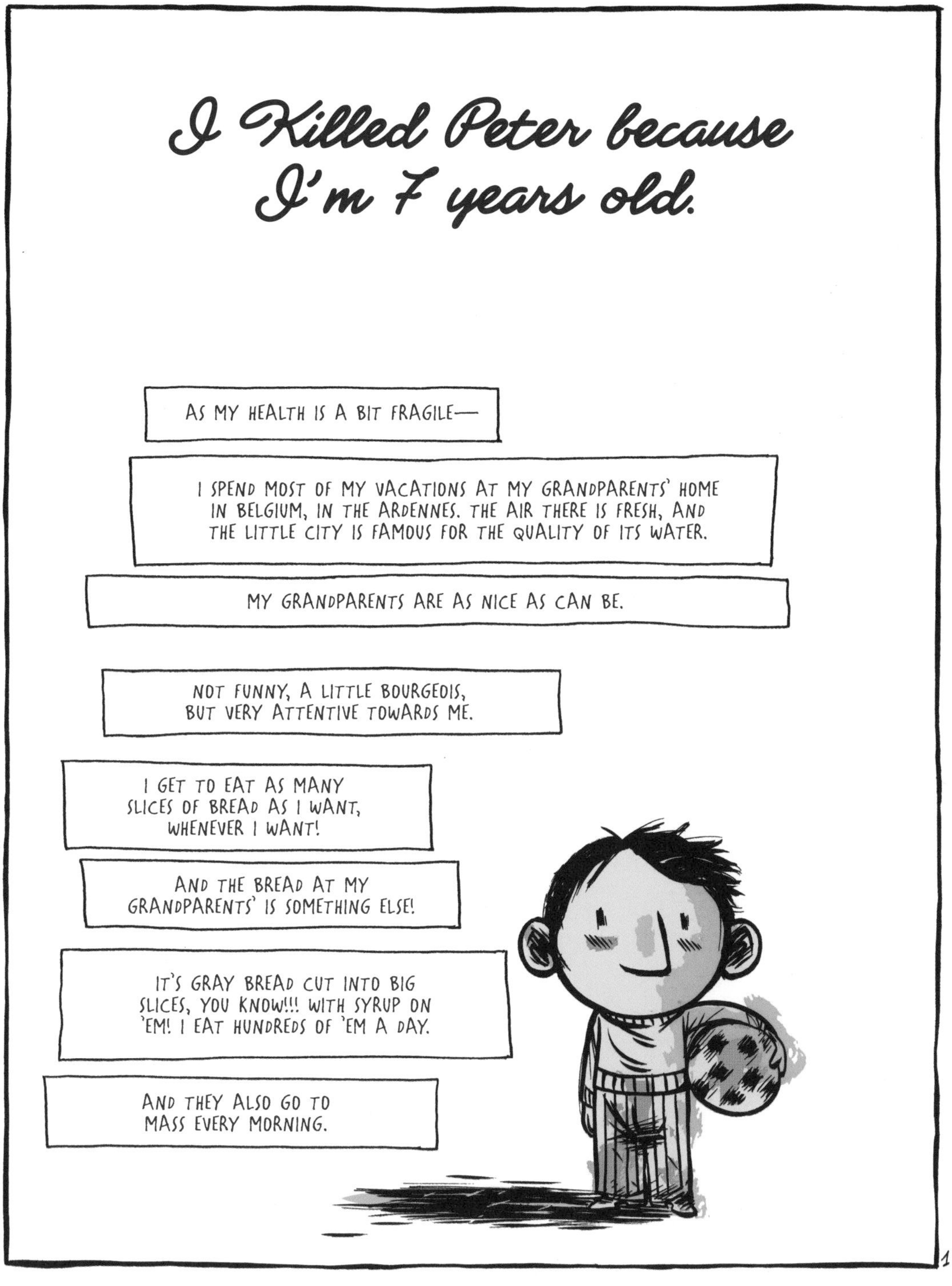
I Killed Peter because I'm 7 years old.
AS MY HEALTH IS A BIT FRAGILE—
I SPEND MOST OF MY VACATIONS AT MY GRANDPARENTS' HOME IN BELGIUM, IN THE ARDENNES. THE AIR THERE IS FRESH, AND THE LITTLE CITY IS FAMOUS FOR THE QUALITY OF ITS WATER.
MY GRANDPARENTS ARE AS NICE AS CAN BE.
NOT FUNNY, A LITTLE BOURGEOIS, BUT VERY ATTENTIVE TOWARDS ME.
I GET TO EAT AS MANY SLICES OF BREAD AS I WANT, WHENEVER I WANT!
AND THE BREAD AT MY GRANDPARENTS' IS SOMETHING ELSE!
IT'S GRAY BREAD CUT INTO BIG SLICES, YOU KNOW!!! WITH SYRUP ON 'EM! I EAT HUNDREDS OF 'EM A DAY.
AND THEY ALSO GO TO MASS EVERY MORNING.
1

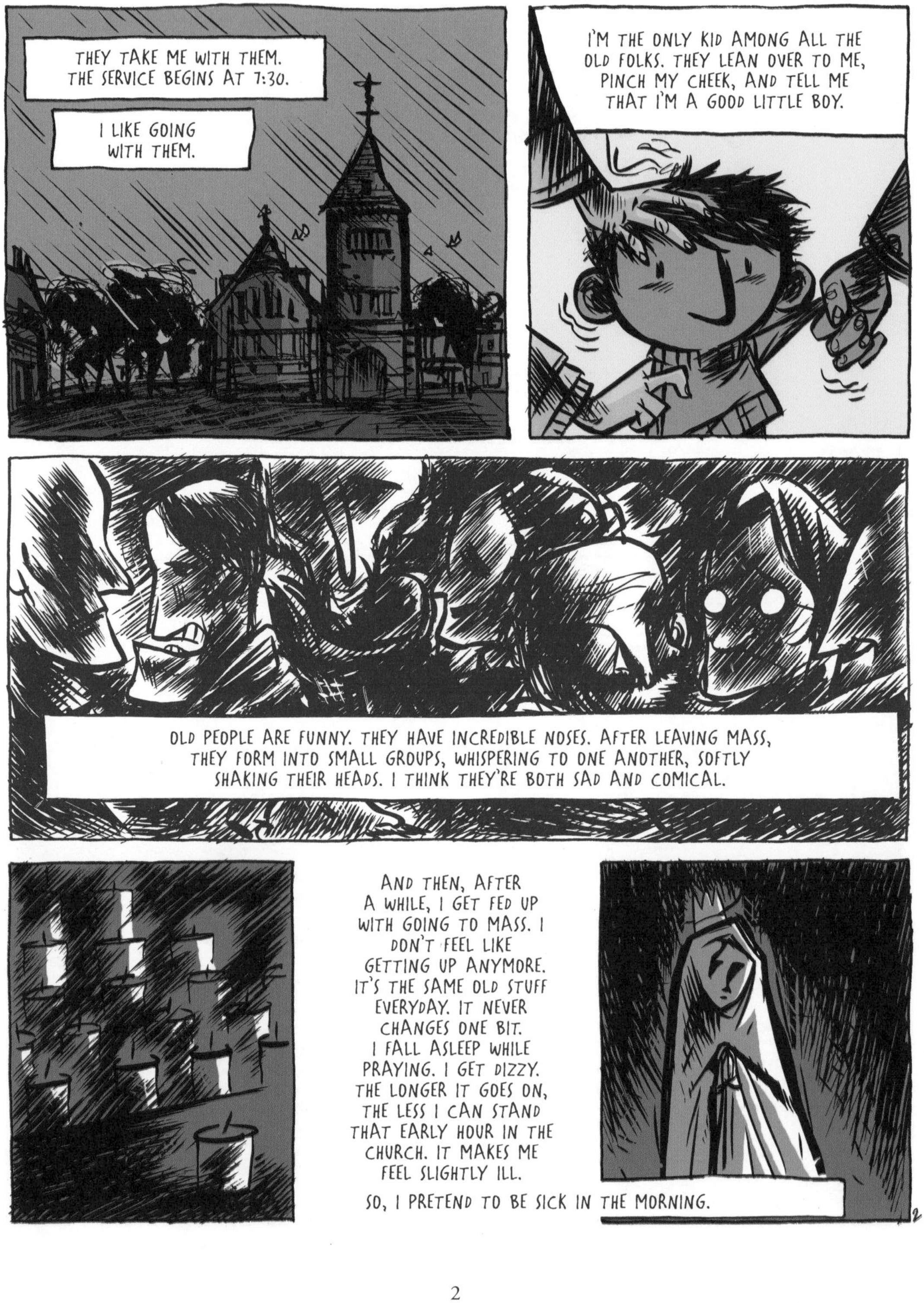
THEY TAKE ME WITH THEM. THE SERVICE BEGINS AT 7:30.
I LIKE GOING WITH THEM.
I'M THE ONLY KID AMONG ALL THE OLD FOLKS. THEY LEAN OVER TO ME, PINCH MY CHEEK, AND TELL ME THAT I'M A GOOD LITTLE BOY.
OLD PEOPLE ARE FUNNY. THEY HAVE INCREDIBLE NOSES. AFTER LEAVING MASS, THEY FORM INTO SMALL GROUPS, WHISPERING TO ONE ANOTHER, SOFTLY SHAKING THEIR HEADS. I THINK THEY'RE BOTH SAD AND COMICAL.
AND THEN, AFTER A WHILE, I GET FED UP WITH GOING TO MASS. I DON'T FEEL LIKE GETTING UP ANYMORE. IT'S THE SAME OLD STUFF EVERYDAY. IT NEVER CHANGES ONE BIT. I FALL ASLEEP WHILE PRAYING. I GET DIZZY. THE LONGER IT GOES ON, THE LESS I CAN STAND THAT EARLY HOUR IN THE CHURCH. IT MAKES ME FEEL SLIGHTLY ILL.
SO, I PRETEND TO BE SICK IN THE MORNING.

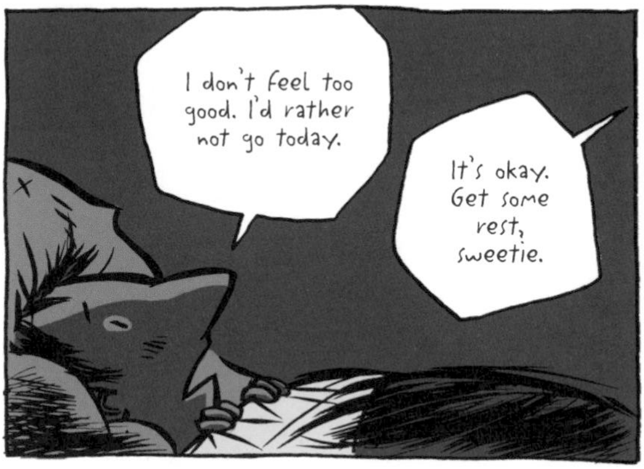
I don't feel too good. I'd rather not go today.
It's okay. Get some rest, sweetie.

I STAY IN MY BED FOR AN HOUR, WITH MY EYES OPEN, WONDERING WHETHER WHAT I'M DOING IS BAD OR VERY BAD.

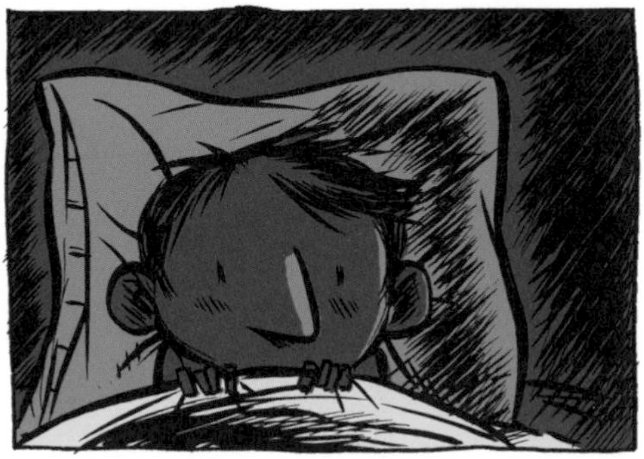

ONE NIGHT, MY GRANNY TALKS TO ME, LEANING OVER MY BED. SHE DESCRIBES HELL TO ME. I ONLY HAVE A VAGUE IDEA WHAT IT IS. SHE PAINTS A TERRIFYING PICTURE FOR ME.

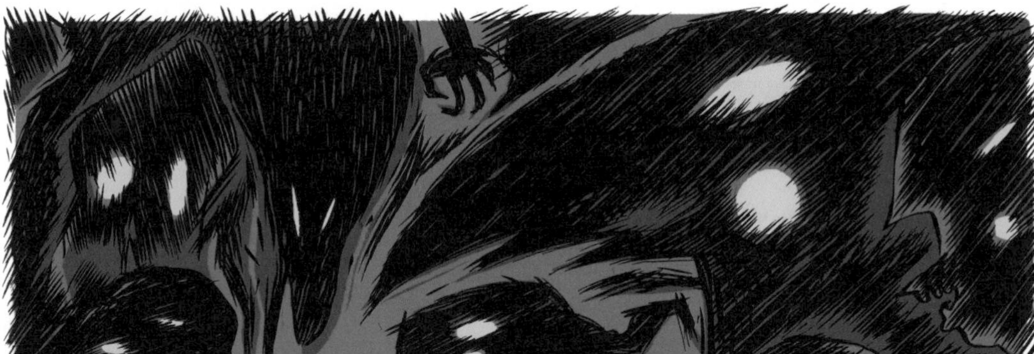

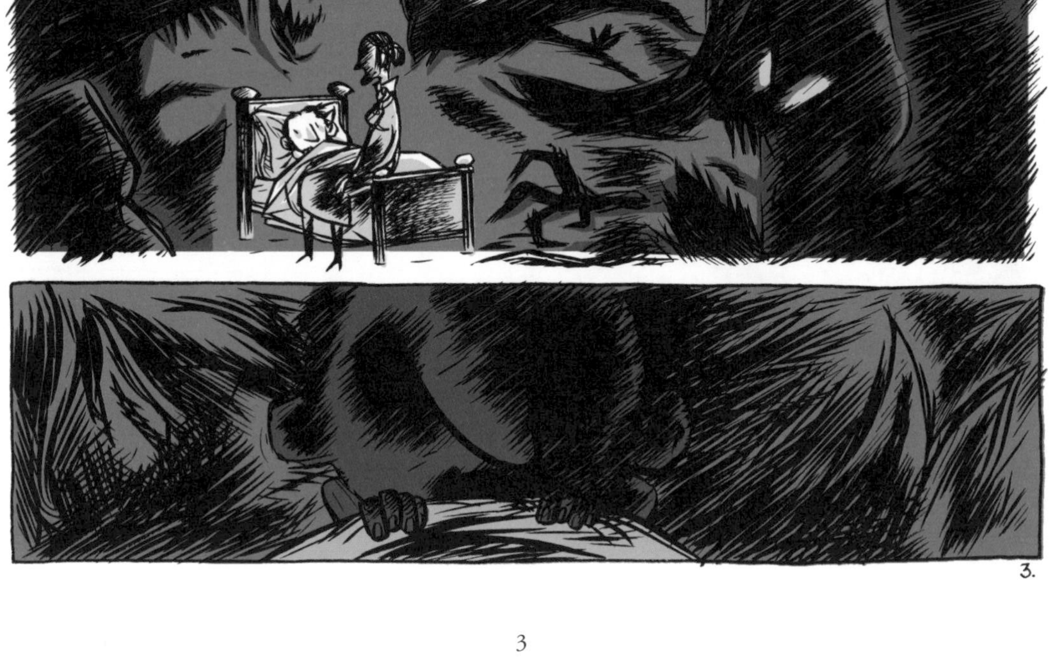

3.

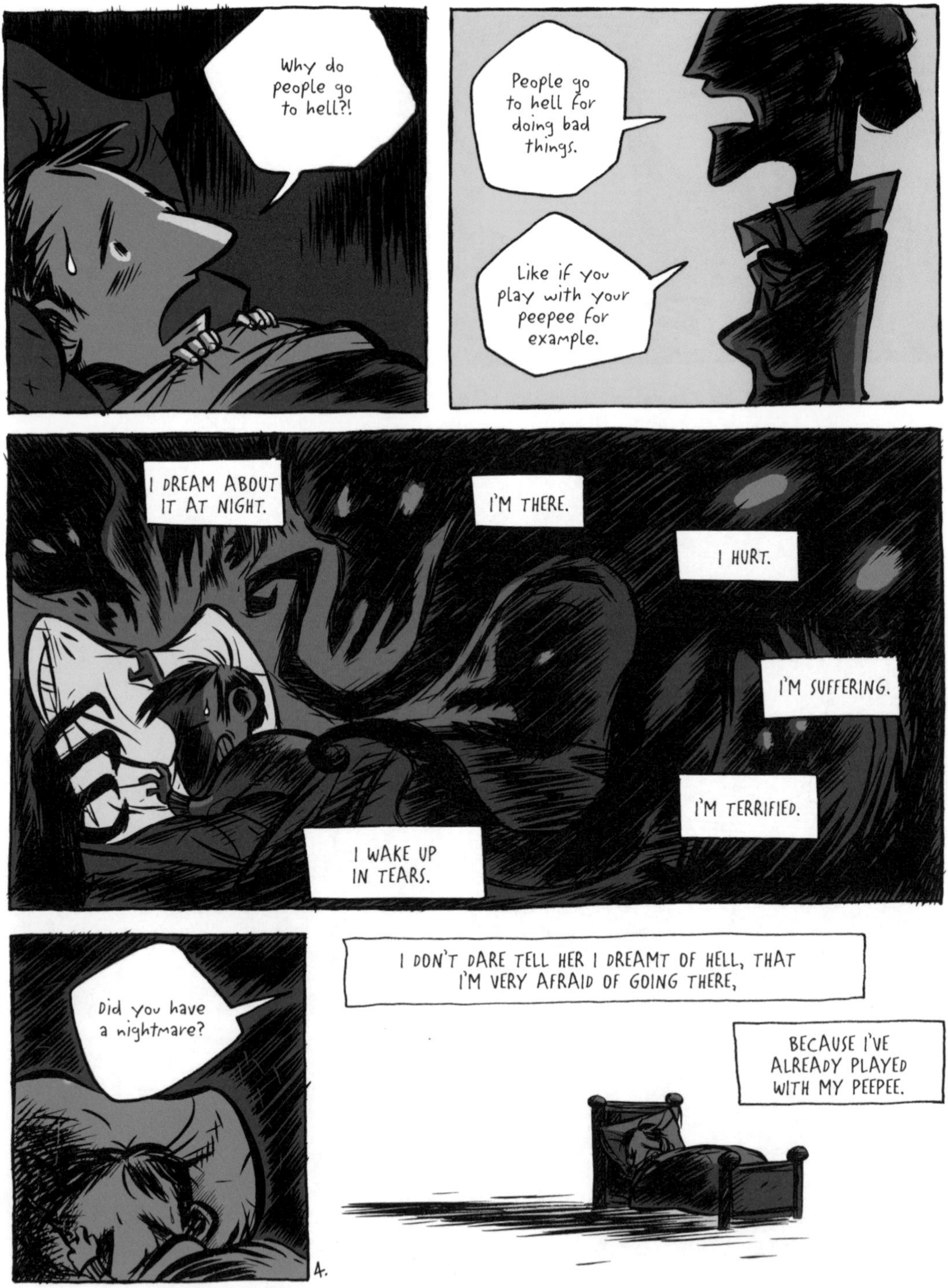
Why do people go to hell?!
People go to hell for doing bad things.
Like if you play with your peepee for example.
I DREAM ABOUT IT AT NIGHT.
I'M THERE.
I HURT.
I'M SUFFERING.
I'M TERRIFIED.
I WAKE UP IN TEARS.
Did you have a nightmare?
4.
I DON'T DARE TELL HER I DREAMT OF HELL, THAT I'M VERY AFRAID OF GOING THERE,
BECAUSE I'VE ALREADY PLAYED WITH MY PEEPEE.

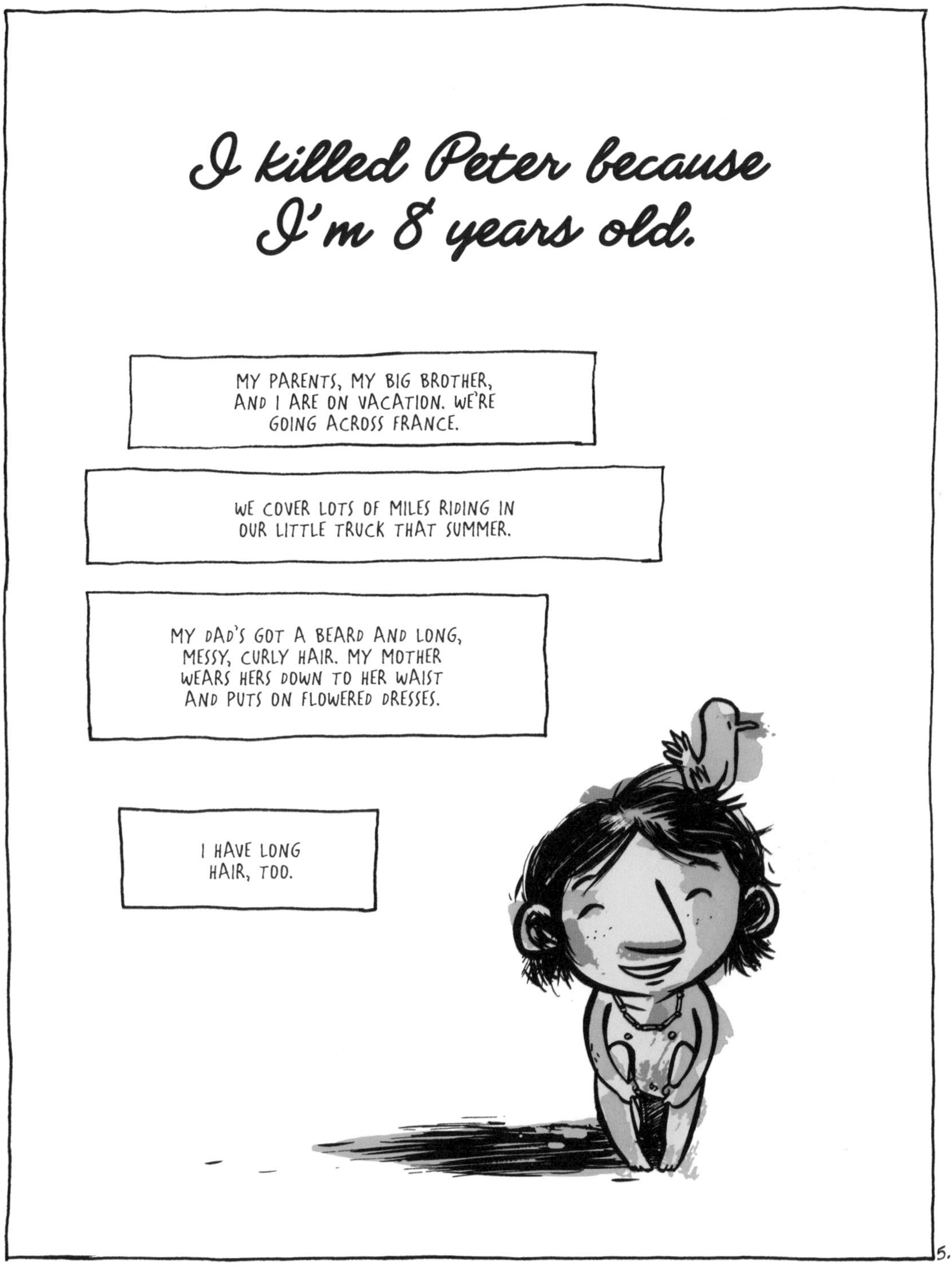
I killed Peter because I'm 8 years old.
MY PARENTS, MY BIG BROTHER, AND I ARE ON VACATION. WE'RE GOING ACROSS FRANCE.
WE COVER LOTS OF MILES RIDING IN OUR LITTLE TRUCK THAT SUMMER.
MY DAD'S GOT A BEARD AND LONG, MESSY, CURLY HAIR. MY MOTHER WEARS HERS DOWN TO HER WAIST AND PUTS ON FLOWERED DRESSES.
I HAVE LONG HAIR, TOO.
5.

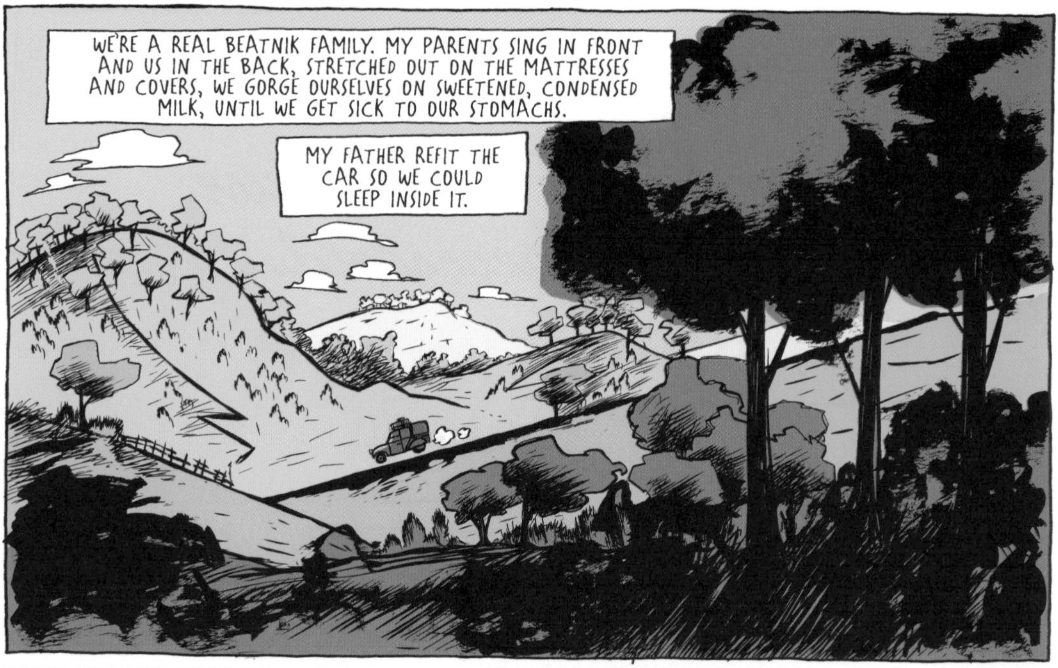
WE'RE A REAL BEATNIK FAMILY. MY PARENTS SING IN FRONT AND US IN THE BACK, STRETCHED OUT ON THE MATTRESSES AND COVERS, WE GORGE OURSELVES ON SWEETENED, CONDENSED MILK, UNTIL WE GET SICK TO OUR STOMACHS.
MY FATHER REFIT THE CAR SO WE COULD SLEEP INSIDE IT.

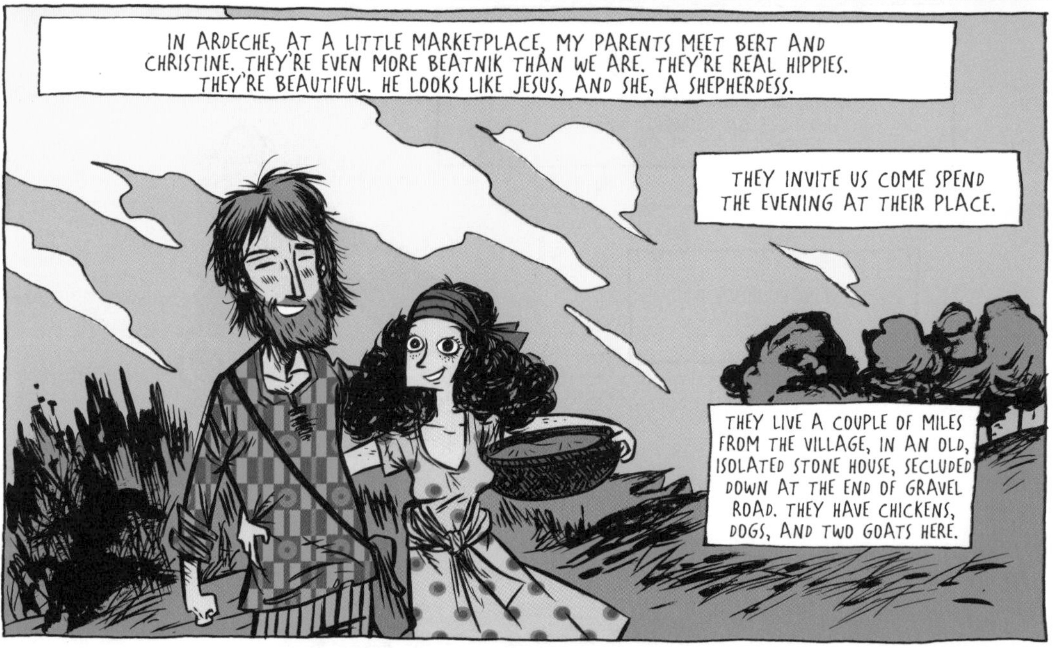
IN ARDECHE, AT A LITTLE MARKETPLACE, MY PARENTS MEET BERT AND CHRISTINE. THEY'RE EVEN MORE BEATNIK THAN WE ARE. THEY'RE REAL HIPPIES. THEY'RE BEAUTIFUL. HE LOOKS LIKE JESUS, AND SHE, A SHEPHERDESS.
THEY INVITE US COME SPEND THE EVENING AT THEIR PLACE.
THEY LIVE A COUPLE OF MILES FROM THE VILLAGE, IN AN OLD, ISOLATED STONE HOUSE, SECLUDED DOWN AT THE END OF GRAVEL ROAD. THEY HAVE CHICKENS, DOGS, AND TWO GOATS HERE.

MY MOM EXPLAINS TO ME THAT BERT AND CHRISTINE LIVE WITHOUT ELECTRICITY, THAT THEY NEED HARDLY ANY MONEY. THE CHEESE THEY SELL AT THE MARKET MAKES THEM ENOUGH TO LIVE. THEY MAKE ALL THEY NEED FOR THEMSELVES. THEY LOVE ONE ANOTHER, THEY DON'T NEED ANYTHING ELSE. WHILE SAYING SO, HER EYES GET BRIGHTER AND BRIGHTER, BERT AND CHRISTINE SYMBOLIZE HER IDEAL LIFE. AND MINE TOO, FROM NOW ON.

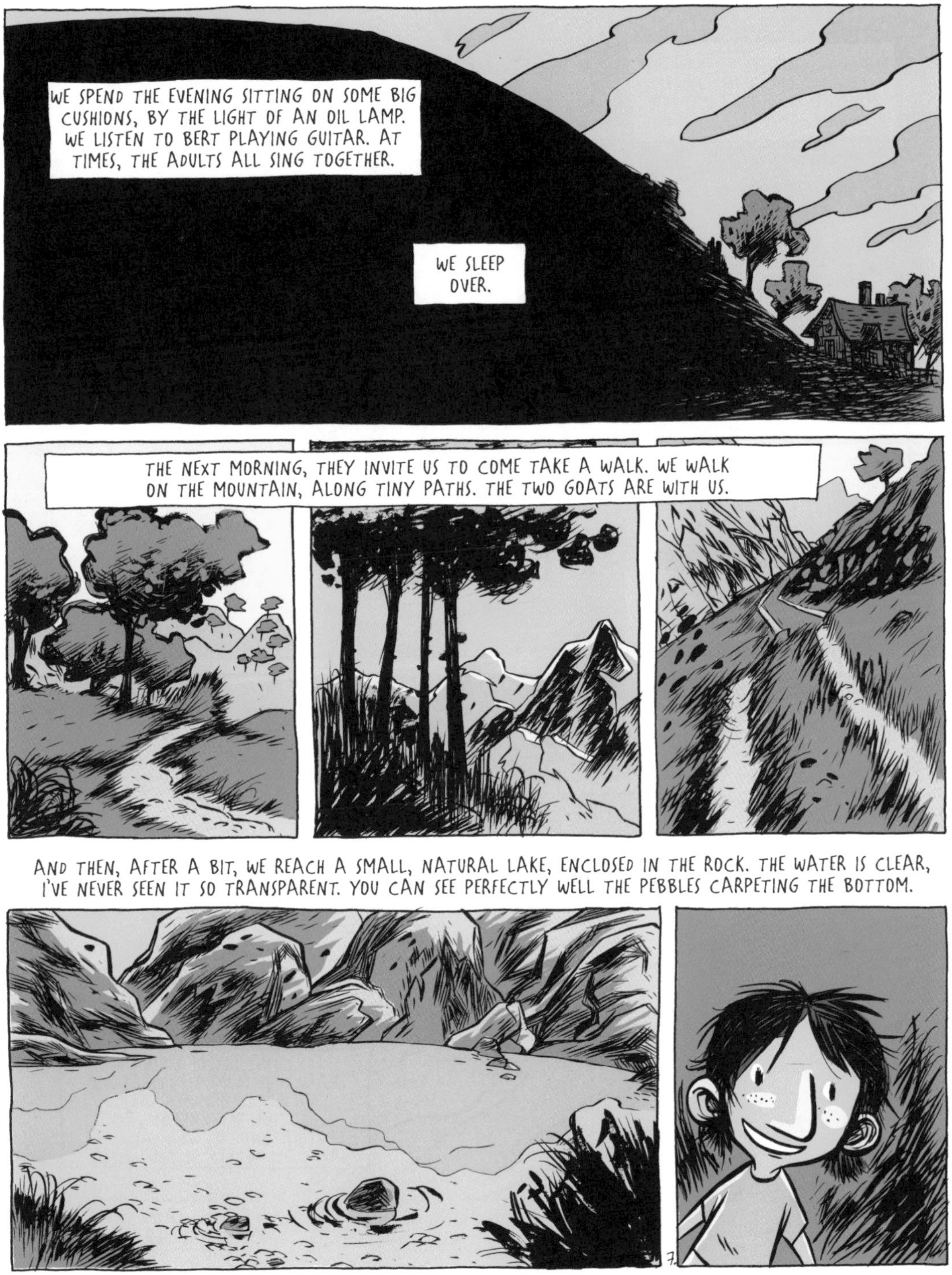
WE SPEND THE EVENING SITTING ON SOME BIG CUSHIONS, BY THE LIGHT OF AN OIL LAMP. WE LISTEN TO BERT PLAYING GUITAR. AT TIMES, THE ADULTS ALL SING TOGETHER.
WE SLEEP OVER.
THE NEXT MORNING, THEY INVITE US TO COME TAKE A WALK. WE WALK ON THE MOUNTAIN, ALONG TINY PATHS. THE TWO GOATS ARE WITH US.
AND THEN, AFTER A BIT, WE REACH A SMALL, NATURAL LAKE, ENCLOSED IN THE ROCK. THE WATER IS CLEAR, I'VE NEVER SEEN IT SO TRANSPARENT. YOU CAN SEE PERFECTLY WELL THE PEBBLES CARPETING THE BOTTOM.

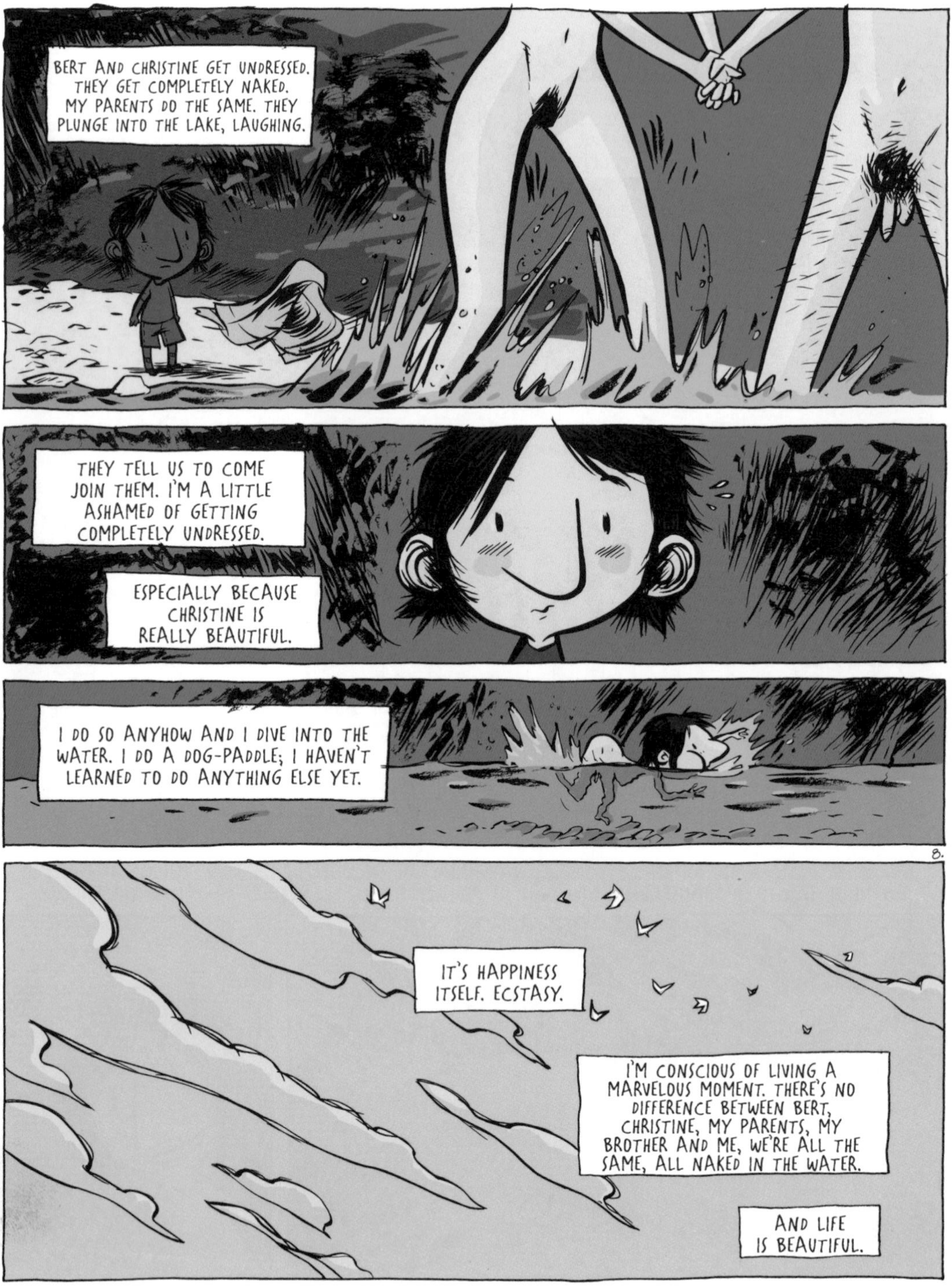
BERT AND CHRISTINE GET UNDRESSED. THEY GET COMPLETELY NAKED. MY PARENTS DO THE SAME. THEY PLUNGE INTO THE LAKE, LAUGHING.
THEY TELL US TO COME JOIN THEM. I'M A LITTLE ASHAMED OF GETTING COMPLETELY UNDRESSED.
ESPECIALLY BECAUSE CHRISTINE IS REALLY BEAUTIFUL.
I DO SO ANYHOW AND I DIVE INTO THE WATER. I DO A DOG-PADDLE; I HAVEN'T LEARNED TO DO ANYTHING ELSE YET.
IT'S HAPPINESS ITSELF. ECSTASY.
I'M CONSCIOUS OF LIVING A MARVELOUS MOMENT. THERE'S NO DIFFERENCE BETWEEN BERT, CHRISTINE, MY PARENTS, MY BROTHER AND ME, WE'RE ALL THE SAME, ALL NAKED IN THE WATER.
AND LIFE IS BEAUTIFUL.

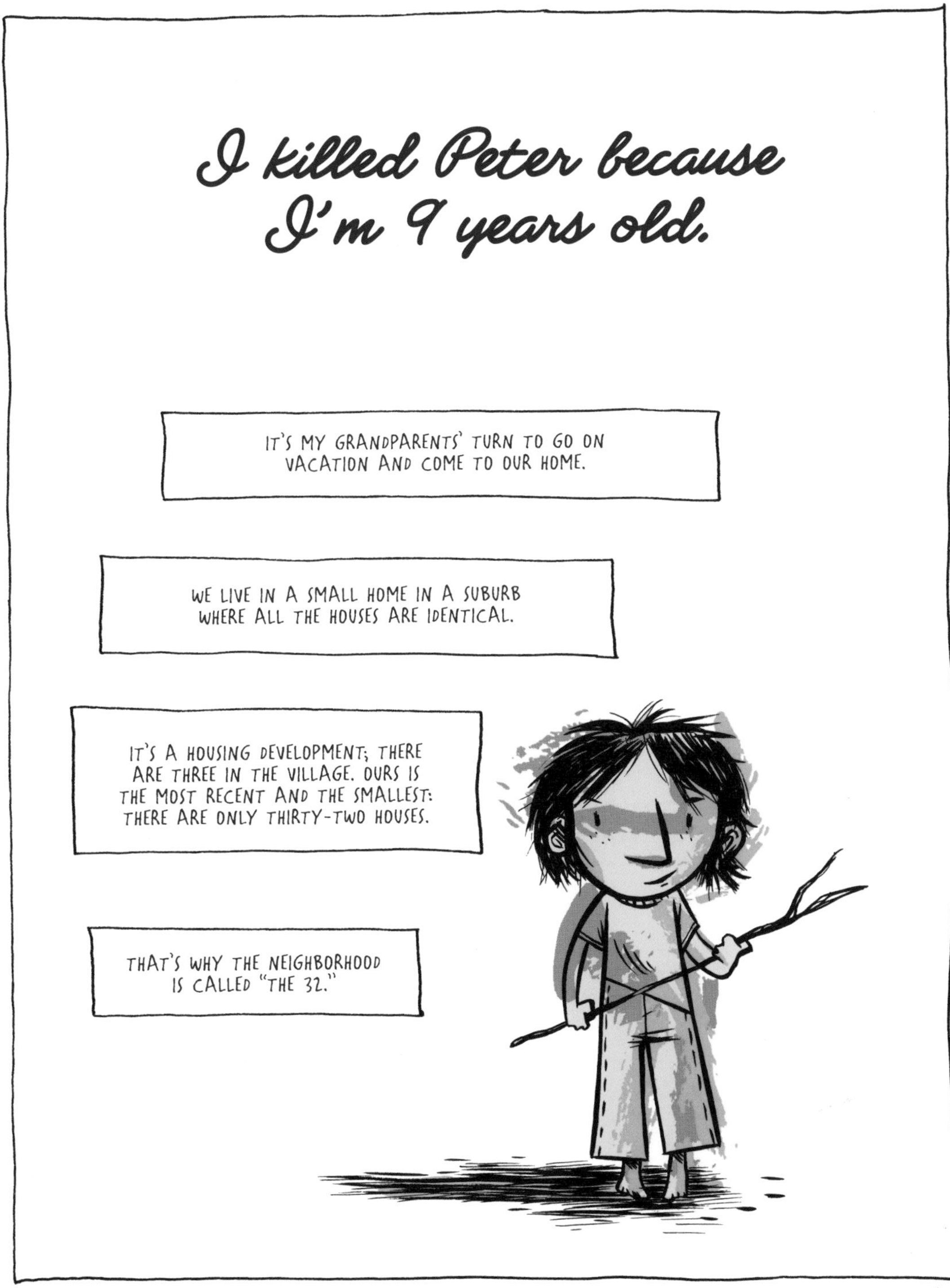
I killed Peter because I'm 9 years old.
IT'S MY GRANDPARENTS' TURN TO GO ON VACATION AND COME TO OUR HOME.
WE LIVE IN A SMALL HOME IN A SUBURB WHERE ALL THE HOUSES ARE IDENTICAL.
IT'S A HOUSING DEVELOPMENT; THERE ARE THREE IN THE VILLAGE. OURS IS THE MOST RECENT AND THE SMALLEST: THERE ARE ONLY THIRTY-TWO HOUSES.
THAT'S WHY THE NEIGHBORHOOD IS CALLED "THE 32."
9.

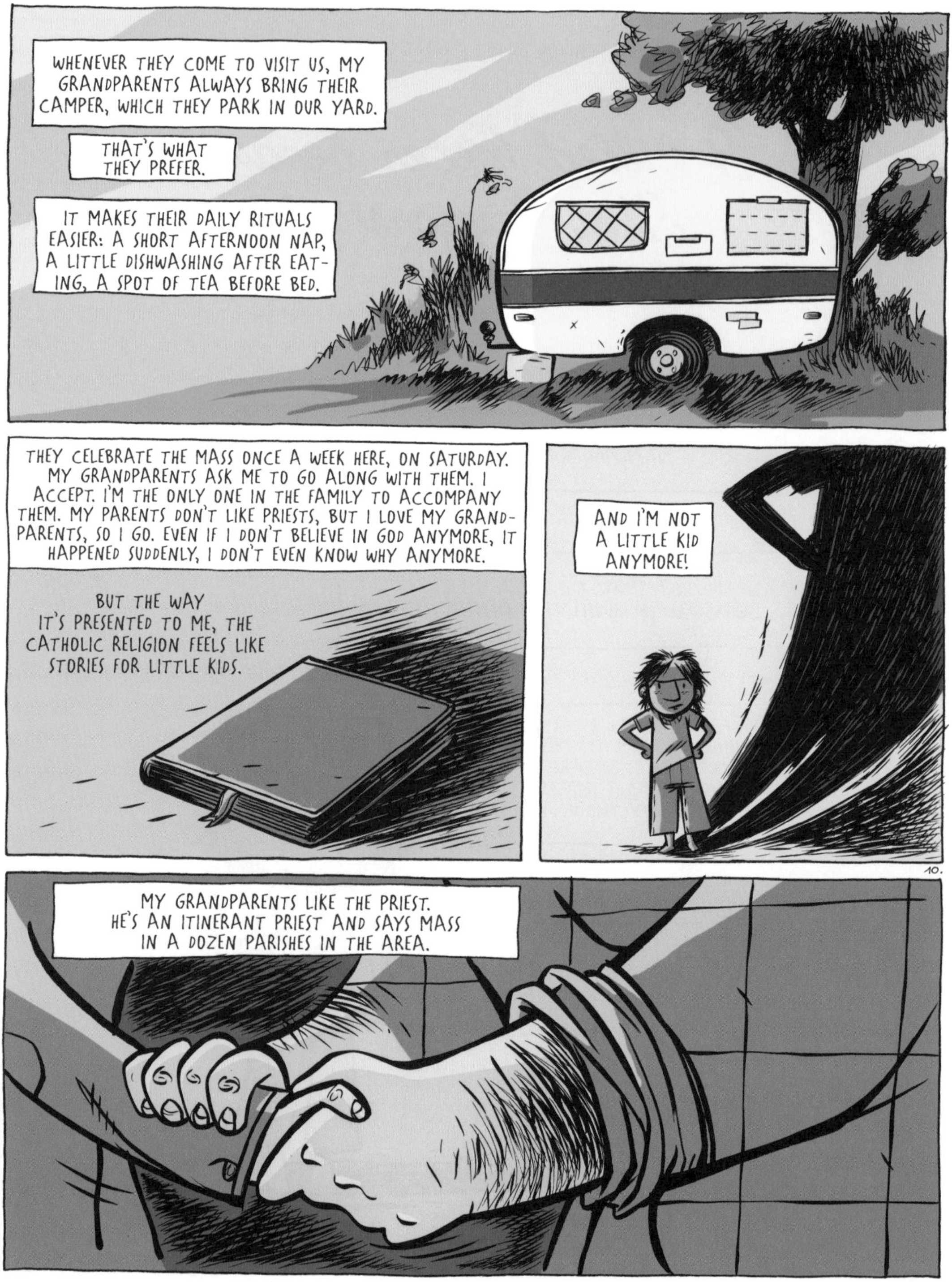
WHENEVER THEY COME TO VISIT US, MY GRANDPARENTS ALWAYS BRING THEIR CAMPER, WHICH THEY PARK IN OUR YARD.
THAT'S WHAT THEY PREFER.
IT MAKES THEIR DAILY RITUALS EASIER: A SHORT AFTERNOON NAP, A LITTLE DISHWASHING AFTER EATING, A SPOT OF TEA BEFORE BED.
THEY CELEBRATE THE MASS ONCE A WEEK HERE, ON SATURDAY. MY GRANDPARENTS ASK ME TO GO ALONG WITH THEM. I ACCEPT. I'M THE ONLY ONE IN THE FAMILY TO ACCOMPANY THEM. MY PARENTS DON'T LIKE PRIESTS, BUT I LOVE MY GRANDPARENTS, SO I GO. EVEN IF I DON'T BELIEVE IN GOD ANYMORE, IT HAPPENED SUDDENLY, I DON'T EVEN KNOW WHY ANYMORE.
BUT THE WAY IT'S PRESENTED TO ME, THE CATHOLIC RELIGION FEELS LIKE STORIES FOR LITTLE KIDS.
AND I'M NOT A LITTLE KID ANYMORE!
MY GRANDPARENTS LIKE THE PRIEST. HE'S AN ITINERANT PRIEST AND SAYS MASS IN A DOZEN PARISHES IN THE AREA.

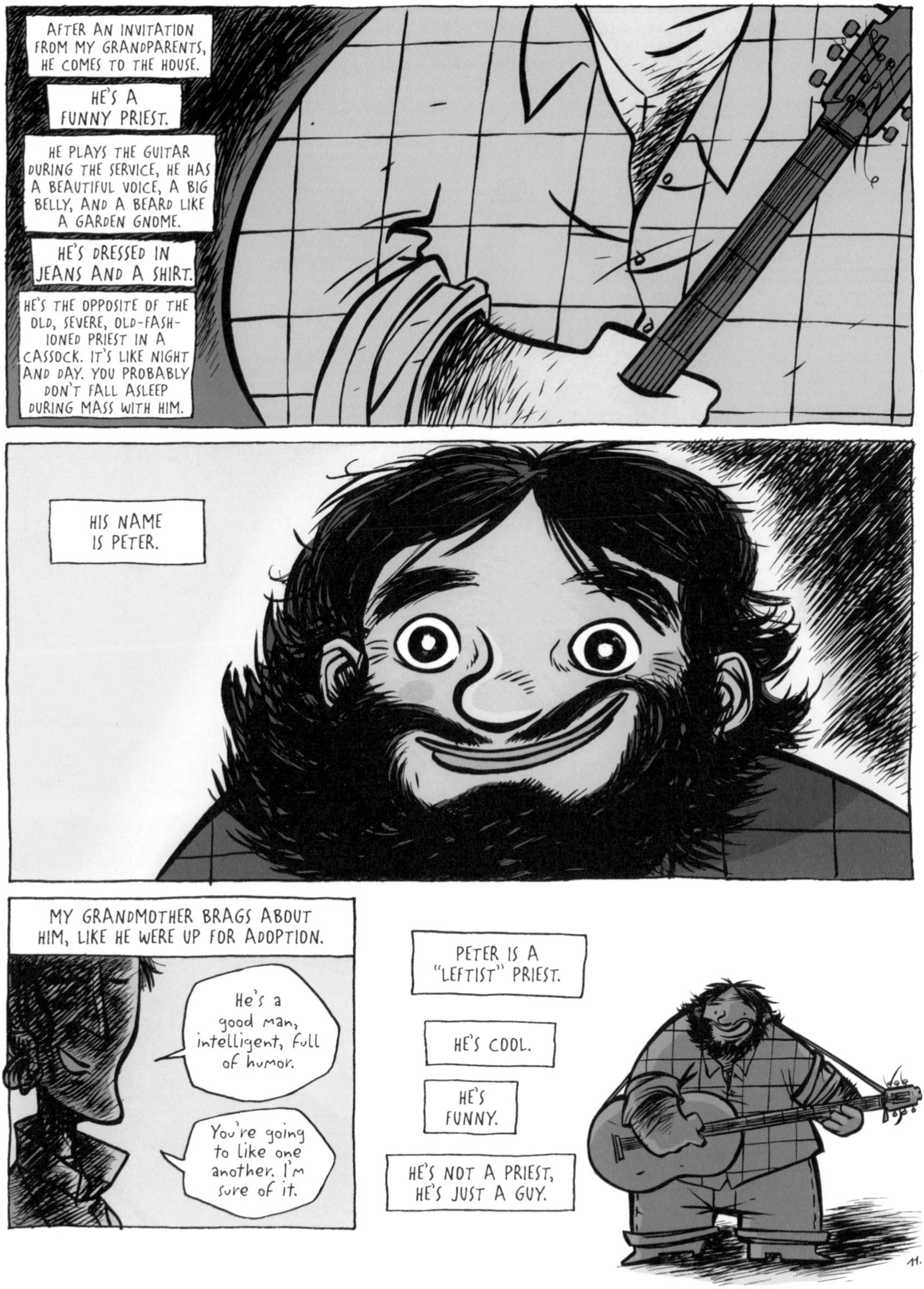

AFTER AN INVITATION FROM MY GRANDPARENTS, HE COMES TO THE HOUSE.
HE'S A FUNNY PRIEST.
HE PLAYS THE GUITAR DURING THE SERVICE, HE HAS A BEAUTIFUL VOICE, A BIG BELLY, AND A BEARD LIKE A GARDEN GNOME.
HE'S DRESSED IN JEANS AND A SHIRT.
HE'S THE OPPOSITE OF THE OLD, SEVERE, OLD-FASHIONED PRIEST IN A CASSOCK. IT'S LIKE NIGHT AND DAY. YOU PROBABLY DON'T FALL ASLEEP DURING MASS WITH HIM.
HIS NAME IS PETER.
MY GRANDMOTHER BRAGS ABOUT HIM, LIKE HE WERE UP FOR ADOPTION.
He's a good man, intelligent, full of humor.
You're going to like one another. I'm sure of it.
PETER IS A "LEFTIST" PRIEST.
HE'S COOL.
HE'S FUNNY.
HE'S NOT A PRIEST, HE'S JUST A GUY.
11.

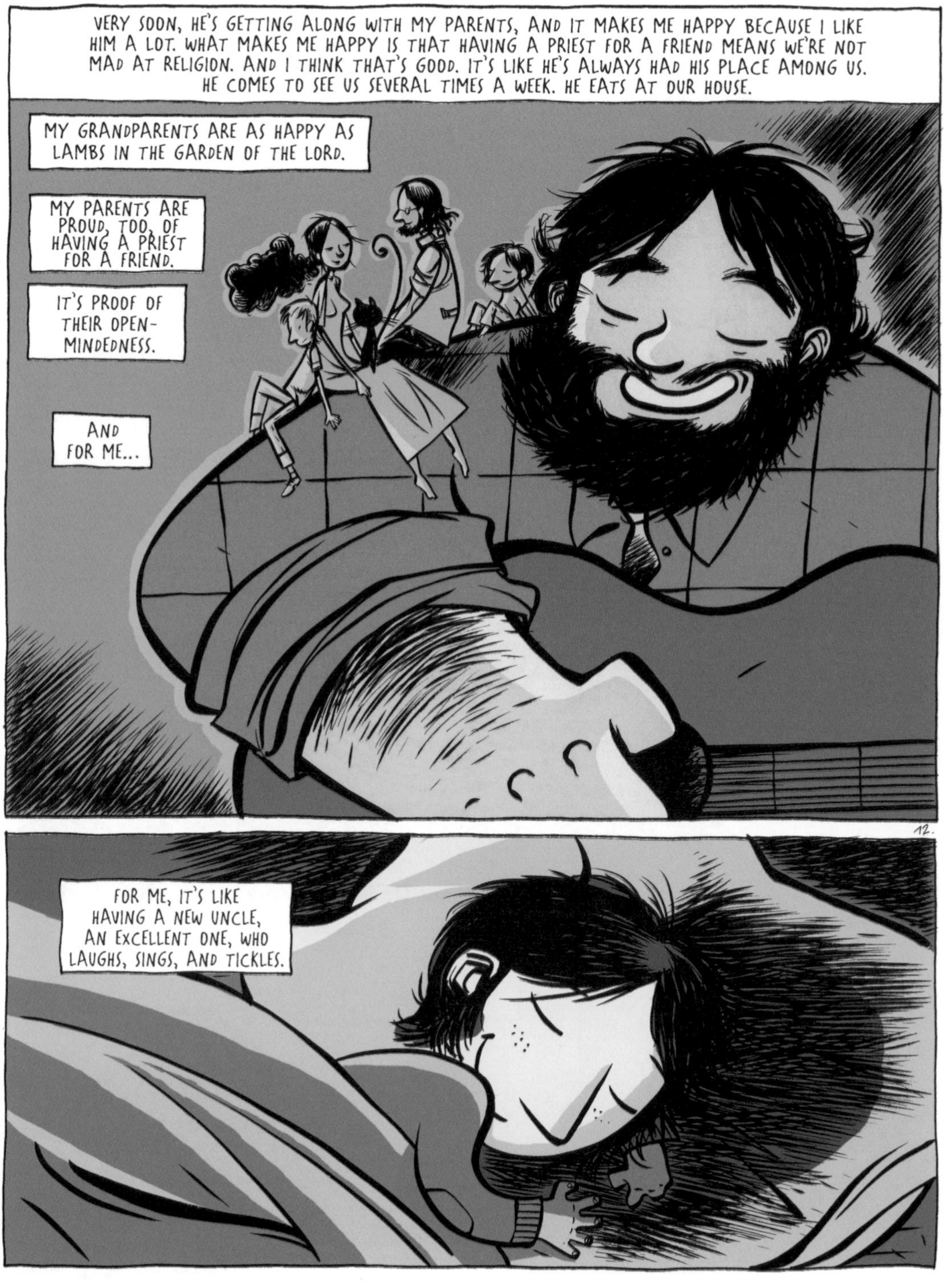
VERY SOON, HE'S GETTING ALONG WITH MY PARENTS, AND IT MAKES ME HAPPY BECAUSE I LIKE HIM A LOT. WHAT MAKES ME HAPPY IS THAT HAVING A PRIEST FOR A FRIEND MEANS WE'RE NOT MAD AT RELIGION. AND I THINK THAT'S GOOD. IT'S LIKE HE'S ALWAYS HAD HIS PLACE AMONG US. HE COMES TO SEE US SEVERAL TIMES A WEEK. HE EATS AT OUR HOUSE.
MY GRANDPARENTS ARE AS HAPPY AS LAMBS IN THE GARDEN OF THE LORD.
MY PARENTS ARE PROUD, TOO, OF HAVING A PRIEST FOR A FRIEND.
IT'S PROOF OF THEIR OPEN-MINDEDNESS.
AND FOR ME...
12.
FOR ME, IT'S LIKE HAVING A NEW UNCLE, AN EXCELLENT ONE, WHO LAUGHS, SINGS, AND TICKLES.

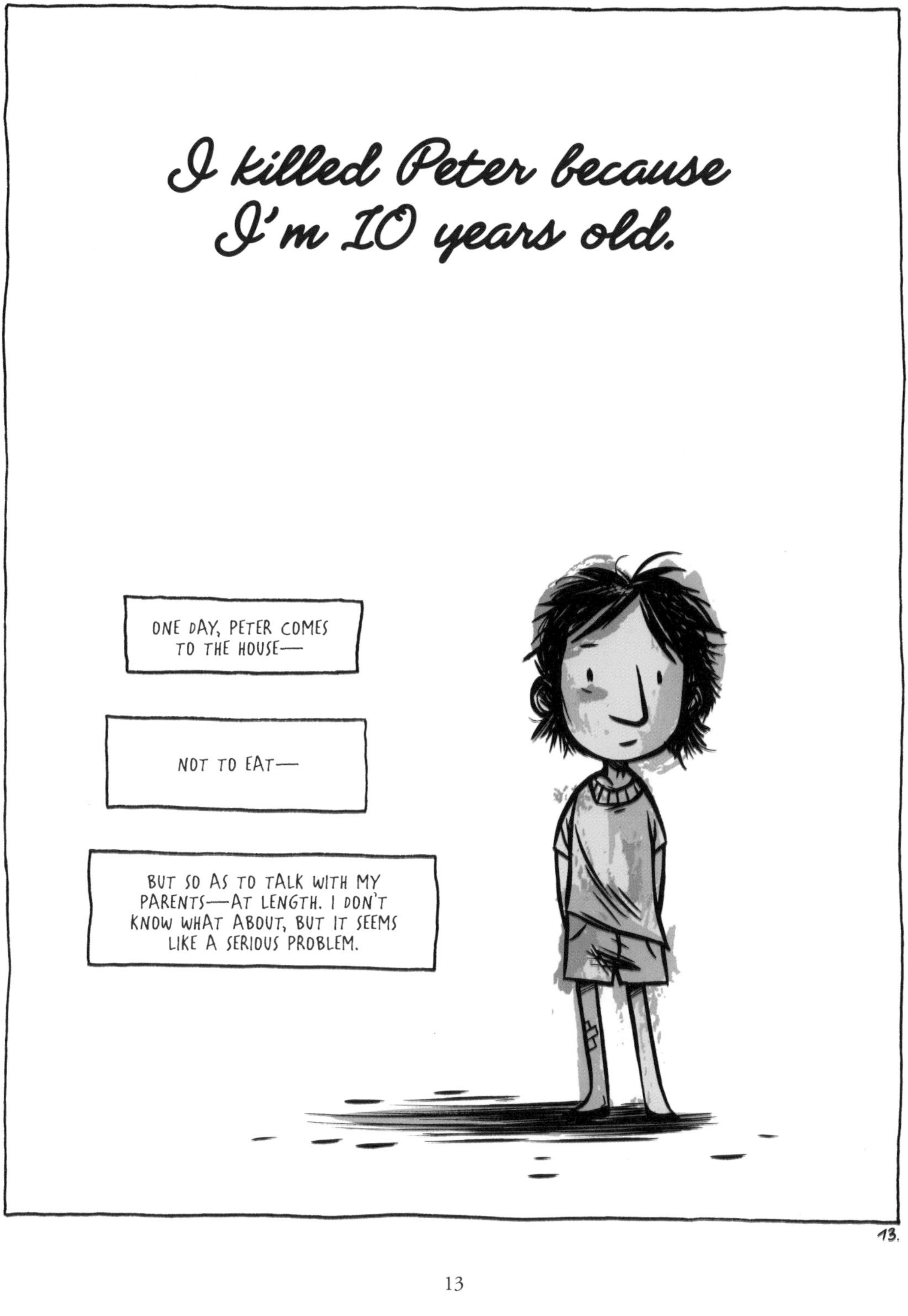
I killed Peter because I'm 10 years old.
ONE DAY, PETER COMES TO THE HOUSE—
NOT TO EAT—
BUT SO AS TO TALK WITH MY PARENTS—AT LENGTH. I DON'T KNOW WHAT ABOUT, BUT IT SEEMS LIKE A SERIOUS PROBLEM.

13.

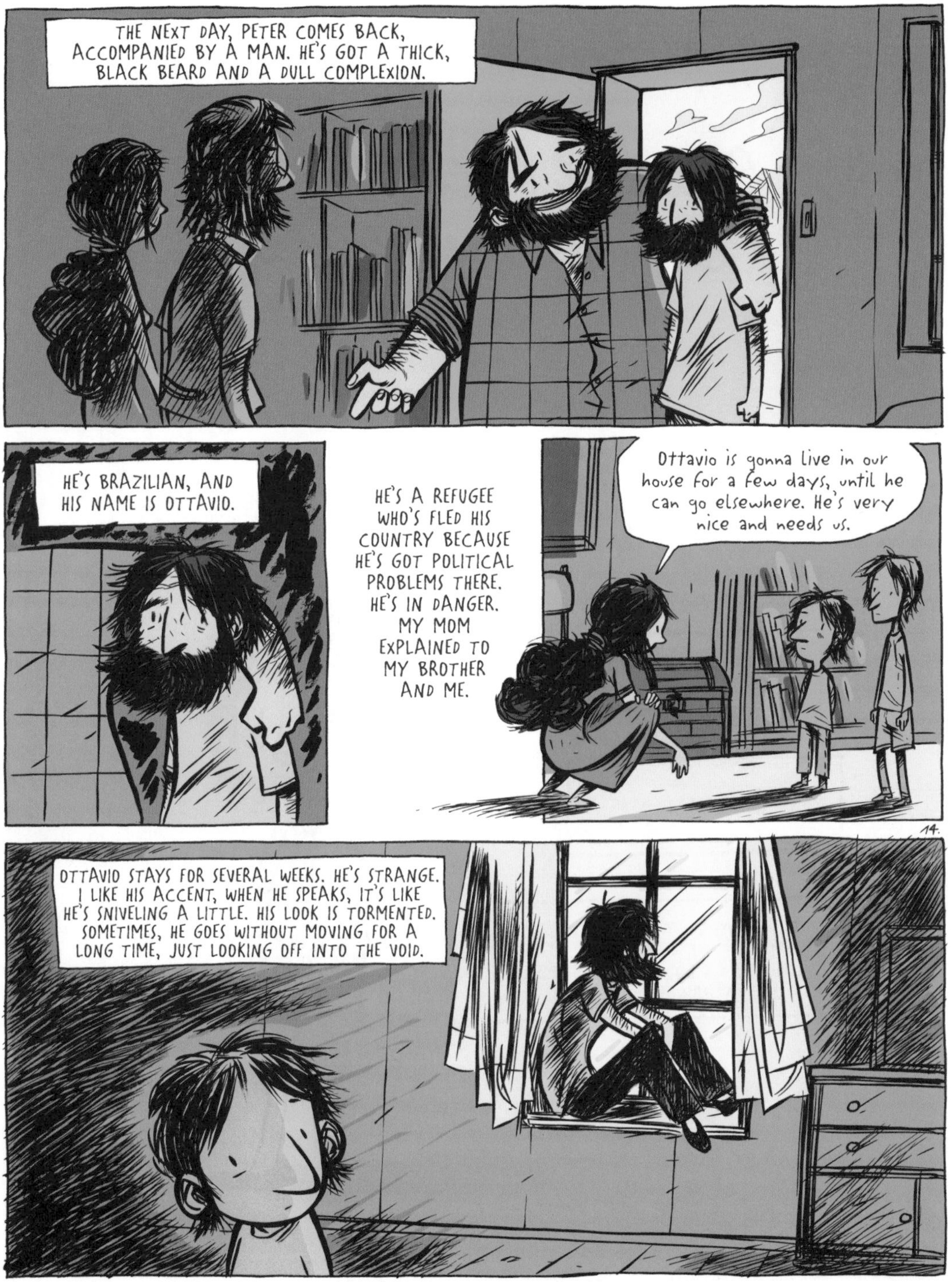
THE NEXT DAY, PETER COMES BACK, ACCOMPANIED BY A MAN. HE'S GOT A THICK, BLACK BEARD AND A DULL COMPLEXION.
HE'S BRAZILIAN, AND HIS NAME IS OTTAVIO.
HE'S A REFUGEE WHO'S FLED HIS COUNTRY BECAUSE HE'S GOT POLITICAL PROBLEMS THERE. HE'S IN DANGER. MY MOM EXPLAINED TO MY BROTHER AND ME.
Ottavio is gonna live in our house for a few days, until he can go elsewhere. He's very nice and needs us.
14.
OTTAVIO STAYS FOR SEVERAL WEEKS. HE'S STRANGE. I LIKE HIS ACCENT, WHEN HE SPEAKS, IT'S LIKE HE'S SNIVELING A LITTLE. HIS LOOK IS TORMENTED. SOMETIMES, HE GOES WITHOUT MOVING FOR A LONG TIME, JUST LOOKING OFF INTO THE VOID.

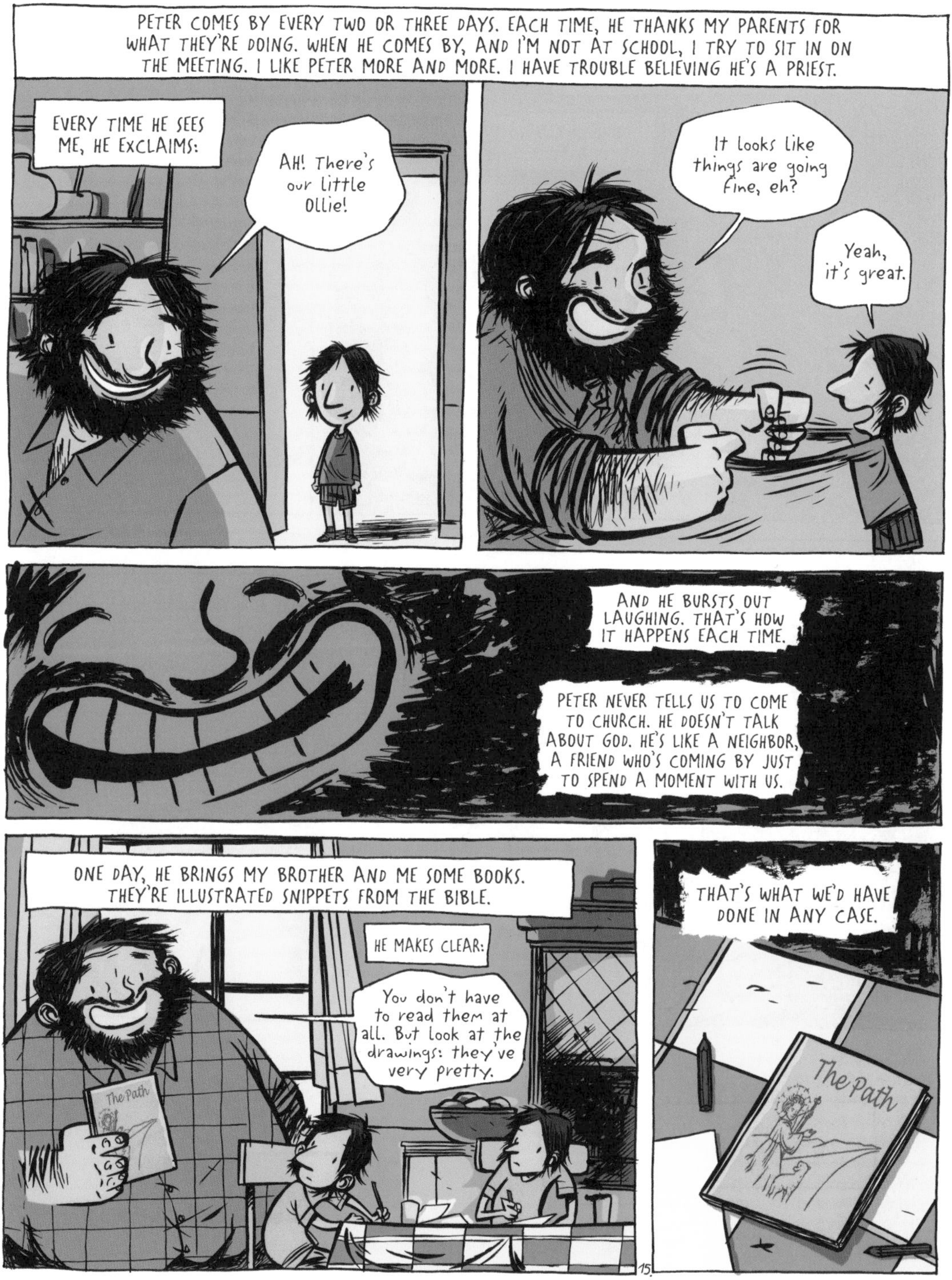
PETER COMES BY EVERY TWO OR THREE DAYS. EACH TIME, HE THANKS MY PARENTS FOR WHAT THEY'RE DOING. WHEN HE COMES BY, AND I'M NOT AT SCHOOL, I TRY TO SIT IN ON THE MEETING. I LIKE PETER MORE AND MORE. I HAVE TROUBLE BELIEVING HE'S A PRIEST.
EVERY TIME HE SEES ME, HE EXCLAIMS:
AH! There's our little Ollie!
It looks like things are going fine, eh?
Yeah, it's great.
AND HE BURSTS OUT LAUGHING. THAT'S HOW IT HAPPENS EACH TIME.
PETER NEVER TELLS US TO COME TO CHURCH. HE DOESN'T TALK ABOUT GOD. HE'S LIKE A NEIGHBOR, A FRIEND WHO'S COMING BY JUST TO SPEND A MOMENT WITH US.
ONE DAY, HE BRINGS MY BROTHER AND ME SOME BOOKS. THEY'RE ILLUSTRATED SNIPPETS FROM THE BIBLE.
HE MAKES CLEAR:
You don't have to read them at all. But look at the drawings: they've very pretty.
The Path
THAT'S WHAT WE'D HAVE DONE IN ANY CASE.
The Path
15

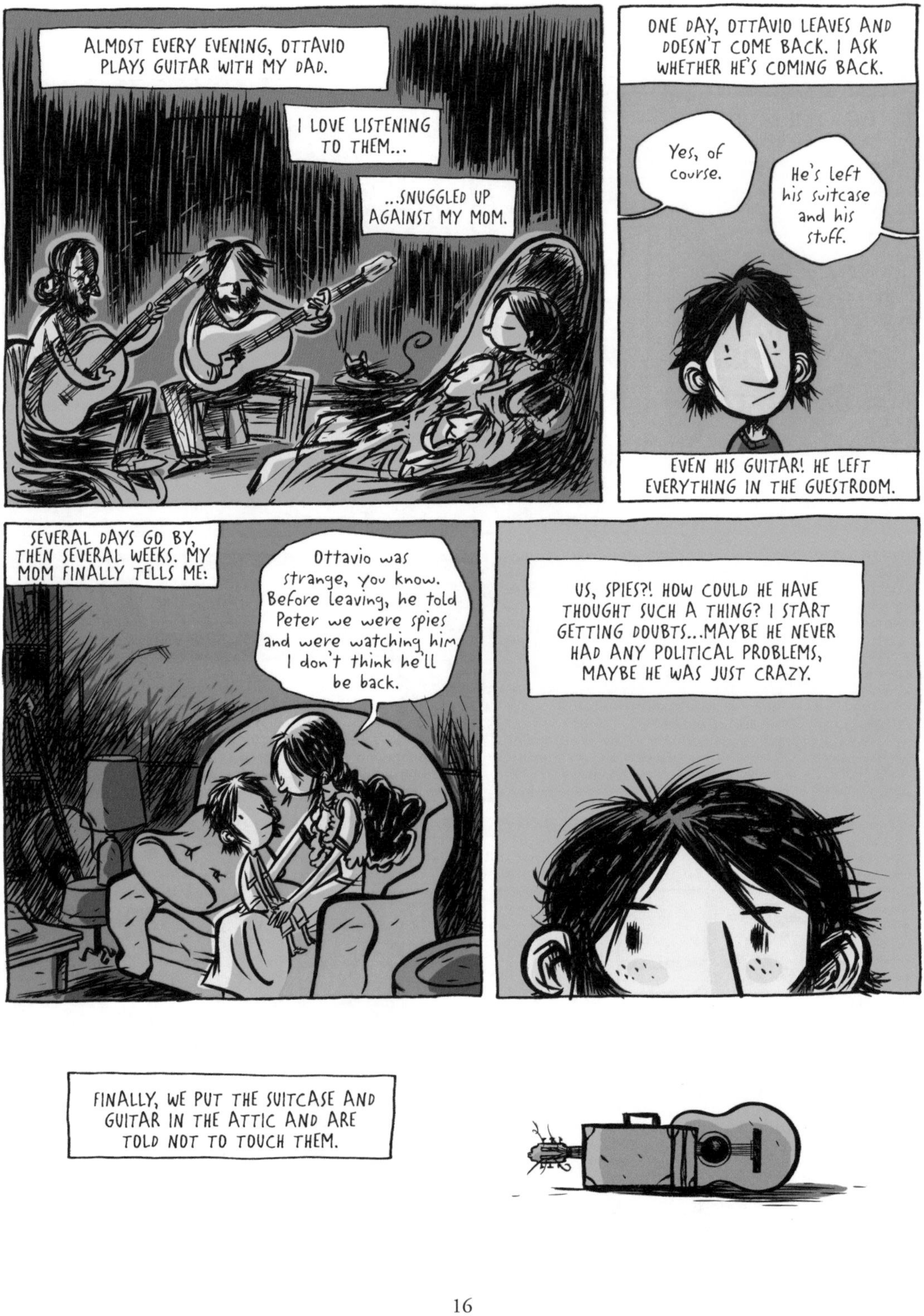

ALMOST EVERY EVENING, OTTAVIO PLAYS GUITAR WITH MY DAD.
I LOVE LISTENING TO THEM...
...SNUGGLED UP AGAINST MY MOM.
ONE DAY, OTTAVIO LEAVES AND DOESN'T COME BACK. I ASK WHETHER HE'S COMING BACK.
Yes, of course.
He's left his suitcase and his stuff.
EVEN HIS GUITAR! HE LEFT EVERYTHING IN THE GUESTROOM.
SEVERAL DAYS GO BY, THEN SEVERAL WEEKS. MY MOM FINALLY TELLS ME:
Ottavio was strange, you know. Before leaving, he told Peter we were spies and were watching him. I don't think he'll be back.
US, SPIES?! HOW COULD HE HAVE THOUGHT SUCH A THING? I START GETTING DOUBTS...MAYBE HE NEVER HAD ANY POLITICAL PROBLEMS, MAYBE HE WAS JUST CRAZY.
FINALLY, WE PUT THE SUITCASE AND GUITAR IN THE ATTIC AND ARE TOLD NOT TO TOUCH THEM.

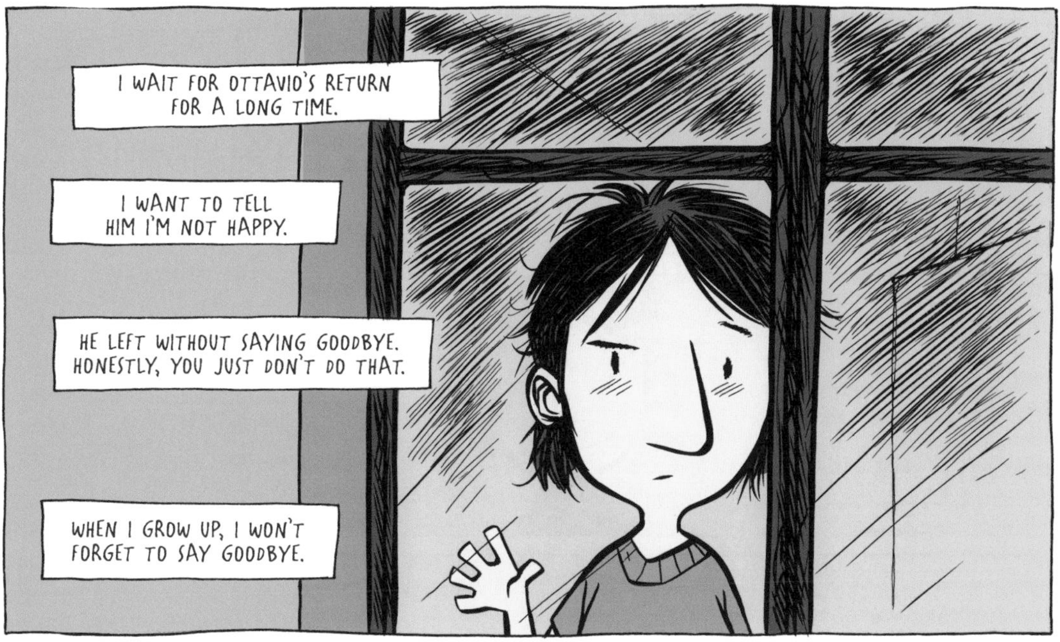
I WAIT FOR OTTAVIO'S RETURN FOR A LONG TIME.
I WANT TO TELL HIM I'M NOT HAPPY.
HE LEFT WITHOUT SAYING GOODBYE. HONESTLY, YOU JUST DON'T DO THAT.
WHEN I GROW UP, I WON'T FORGET TO SAY GOODBYE.

PETER INVITES US, MY BROTHER AND I, TO HIS SUMMER CAMP. MY BROTHER CAN'T AS HE HAS PLANS TO VISIT HIS FRIEND.BUT I'M ALL EXCITED, NEVER BEEN TO A CAMP BEFORE, AND WHAT A CHANGE IT WILL BE FROM SUMMERS IN THE CITY WITHOUT ANY BUD TO PLAY WITH. PETER CREATED HIS OWN SUMMER CAMP A FEW YEARS AGO.

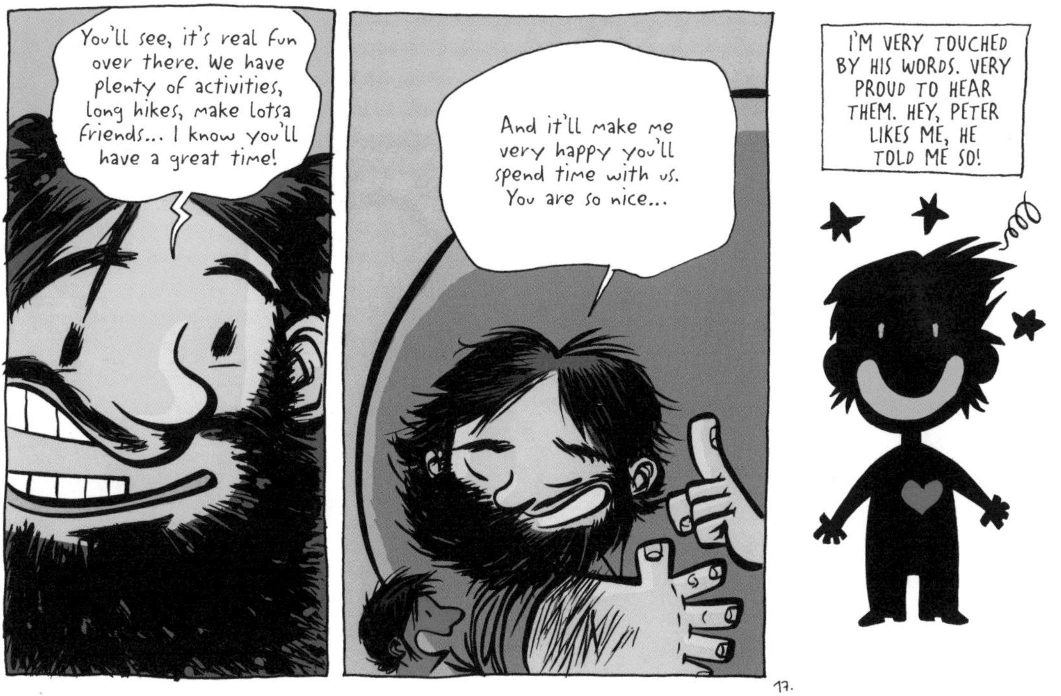
You'll see, it's real fun over there. We have plenty of activities, long hikes, make lotsa friends... I know you'll have a great time!
And it'll make me very happy you'll spend time with us. You are so nice...
I'M VERY TOUCHED BY HIS WORDS. VERY PROUD TO HEAR THEM. HEY, PETER LIKES ME, HE TOLD ME SO!
17.

I'M GOING TO CAMP.

ALL ALONE. WITHOUT MY PARENTS, WITHOUT MY BIG BROTHER.

I'M GONNA MAKE SOME FRIENDS. AND GO OUT WITH SOME GIRLS, MAYBE. LIKE MY DAD.

MY DAD HAS GIRLFRIENDS. EVERYBODY KNOWS. EVEN MY MOM. IT'S NO BIG DEAL.

HAVING GIRLFRIENDS IS COOL!!

HE SOMETIMES SPENDS EVENINGS AND NIGHTS IN PARIS WITH HIS "HARA-KIRI"* BUDDIES.

I TOTALLY ACCEPT MY DAD'S WAY OF LIFE. WHAT'S MORE, I ADMIRE HIM!

MY DAD IS SOMEBODY.

I FEEL CLOSE TO HIM. WHEN I'M HIS AGE, I'LL BE LIKE HIM, THE SAME KIND OF GUY. MY MOM NEVER SHOWS ANY SIGNS OF DISTRESS OR DISAGREEMENT ABOUT THIS LIFESTYLE.

SO IT'S A GOOD ONE. THE HEALTHIEST ONE.

18.

MY DAD'S GETTING LAID RIGHT AND LEFT, BUT AT NO TIME DO I HAVE A FEELING OF DECEPTION OR INFIDELITY.

JUST A WAY OF BEING COOL.

I FIGURE IT'S THE SAME IN ALL FAMILIES, OR ALMOST...

* A POPULAR SATIRE MAGAZINE

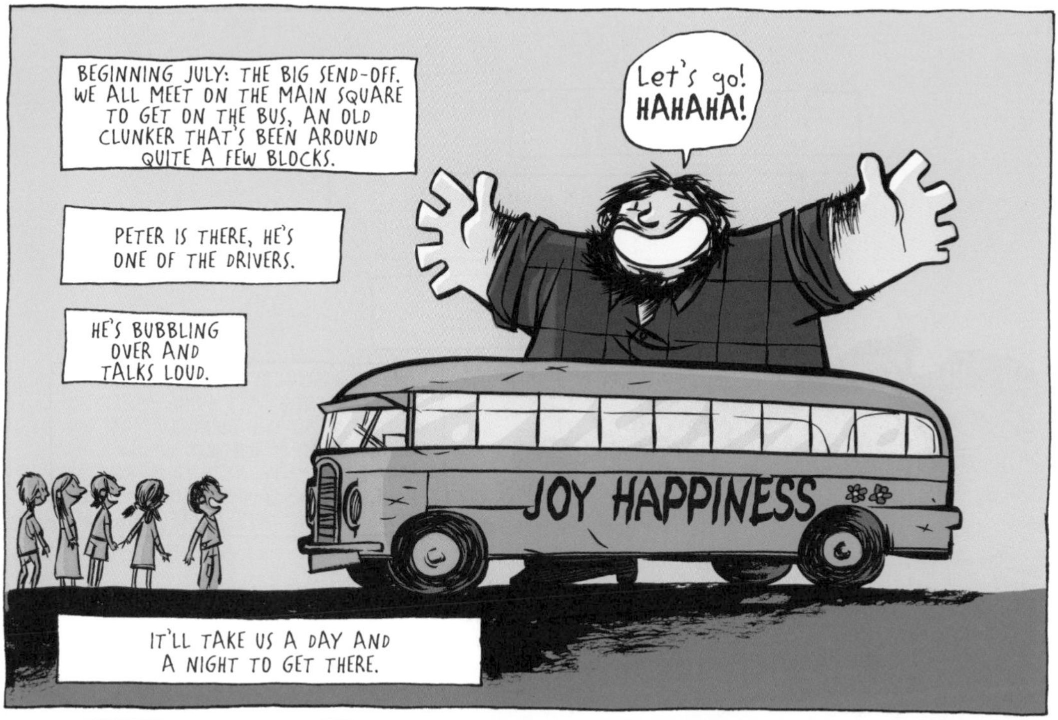
BEGINNING JULY: THE BIG SEND-OFF. WE ALL MEET ON THE MAIN SQUARE TO GET ON THE BUS, AN OLD CLUNKER THAT'S BEEN AROUND QUITE A FEW BLOCKS.
Let's go! HAHAHA!
PETER IS THERE, HE'S ONE OF THE DRIVERS.
HE'S BUBBLING OVER AND TALKS LOUD.
JOY HAPPINESS
IT'LL TAKE US A DAY AND A NIGHT TO GET THERE.

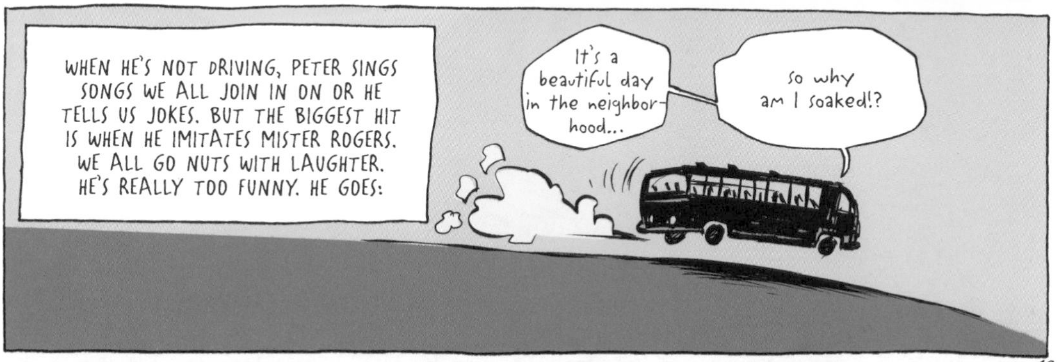
WHEN HE'S NOT DRIVING, PETER SINGS SONGS WE ALL JOIN IN ON OR HE TELLS US JOKES. BUT THE BIGGEST HIT IS WHEN HE IMITATES MISTER ROGERS. WE ALL GO NUTS WITH LAUGHTER. HE'S REALLY TOO FUNNY. HE GOES:
It's a beautiful day in the neighbor-hood...
so why am I soaked!?

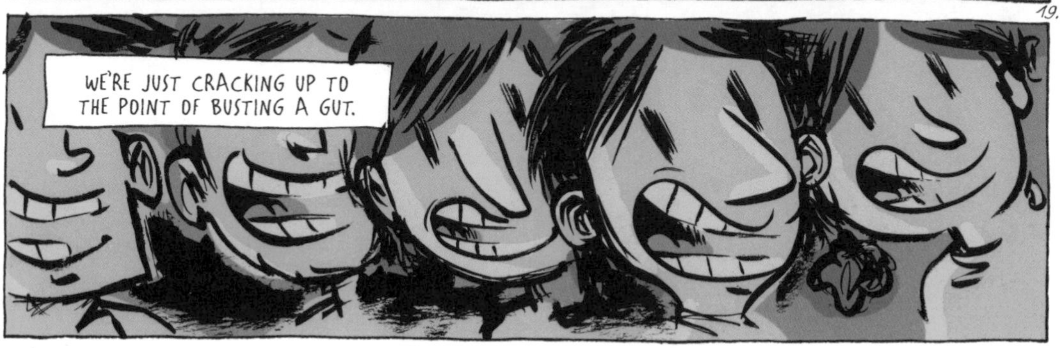
19.
WE'RE JUST CRACKING UP TO THE POINT OF BUSTING A GUT.

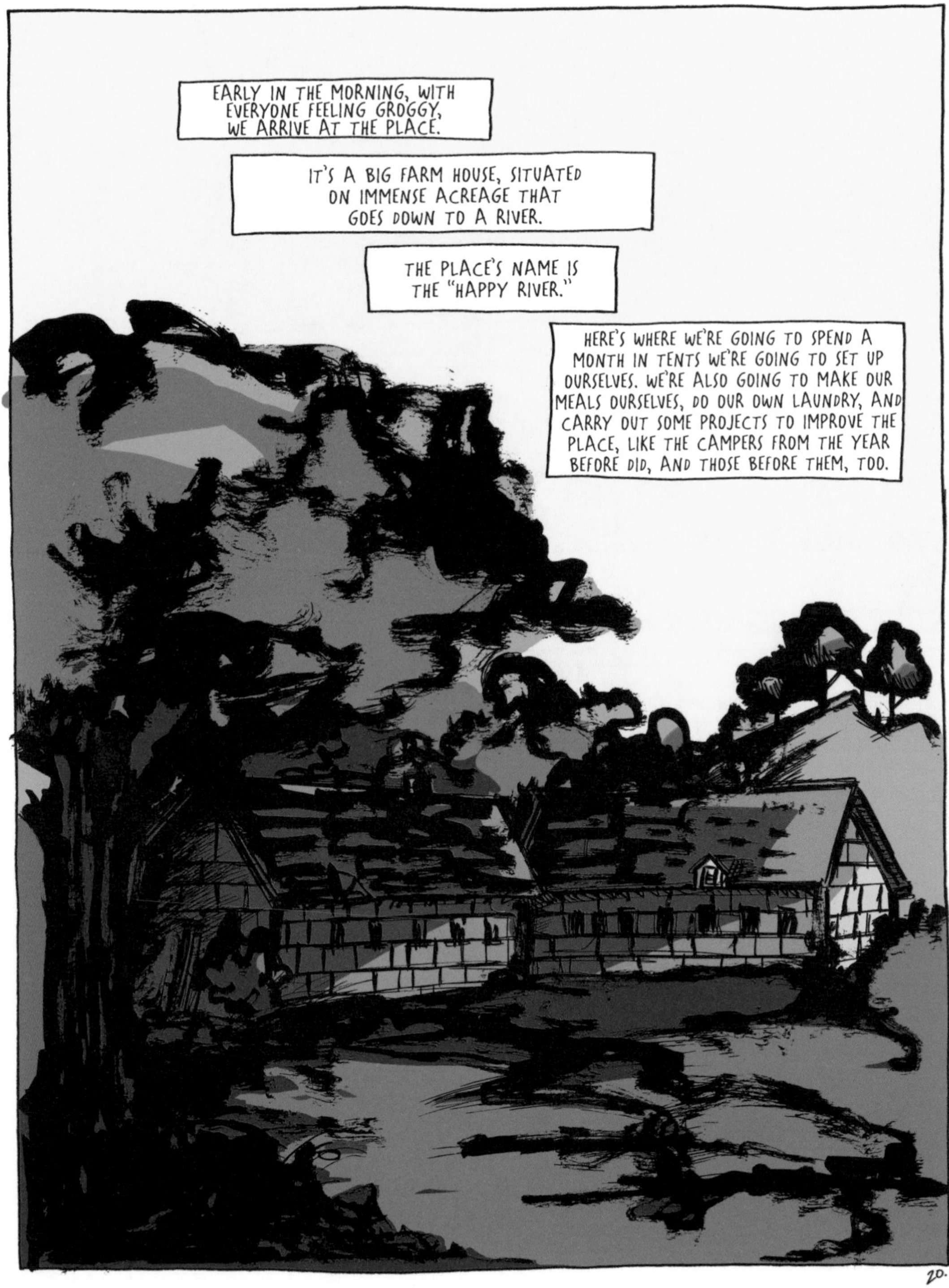
EARLY IN THE MORNING, WITH EVERYONE FEELING GROGGY, WE ARRIVE AT THE PLACE.
IT'S A BIG FARM HOUSE, SITUATED ON IMMENSE ACREAGE THAT GOES DOWN TO A RIVER.
THE PLACE'S NAME IS THE "HAPPY RIVER."
HERE'S WHERE WE'RE GOING TO SPEND A MONTH IN TENTS WE'RE GOING TO SET UP OURSELVES. WE'RE ALSO GOING TO MAKE OUR MEALS OURSELVES, DO OUR OWN LAUNDRY, AND CARRY OUT SOME PROJECTS TO IMPROVE THE PLACE, LIKE THE CAMPERS FROM THE YEAR BEFORE DID, AND THOSE BEFORE THEM, TOO.
20.

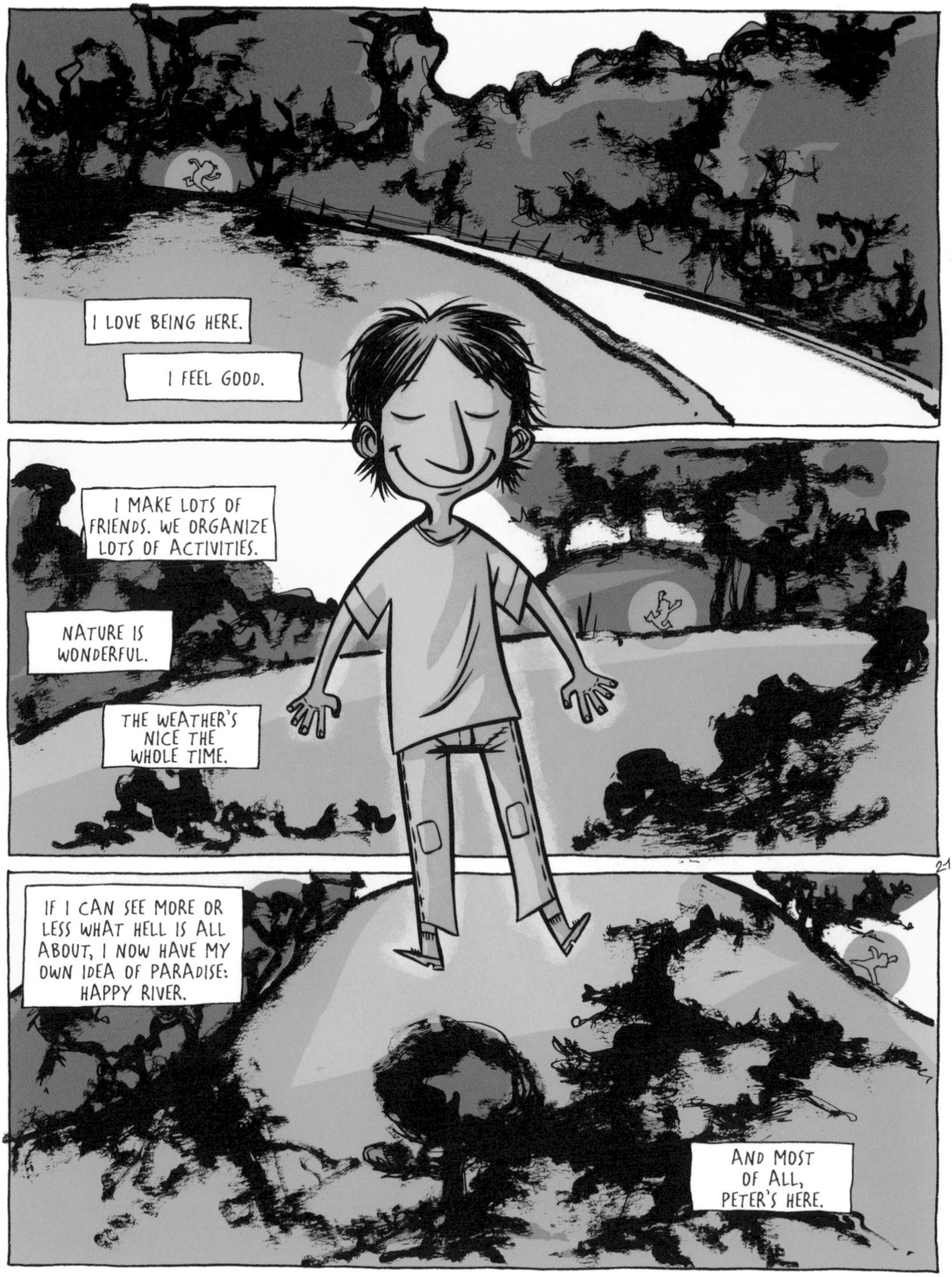
I LOVE BEING HERE.
I FEEL GOOD.
I MAKE LOTS OF FRIENDS. WE ORGANIZE LOTS OF ACTIVITIES.
NATURE IS WONDERFUL.
THE WEATHER'S NICE THE WHOLE TIME.
IF I CAN SEE MORE OR LESS WHAT HELL IS ALL ABOUT, I NOW HAVE MY OWN IDEA OF PARADISE: HAPPY RIVER.
AND MOST OF ALL, PETER'S HERE.

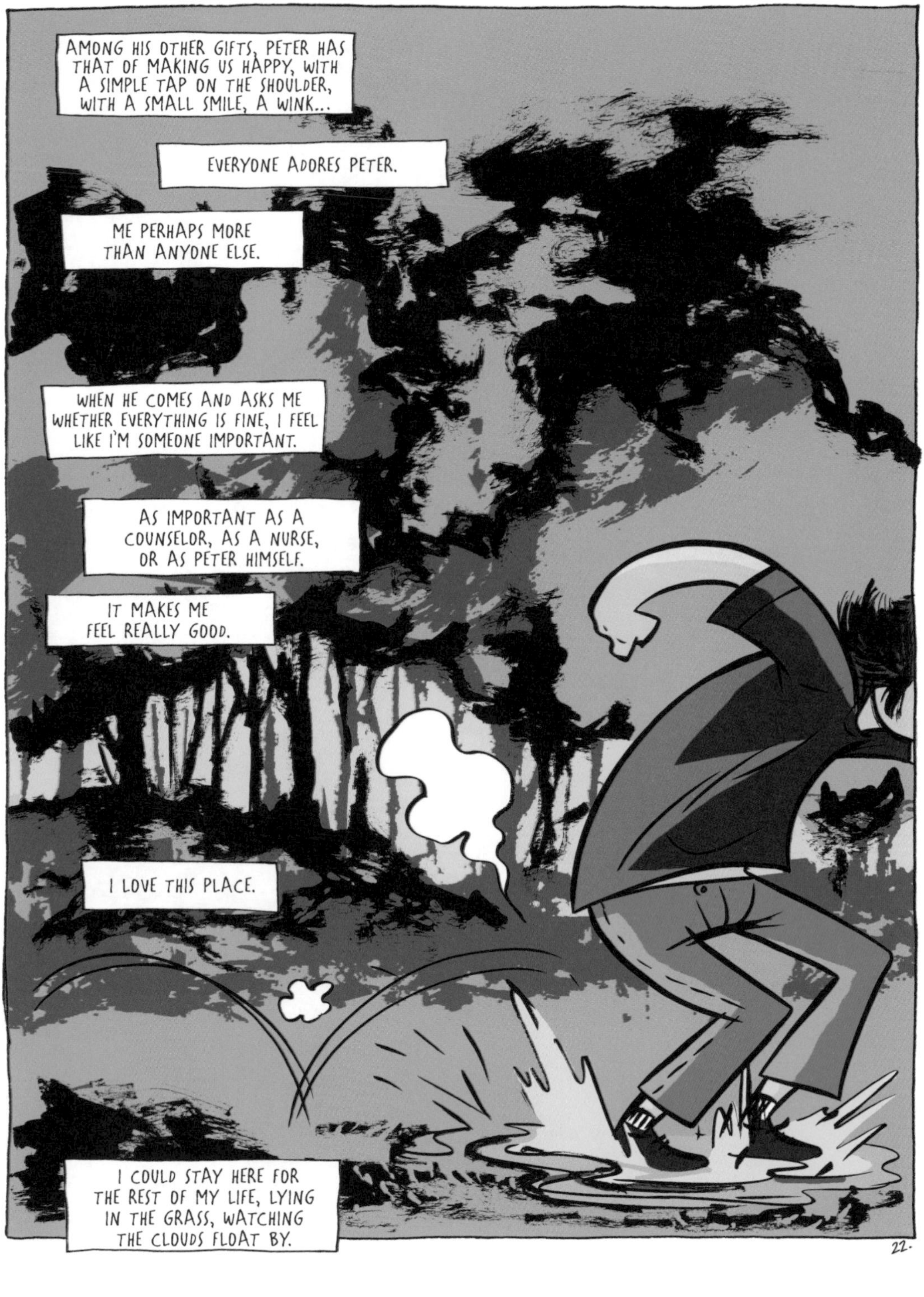
AMONG HIS OTHER GIFTS, PETER HAS THAT OF MAKING US HAPPY, WITH A SIMPLE TAP ON THE SHOULDER, WITH A SMALL SMILE, A WINK...
EVERYONE ADORES PETER.
ME PERHAPS MORE THAN ANYONE ELSE.
WHEN HE COMES AND ASKS ME WHETHER EVERYTHING IS FINE, I FEEL LIKE I'M SOMEONE IMPORTANT.
AS IMPORTANT AS A COUNSELOR, AS A NURSE, OR AS PETER HIMSELF.
IT MAKES ME FEEL REALLY GOOD.
I LOVE THIS PLACE.
I COULD STAY HERE FOR THE REST OF MY LIFE, LYING IN THE GRASS, WATCHING THE CLOUDS FLOAT BY.
22.

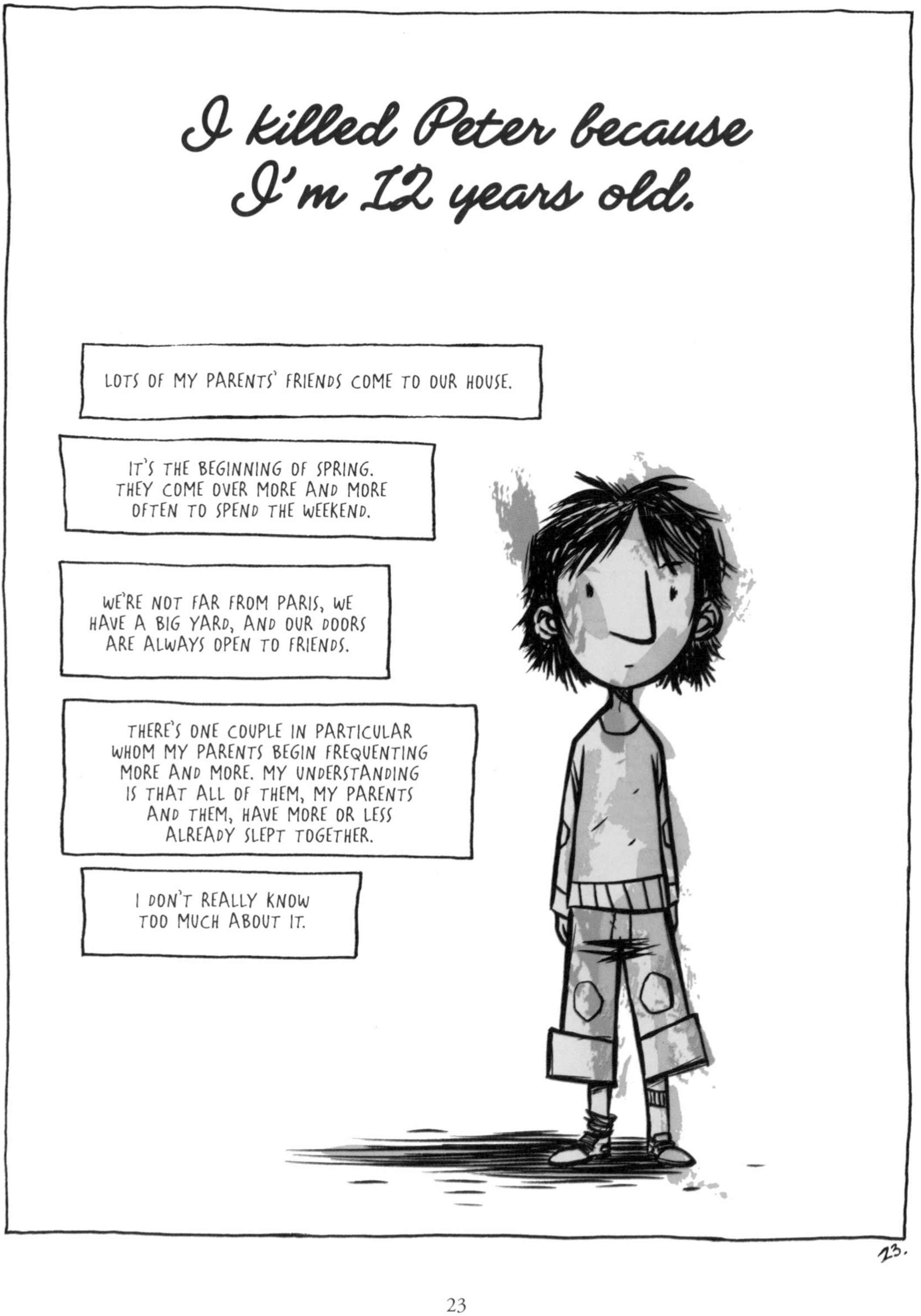
I killed Peter because I'm 12 years old.
LOTS OF MY PARENTS' FRIENDS COME TO OUR HOUSE.
IT'S THE BEGINNING OF SPRING. THEY COME OVER MORE AND MORE OFTEN TO SPEND THE WEEKEND.
WE'RE NOT FAR FROM PARIS, WE HAVE A BIG YARD, AND OUR DOORS ARE ALWAYS OPEN TO FRIENDS.
THERE'S ONE COUPLE IN PARTICULAR WHOM MY PARENTS BEGIN FREQUENTING MORE AND MORE. MY UNDERSTANDING IS THAT ALL OF THEM, MY PARENTS AND THEM, HAVE MORE OR LESS ALREADY SLEPT TOGETHER.
I DON'T REALLY KNOW TOO MUCH ABOUT IT.

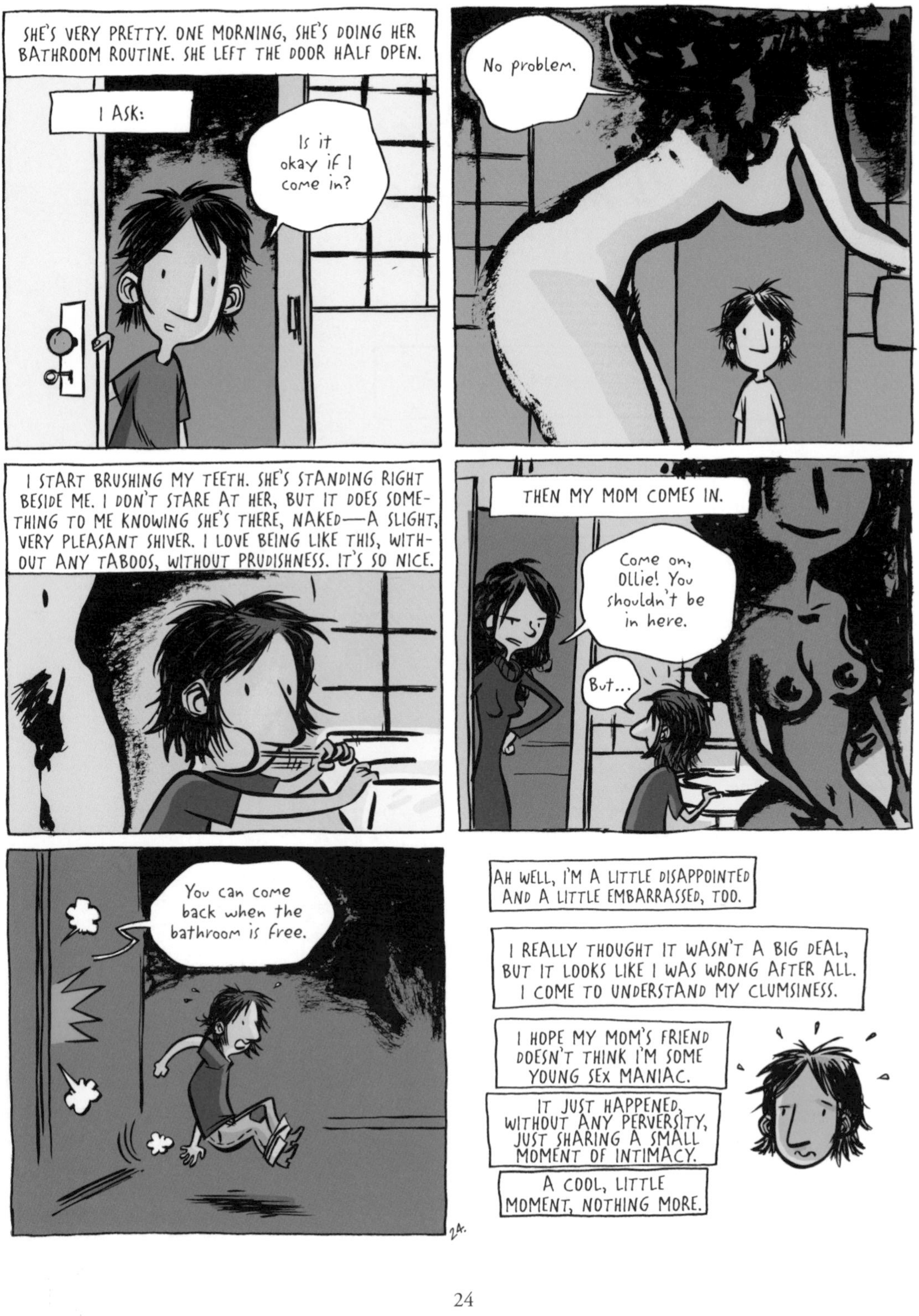
SHE'S VERY PRETTY. ONE MORNING, SHE'S DOING HER BATHROOM ROUTINE. SHE LEFT THE DOOR HALF OPEN.
I ASK:
Is it okay if I come in?
No problem.
I START BRUSHING MY TEETH. SHE'S STANDING RIGHT BESIDE ME. I DON'T STARE AT HER, BUT IT DOES SOMETHING TO ME KNOWING SHE'S THERE, NAKED—A SLIGHT, VERY PLEASANT SHIVER. I LOVE BEING LIKE THIS, WITHOUT ANY TABOOS, WITHOUT PRUDISHNESS. IT'S SO NICE.
THEN MY MOM COMES IN.
Come on, Ollie! You shouldn't be in here.
But...
You can come back when the bathroom is free.
AH WELL, I'M A LITTLE DISAPPOINTED AND A LITTLE EMBARRASSED, TOO.
I REALLY THOUGHT IT WASN'T A BIG DEAL, BUT IT LOOKS LIKE I WAS WRONG AFTER ALL. I COME TO UNDERSTAND MY CLUMSINESS.
I HOPE MY MOM'S FRIEND DOESN'T THINK I'M SOME YOUNG SEX MANIAC.
IT JUST HAPPENED, WITHOUT ANY PERVERSITY, JUST SHARING A SMALL MOMENT OF INTIMACY.
A COOL, LITTLE MOMENT, NOTHING MORE.

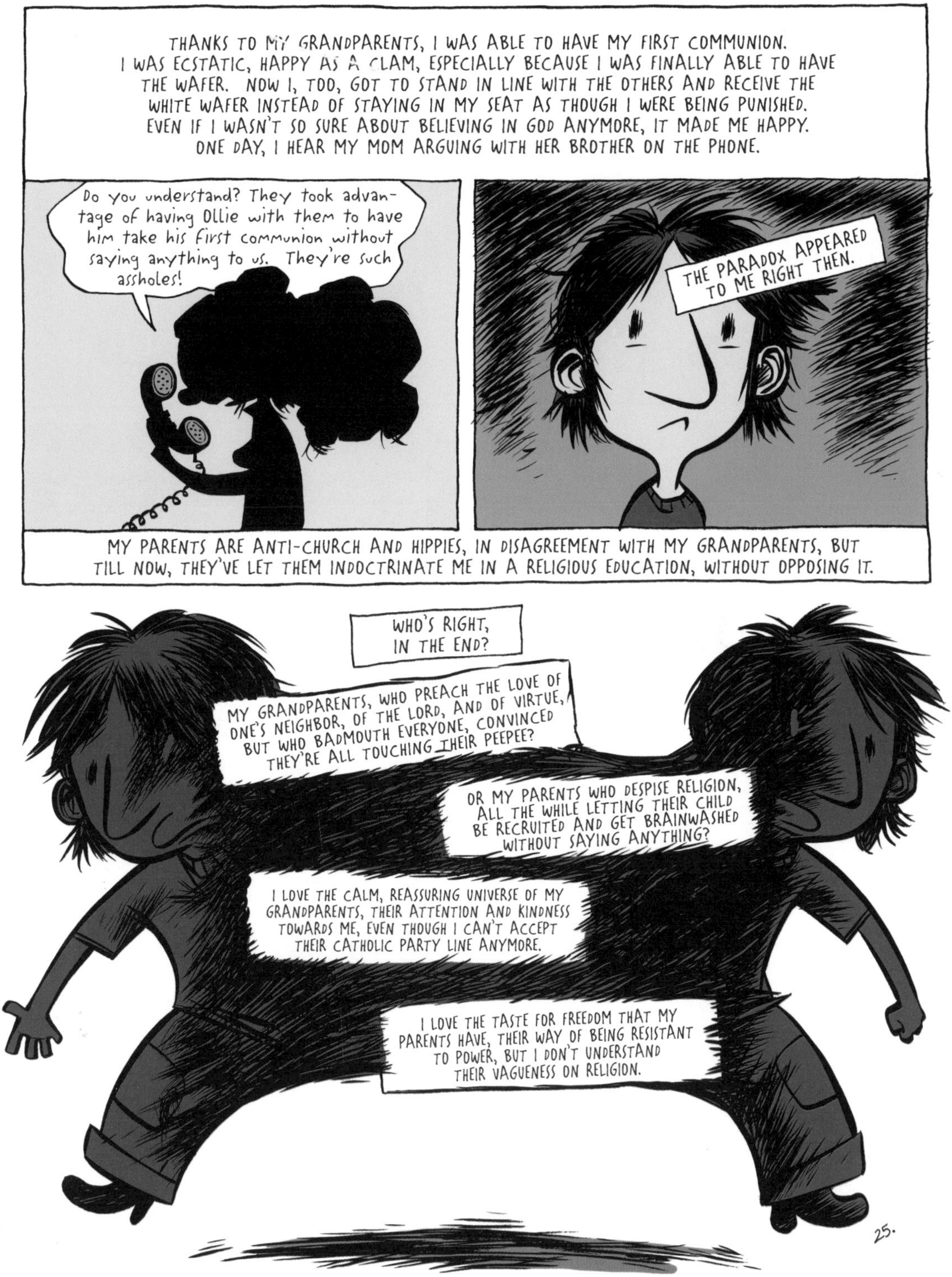
THANKS TO MY GRANDPARENTS, I WAS ABLE TO HAVE MY FIRST COMMUNION. I WAS ECSTATIC, HAPPY AS A CLAM, ESPECIALLY BECAUSE I WAS FINALLY ABLE TO HAVE THE WAFER. NOW I, TOO, GOT TO STAND IN LINE WITH THE OTHERS AND RECEIVE THE WHITE WAFER INSTEAD OF STAYING IN MY SEAT AS THOUGH I WERE BEING PUNISHED. EVEN IF I WASN'T SO SURE ABOUT BELIEVING IN GOD ANYMORE, IT MADE ME HAPPY. ONE DAY, I HEAR MY MOM ARGUING WITH HER BROTHER ON THE PHONE.
Do you understand? They took advantage of having Ollie with them to have him take his first communion without saying anything to us. They're such assholes!
THE PARADOX APPEARED TO ME RIGHT THEN.
MY PARENTS ARE ANTI-CHURCH AND HIPPIES, IN DISAGREEMENT WITH MY GRANDPARENTS, BUT TILL NOW, THEY'VE LET THEM INDOCTRINATE ME IN A RELIGIOUS EDUCATION, WITHOUT OPPOSING IT.
WHO'S RIGHT, IN THE END?
MY GRANDPARENTS, WHO PREACH THE LOVE OF ONE'S NEIGHBOR, OF THE LORD, AND OF VIRTUE, BUT WHO BADMOUTH EVERYONE, CONVINCED THEY'RE ALL TOUCHING THEIR PEEPEE?
OR MY PARENTS WHO DESPISE RELIGION, ALL THE WHILE LETTING THEIR CHILD BE RECRUITED AND GET BRAINWASHED WITHOUT SAYING ANYTHING?
I LOVE THE CALM, REASSURING UNIVERSE OF MY GRANDPARENTS, THEIR ATTENTION AND KINDNESS TOWARDS ME, EVEN THOUGH I CAN'T ACCEPT THEIR CATHOLIC PARTY LINE ANYMORE.
I LOVE THE TASTE FOR FREEDOM THAT MY PARENTS HAVE, THEIR WAY OF BEING RESISTANT TO POWER, BUT I DON'T UNDERSTAND THEIR VAGUENESS ON RELIGION.
25.

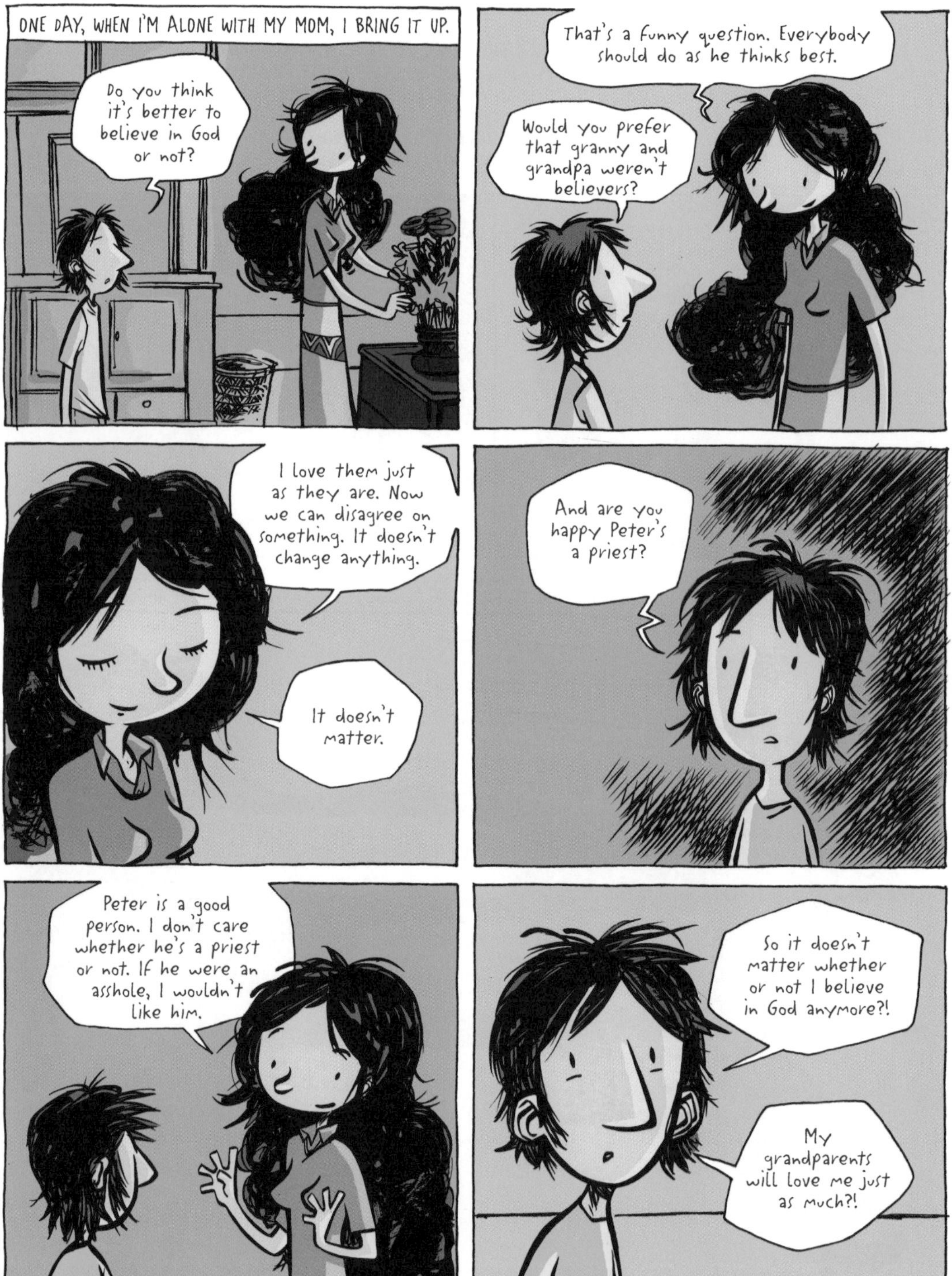
ONE DAY, WHEN I'M ALONE WITH MY MOM, I BRING IT UP.
Do you think it's better to believe in God or not?
That's a funny question. Everybody should do as he thinks best.
Would you prefer that granny and grandpa weren't believers?
I love them just as they are. Now we can disagree on something. It doesn't change anything.
It doesn't matter.
And are you happy Peter's a priest?
Peter is a good person. I don't care whether he's a priest or not. If he were an asshole, I wouldn't like him.
So it doesn't matter whether or not I believe in God anymore?!
My grandparents will love me just as much?!
26.

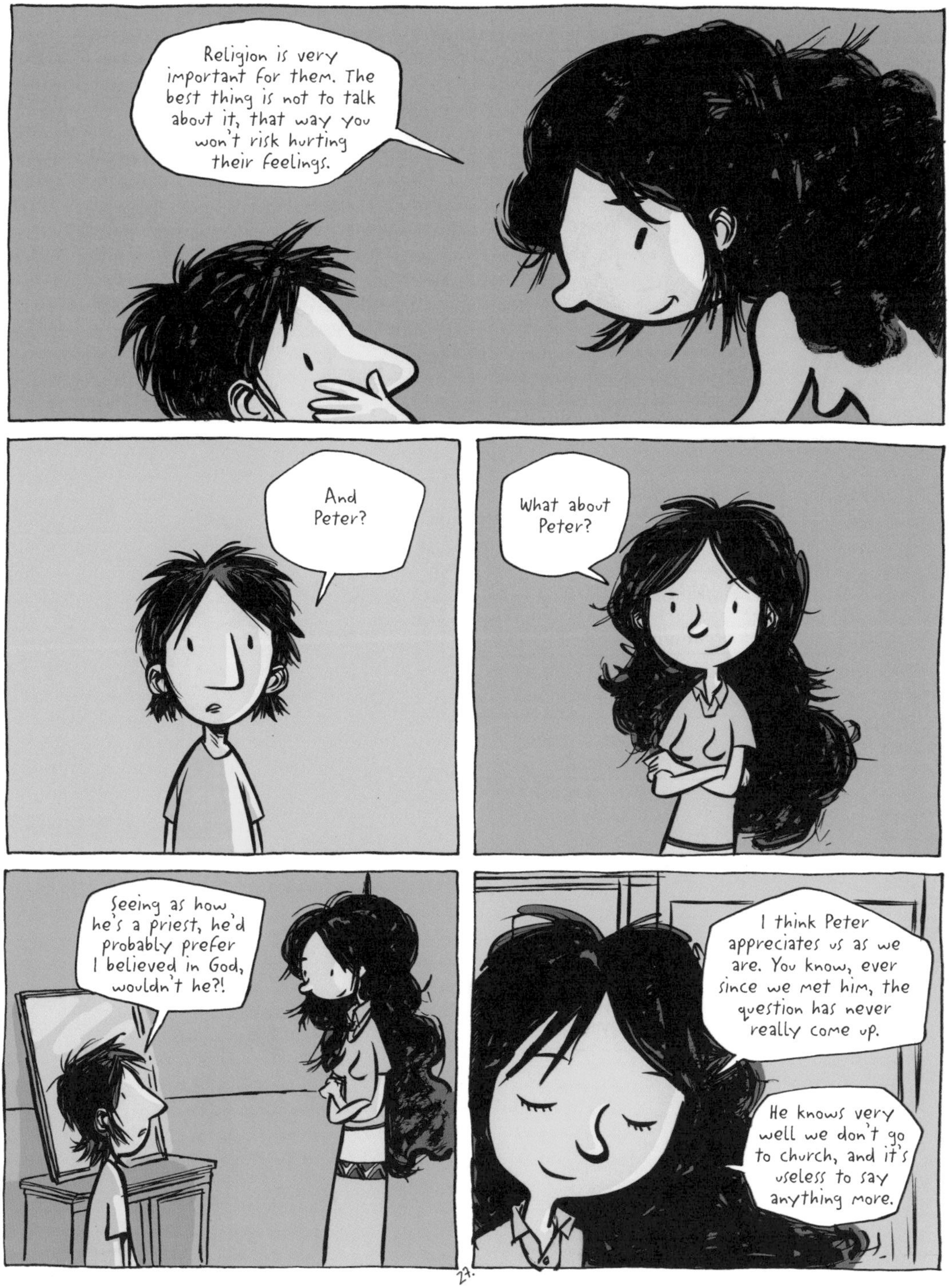
Religion is very important for them. The best thing is not to talk about it, that way you won't risk hurting their feelings.
And Peter?
What about Peter?
Seeing as how he's a priest, he'd probably prefer I believed in God, wouldn't he?!
I think Peter appreciates us as we are. You know, ever since we met him, the question has never really come up.
He knows very well we don't go to church, and it's useless to say anything more.

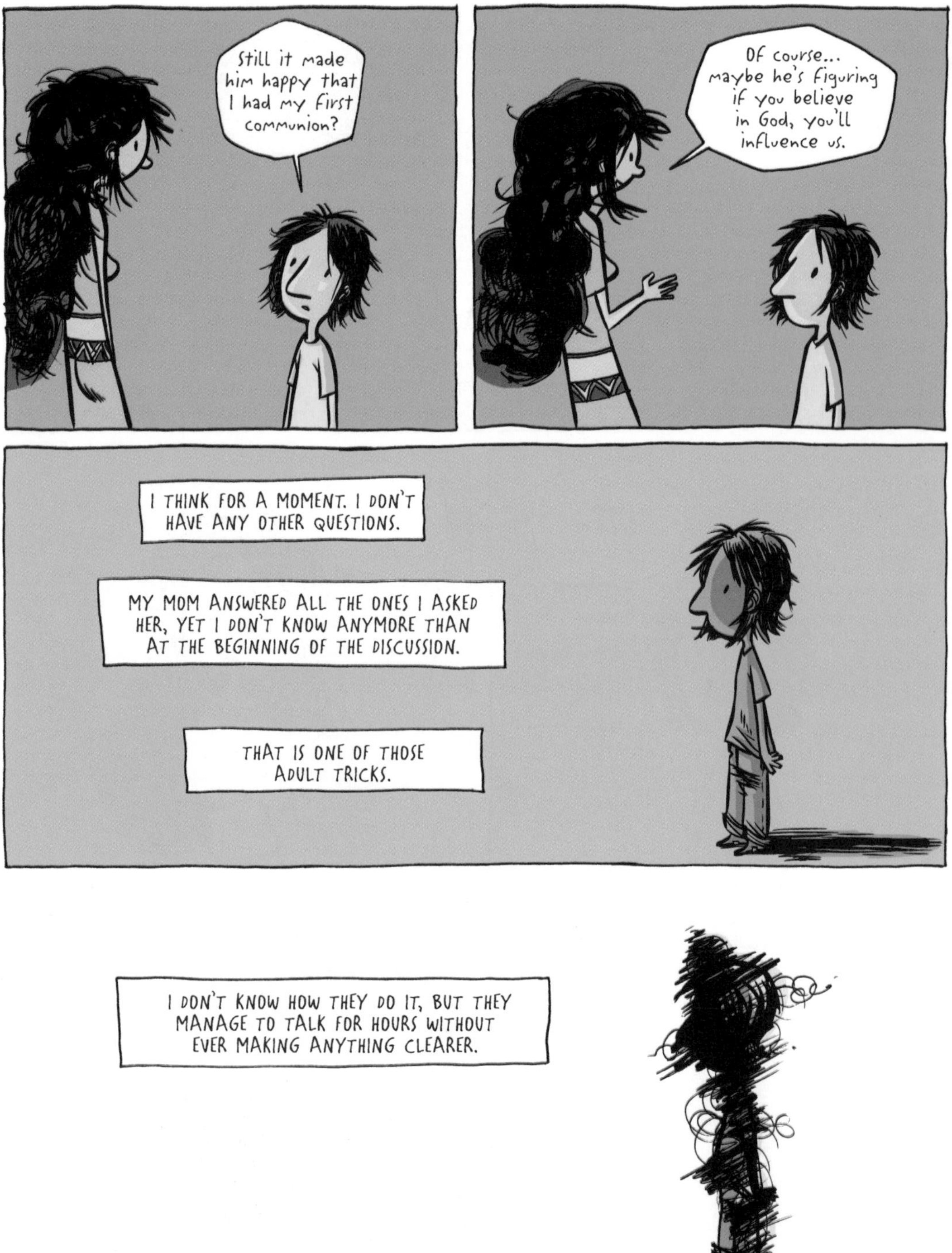
Still it made him happy that I had my first communion?
Of course... maybe he's figuring if you believe in God, you'll influence us.
I THINK FOR A MOMENT. I DON'T HAVE ANY OTHER QUESTIONS.
MY MOM ANSWERED ALL THE ONES I ASKED HER, YET I DON'T KNOW ANYMORE THAN AT THE BEGINNING OF THE DISCUSSION.
THAT IS ONE OF THOSE ADULT TRICKS.
I DON'T KNOW HOW THEY DO IT, BUT THEY MANAGE TO TALK FOR HOURS WITHOUT EVER MAKING ANYTHING CLEARER.
28.

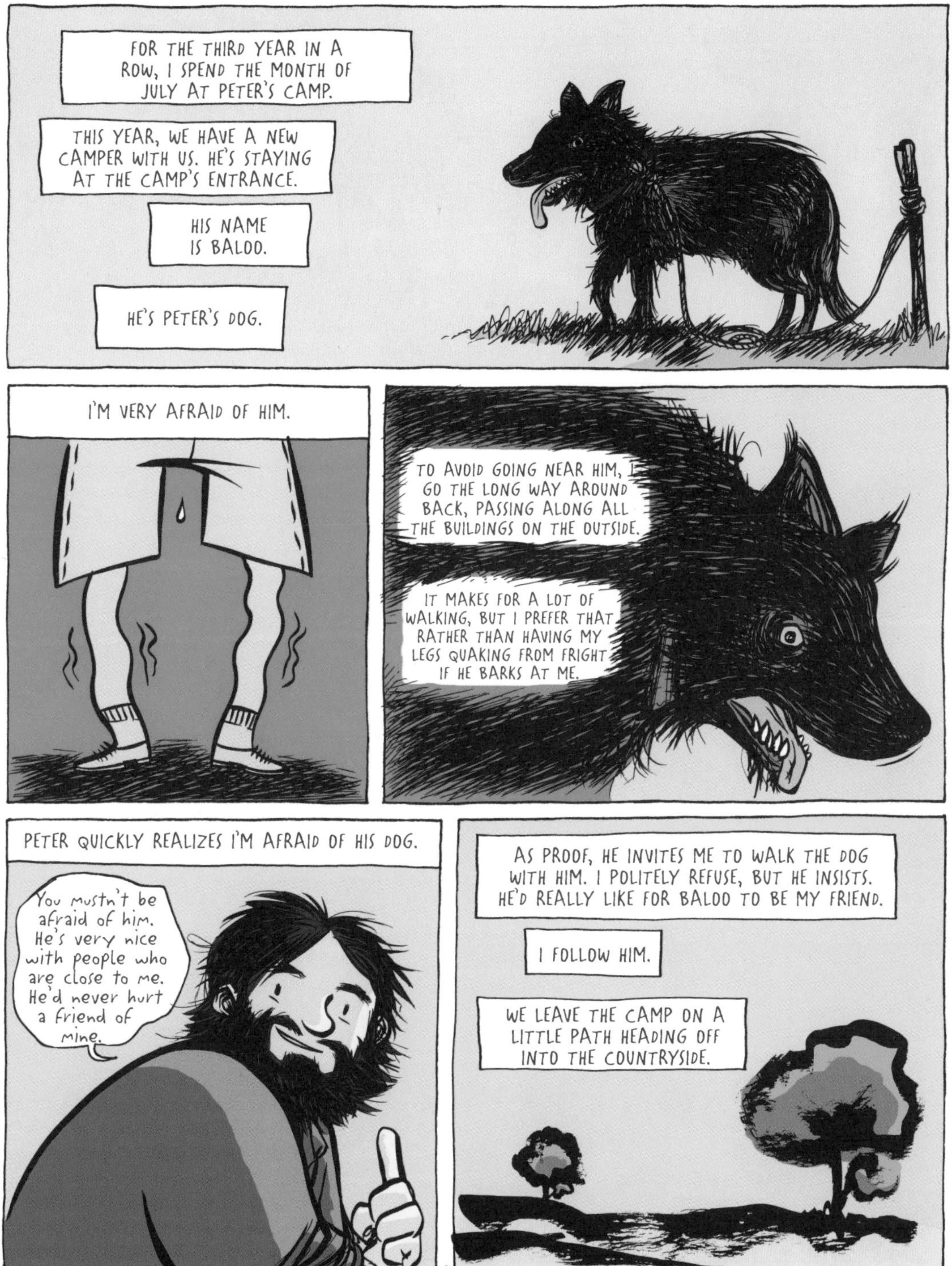
FOR THE THIRD YEAR IN A ROW, I SPEND THE MONTH OF JULY AT PETER'S CAMP.
THIS YEAR, WE HAVE A NEW CAMPER WITH US. HE'S STAYING AT THE CAMP'S ENTRANCE.
HIS NAME IS BALOO.
HE'S PETER'S DOG.
I'M VERY AFRAID OF HIM.
TO AVOID GOING NEAR HIM, I GO THE LONG WAY AROUND BACK, PASSING ALONG ALL THE BUILDINGS ON THE OUTSIDE.
IT MAKES FOR A LOT OF WALKING, BUT I PREFER THAT RATHER THAN HAVING MY LEGS QUAKING FROM FRIGHT IF HE BARKS AT ME.
PETER QUICKLY REALIZES I'M AFRAID OF HIS DOG.
You mustn't be afraid of him. He's very nice with people who are close to me. He'd never hurt a friend of mine.
AS PROOF, HE INVITES ME TO WALK THE DOG WITH HIM. I POLITELY REFUSE, BUT HE INSISTS. HE'D REALLY LIKE FOR BALOO TO BE MY FRIEND.
I FOLLOW HIM.
WE LEAVE THE CAMP ON A LITTLE PATH HEADING OFF INTO THE COUNTRYSIDE.
29

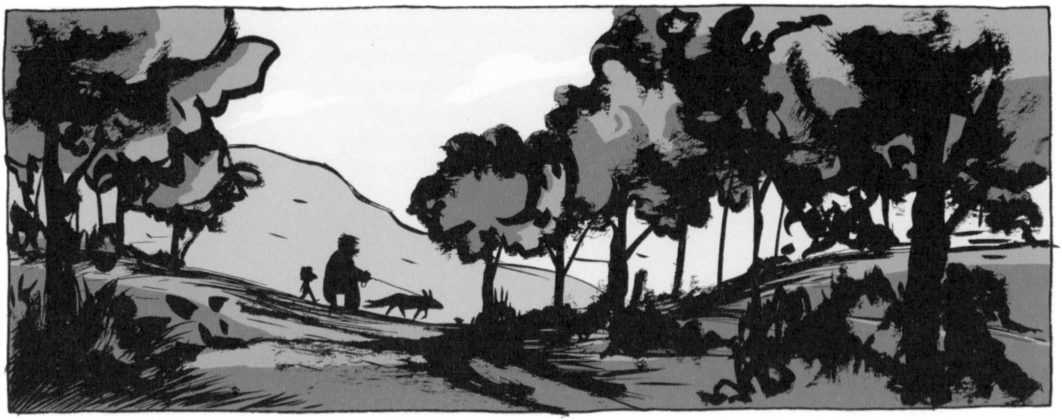

I WALK ALONGSIDE PETER, WATCHING THE ANIMAL OUT OF THE CORNER OF MY EYE.
PETER'S HOLDING HIM ON A LEASH. AFTER A WHILE, HE HANDS ME THE LEASH.
MY STOMACH'S IN KNOTS. IF BALOO TEARS OFF, I'D FLY AWAY LIKE A GLIDER! BUT HE DOESN'T.

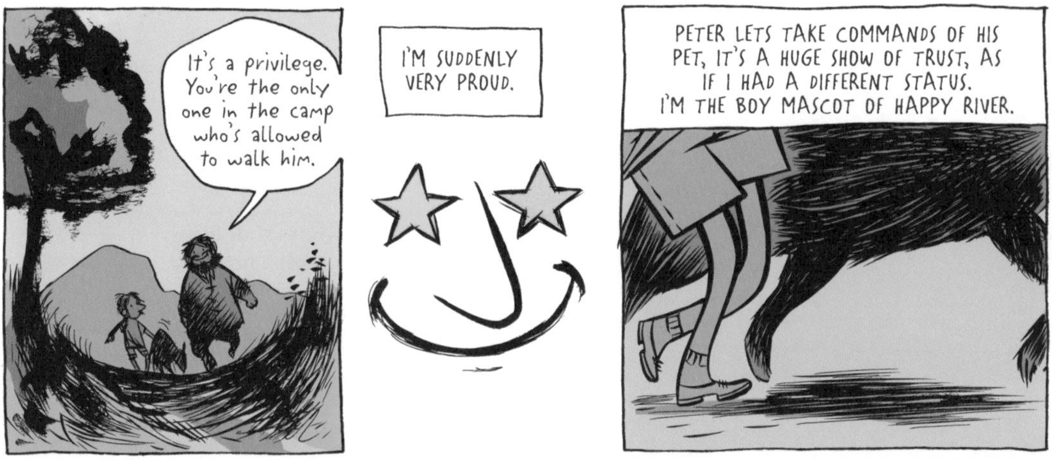
It's a privilege. You're the only one in the camp who's allowed to walk him.
I'M SUDDENLY VERY PROUD.
PETER LETS TAKE COMMANDS OF HIS PET, IT'S A HUGE SHOW OF TRUST, AS IF I HAD A DIFFERENT STATUS. I'M THE BOY MASCOT OF HAPPY RIVER.

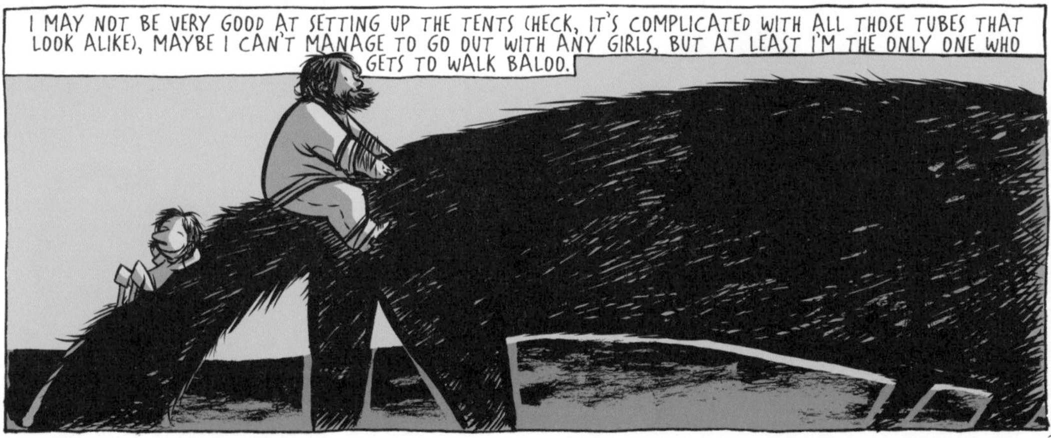
I MAY NOT BE VERY GOOD AT SETTING UP THE TENTS (HECK, IT'S COMPLICATED WITH ALL THOSE TUBES THAT LOOK ALIKE), MAYBE I CAN'T MANAGE TO GO OUT WITH ANY GIRLS, BUT AT LEAST I'M THE ONLY ONE WHO GETS TO WALK BALOO.

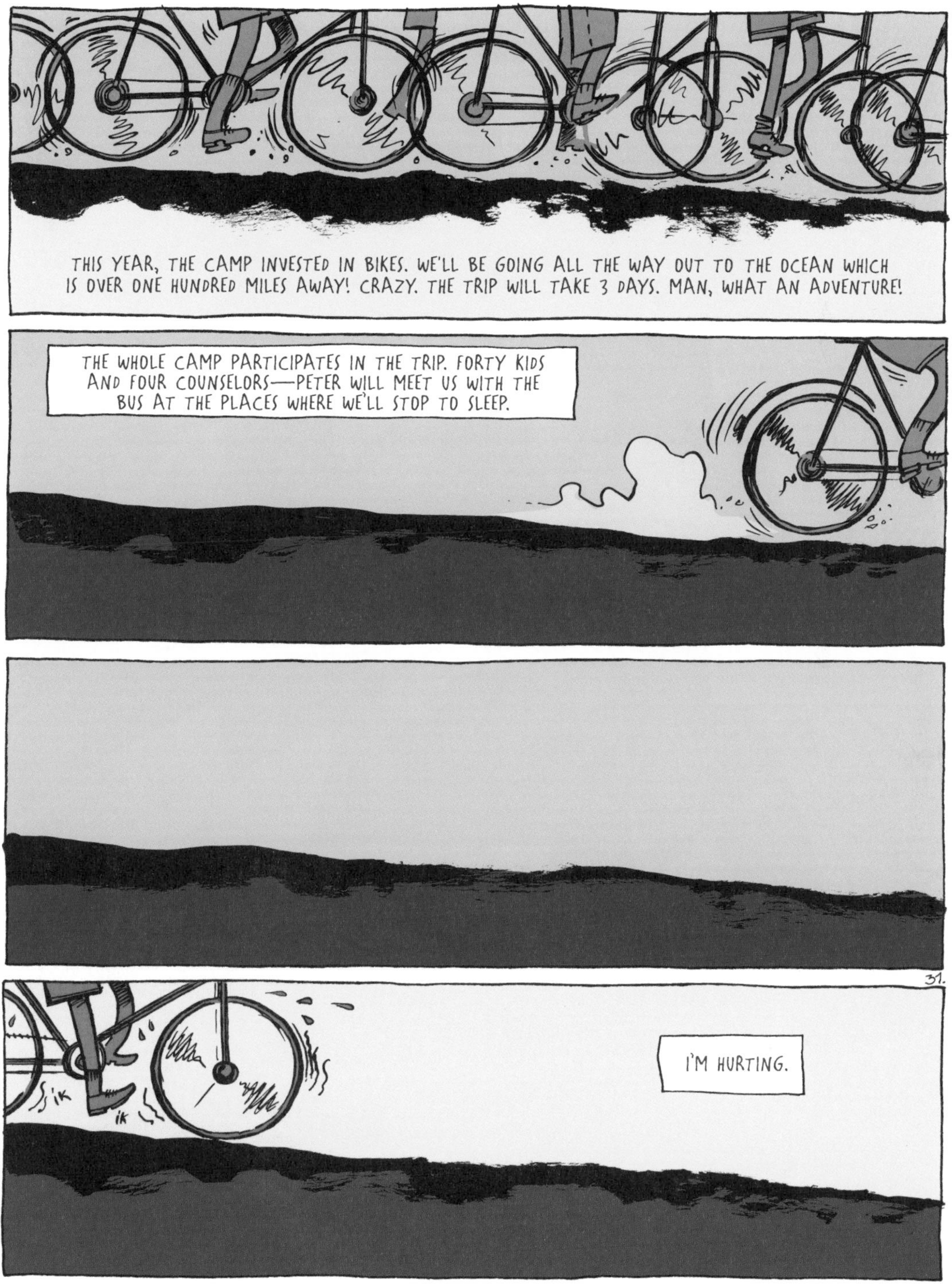
THIS YEAR, THE CAMP INVESTED IN BIKES. WE'LL BE GOING ALL THE WAY OUT TO THE OCEAN WHICH IS OVER ONE HUNDRED MILES AWAY! CRAZY. THE TRIP WILL TAKE 3 DAYS. MAN, WHAT AN ADVENTURE!
THE WHOLE CAMP PARTICIPATES IN THE TRIP. FORTY KIDS AND FOUR COUNSELORS—PETER WILL MEET US WITH THE BUS AT THE PLACES WHERE WE'LL STOP TO SLEEP.
31.
I'M HURTING.

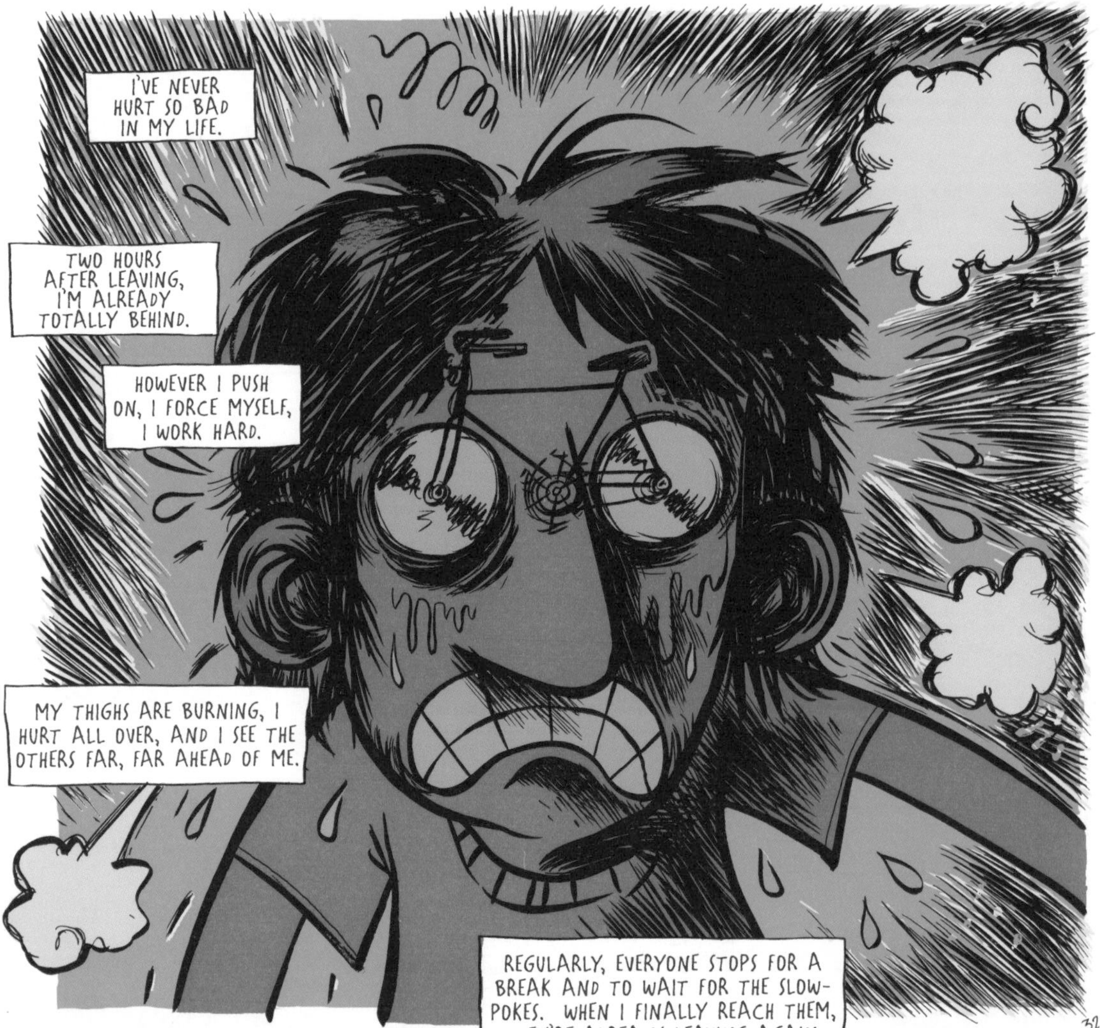
I'VE NEVER HURT SO BAD IN MY LIFE.
TWO HOURS AFTER LEAVING, I'M ALREADY TOTALLY BEHIND.
HOWEVER I PUSH ON, I FORCE MYSELF, I WORK HARD.
MY THIGHS ARE BURNING, I HURT ALL OVER, AND I SEE THE OTHERS FAR, FAR AHEAD OF ME.
REGULARLY, EVERYONE STOPS FOR A BREAK AND TO WAIT FOR THE SLOW-POKES. WHEN I FINALLY REACH THEM, THEY'RE ALREADY LEAVING AGAIN.
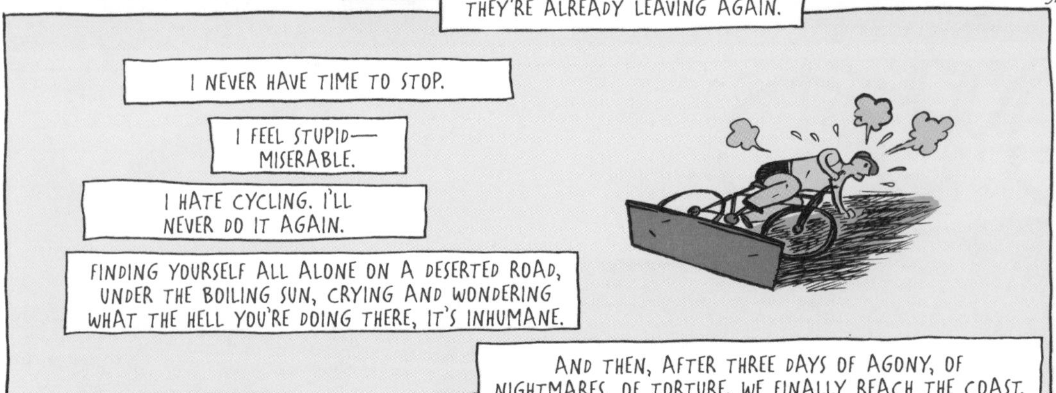
I NEVER HAVE TIME TO STOP.
I FEEL STUPID—MISERABLE.
I HATE CYCLING. I'LL NEVER DO IT AGAIN.
FINDING YOURSELF ALL ALONE ON A DESERTED ROAD, UNDER THE BOILING SUN, CRYING AND WONDERING WHAT THE HELL YOU'RE DOING THERE, IT'S INHUMANE.
AND THEN, AFTER THREE DAYS OF AGONY, OF NIGHTMARES, OF TORTURE, WE FINALLY REACH THE COAST.

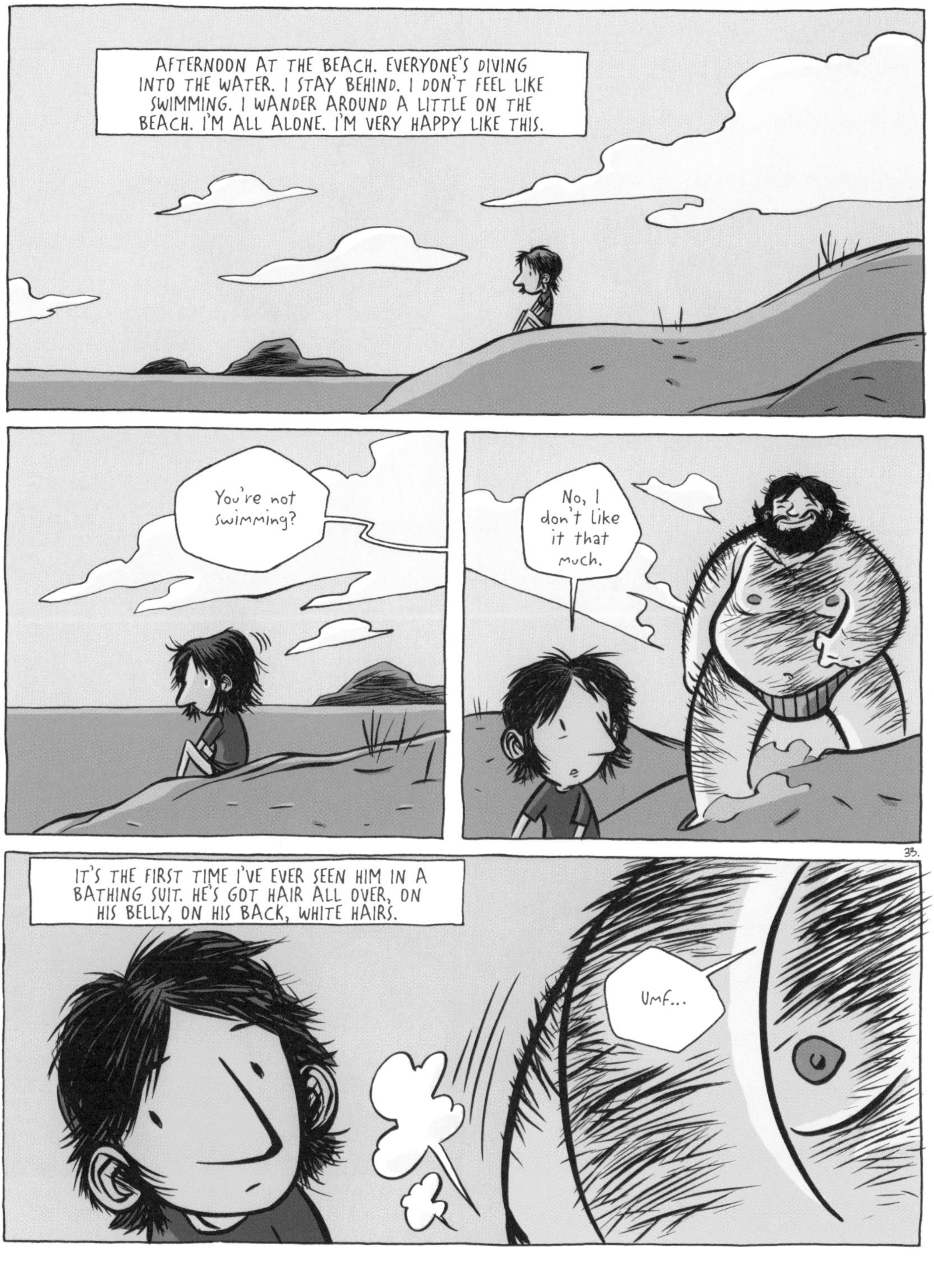
AFTERNOON AT THE BEACH. EVERYONE'S DIVING INTO THE WATER. I STAY BEHIND. I DON'T FEEL LIKE SWIMMING. I WANDER AROUND A LITTLE ON THE BEACH. I'M ALL ALONE. I'M VERY HAPPY LIKE THIS.
You're not swimming?
No, I don't like it that much.
33.
IT'S THE FIRST TIME I'VE EVER SEEN HIM IN A BATHING SUIT. HE'S GOT HAIR ALL OVER, ON HIS BELLY, ON HIS BACK, WHITE HAIRS.
Umf...

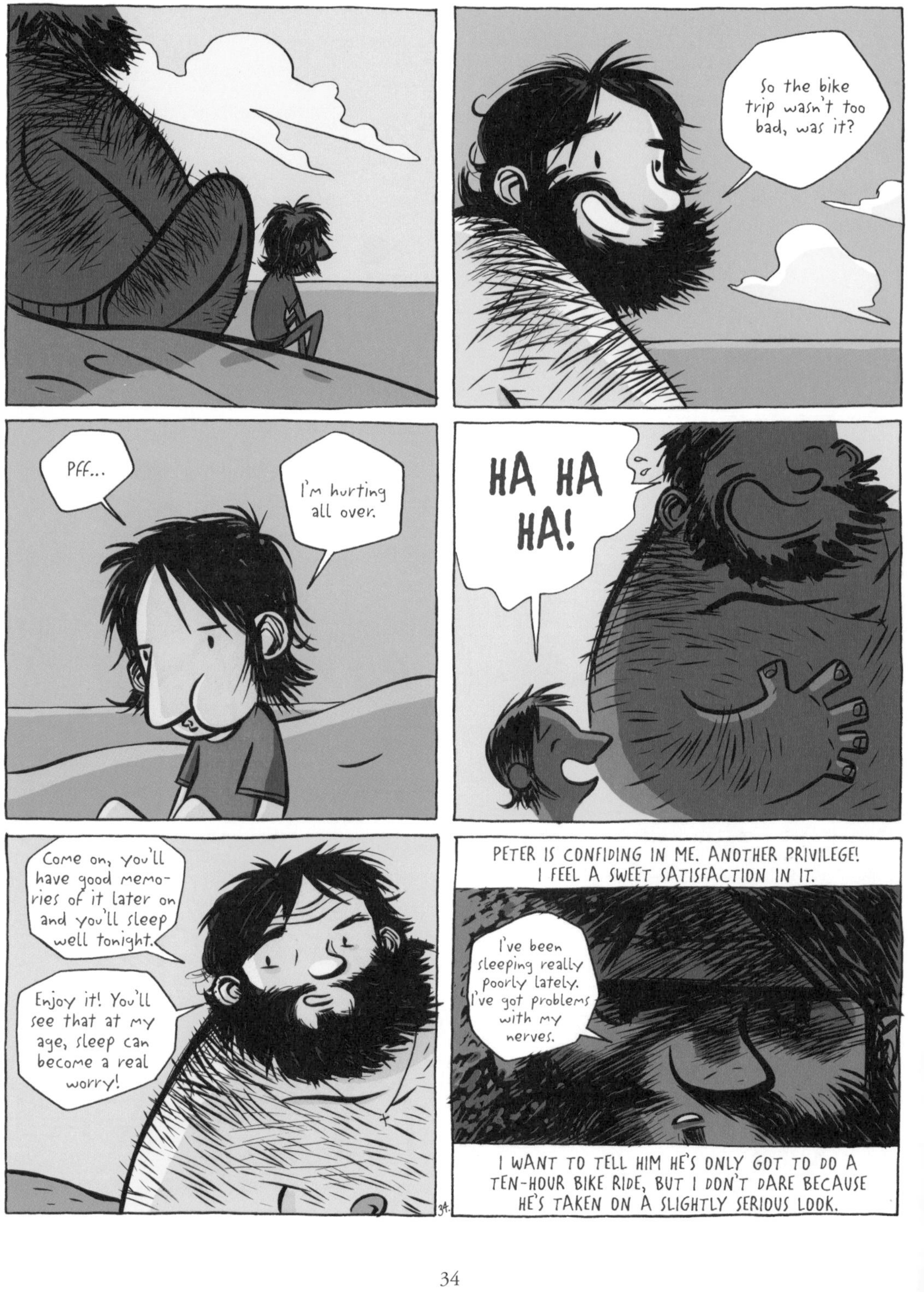
So the bike trip wasn't too bad, was it?
Pff...
I'm hurting all over.
HA HA HA!
Come on, you'll have good memories of it later on and you'll sleep well tonight.
Enjoy it! You'll see that at my age, sleep can become a real worry!
PETER IS CONFIDING IN ME. ANOTHER PRIVILEGE! I FEEL A SWEET SATISFACTION IN IT.
I've been sleeping really poorly lately. I've got problems with my nerves.
I WANT TO TELL HIM HE'S ONLY GOT TO DO A TEN-HOUR BIKE RIDE, BUT I DON'T DARE BECAUSE HE'S TAKEN ON A SLIGHTLY SERIOUS LOOK.
34.

It's annoying, really. I'm tired all the time. It's not very fun.

IT'S TRUE THAT HE LOOKS TIRED. IN PREVIOUS YEARS, HE PLAYED AROUND MORE, HE HAD MORE ENERGY. I FEEL LIKE SAYING SOMETHING NICE TO HIM, BUT NOTHING COMES TO ME. SO I SAY:

Yeah...

Still, it's great to be able to come here, don't you think?

Yeah, it's cool.

Ah, if only I could sleep, it would be perfect,

Mm...

Do you know what they do to babies to help them fall asleep?

...?

They sing a lullaby to them?

Haha! Yes, that's right! But the best way is to rub their belly.

And it's the same thing for adults.

In fact, someone ought to rub my belly at night, just before going to sleep. It would do me a world of good.

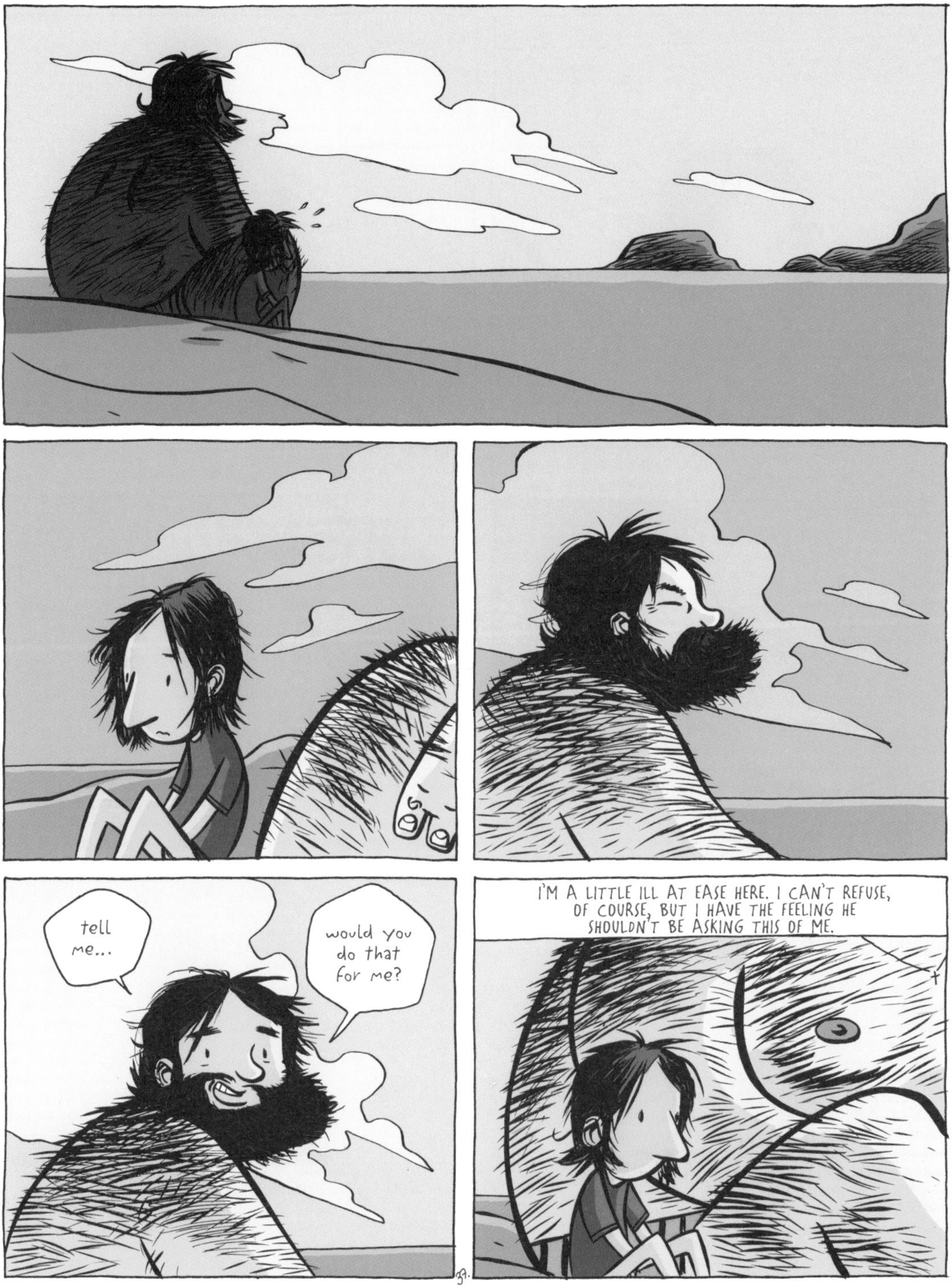
tell me...
would you do that for me?
I'M A LITTLE ILL AT EASE HERE. I CAN'T REFUSE, OF COURSE, BUT I HAVE THE FEELING HE SHOULDN'T BE ASKING THIS OF ME.

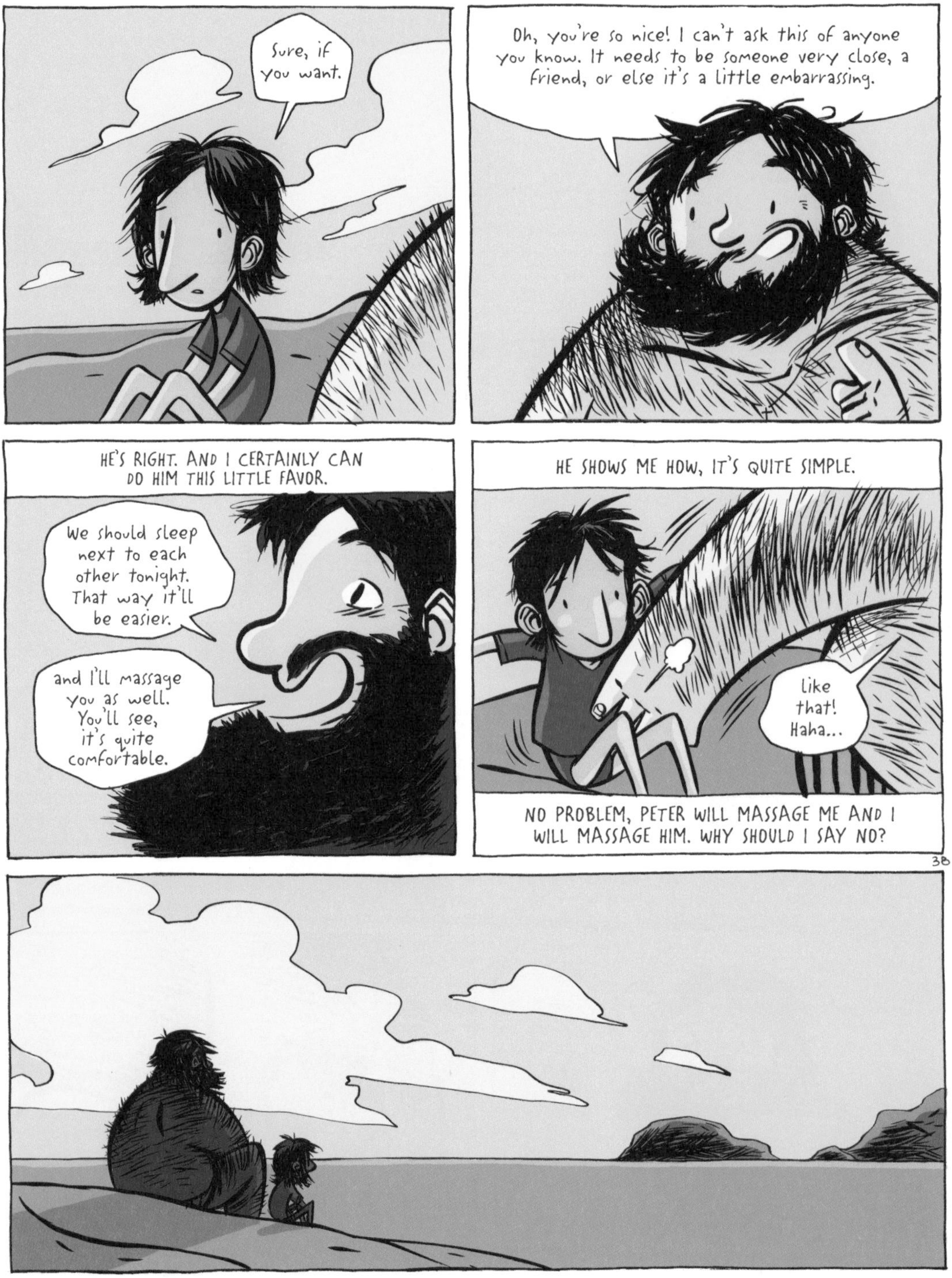
Sure, if you want.
Oh, you're so nice! I can't ask this of anyone you know. It needs to be someone very close, a friend, or else it's a little embarrassing.
HE'S RIGHT. AND I CERTAINLY CAN DO HIM THIS LITTLE FAVOR.
We should sleep next to each other tonight. That way it'll be easier.
and I'll massage you as well. You'll see, it's quite comfortable.
HE SHOWS ME HOW, IT'S QUITE SIMPLE.
Like that! Haha...
NO PROBLEM, PETER WILL MASSAGE ME AND I WILL MASSAGE HIM. WHY SHOULD I SAY NO?
38

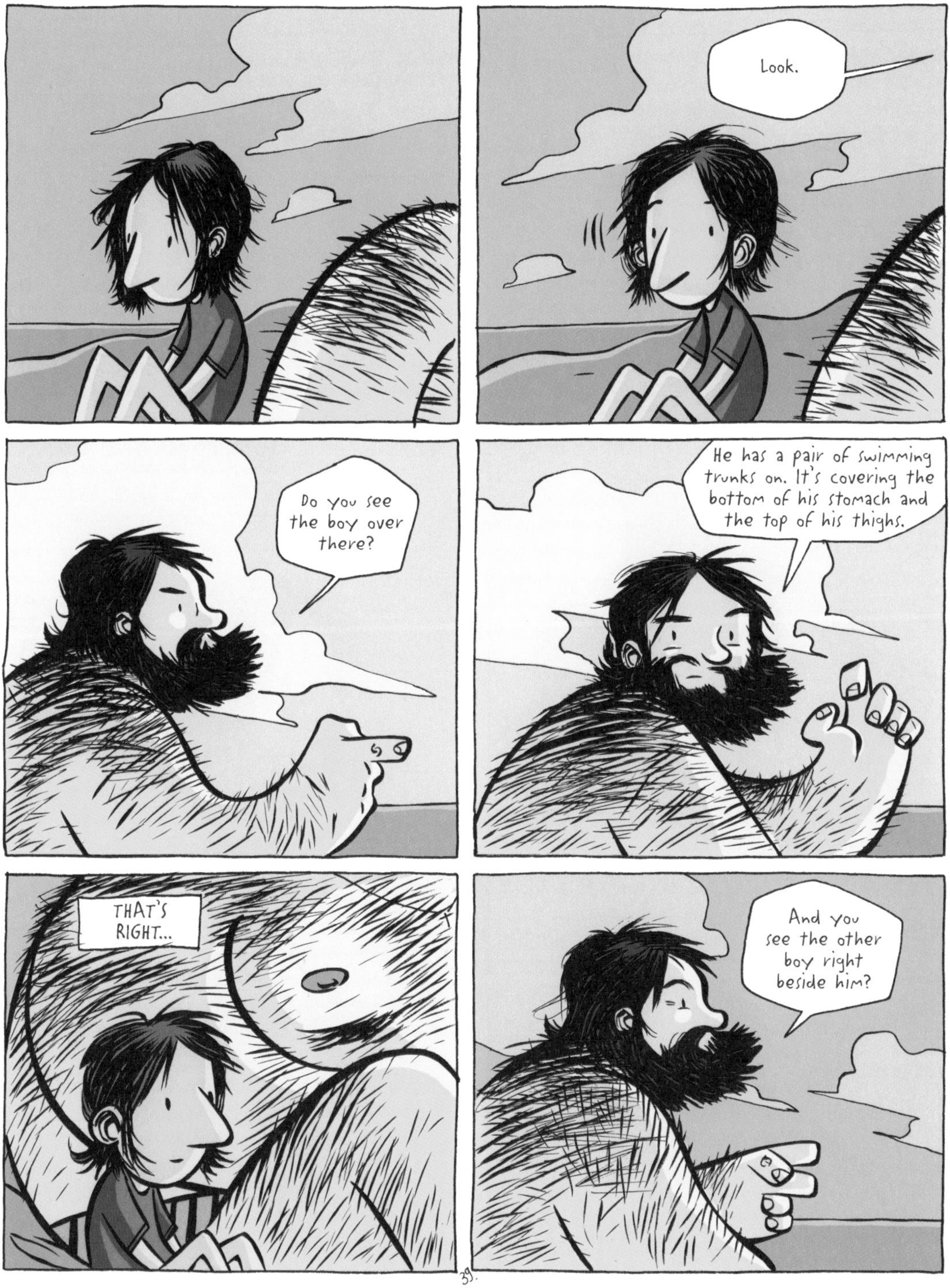
Look.
Do you see the boy over there?
He has a pair of swimming trunks on. It's covering the bottom of his stomach and the top of his thighs.
THAT'S RIGHT...
And you see the other boy right beside him?
39.

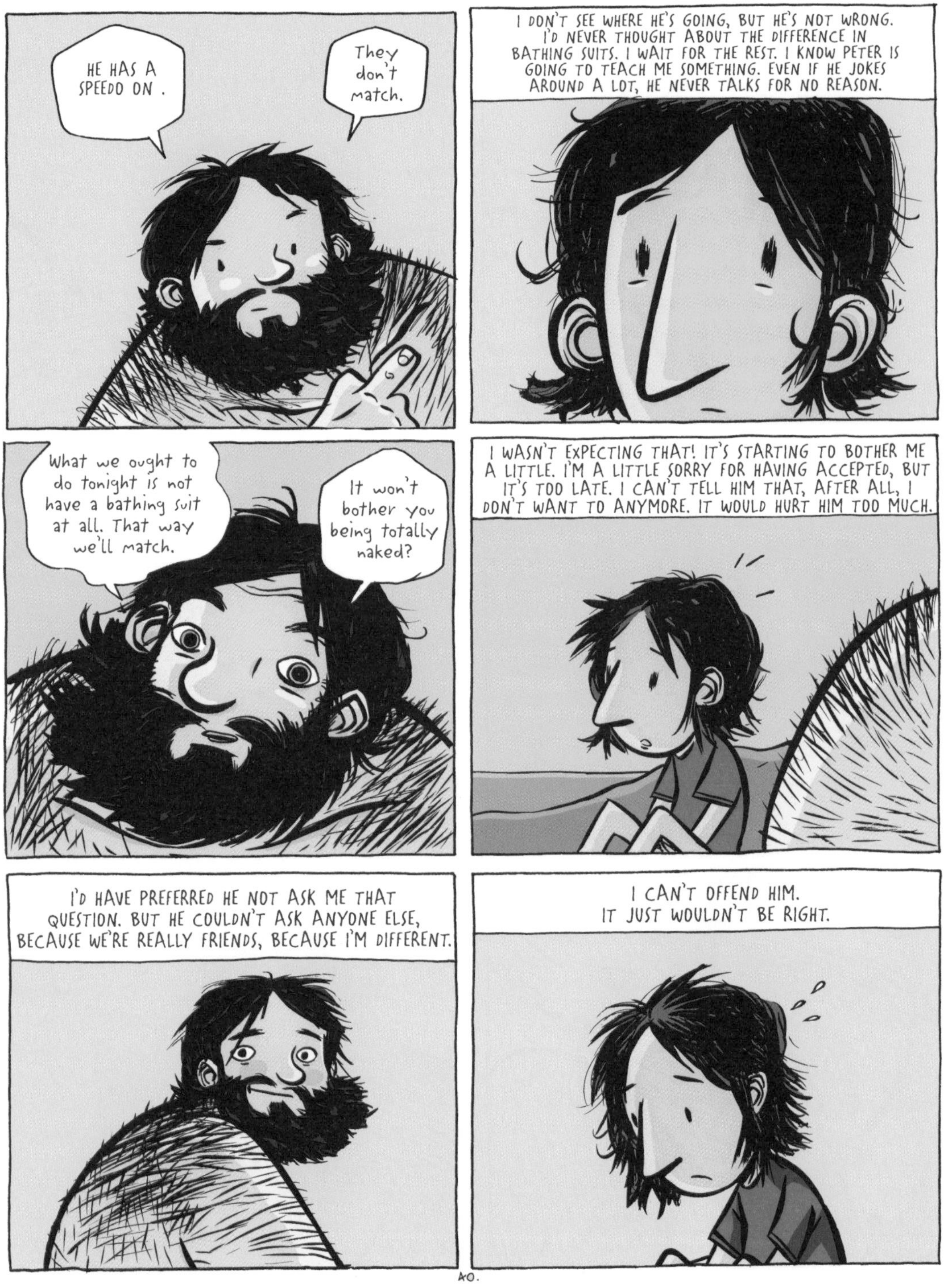
HE HAS A SPEEDO ON .
They don't match.
I DON'T SEE WHERE HE'S GOING, BUT HE'S NOT WRONG. I'D NEVER THOUGHT ABOUT THE DIFFERENCE IN BATHING SUITS. I WAIT FOR THE REST. I KNOW PETER IS GOING TO TEACH ME SOMETHING. EVEN IF HE JOKES AROUND A LOT, HE NEVER TALKS FOR NO REASON.
What we ought to do tonight is not have a bathing suit at all. That way we'll match.
It won't bother you being totally naked?
I WASN'T EXPECTING THAT! IT'S STARTING TO BOTHER ME A LITTLE. I'M A LITTLE SORRY FOR HAVING ACCEPTED, BUT IT'S TOO LATE. I CAN'T TELL HIM THAT, AFTER ALL, I DON'T WANT TO ANYMORE. IT WOULD HURT HIM TOO MUCH.
I'D HAVE PREFERRED HE NOT ASK ME THAT QUESTION. BUT HE COULDN'T ASK ANYONE ELSE, BECAUSE WE'RE REALLY FRIENDS, BECAUSE I'M DIFFERENT.
I CAN'T OFFEND HIM. IT JUST WOULDN'T BE RIGHT.
40.

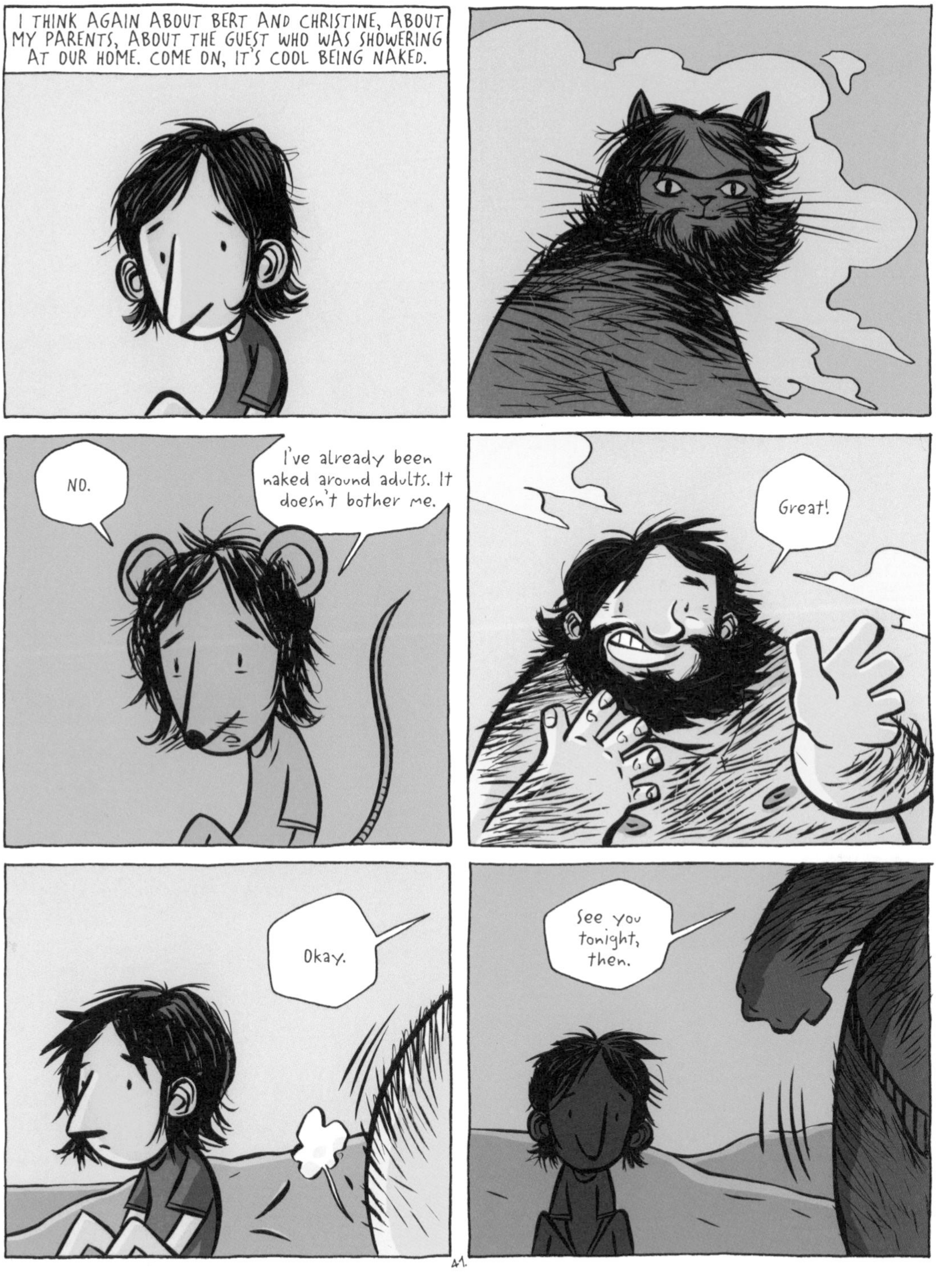

I THINK AGAIN ABOUT BERT AND CHRISTINE, ABOUT MY PARENTS, ABOUT THE GUEST WHO WAS SHOWERING AT OUR HOME. COME ON, IT'S COOL BEING NAKED.
NO.
I've already been naked around adults. It doesn't bother me.
Great!
Okay.
See you tonight, then.
41.

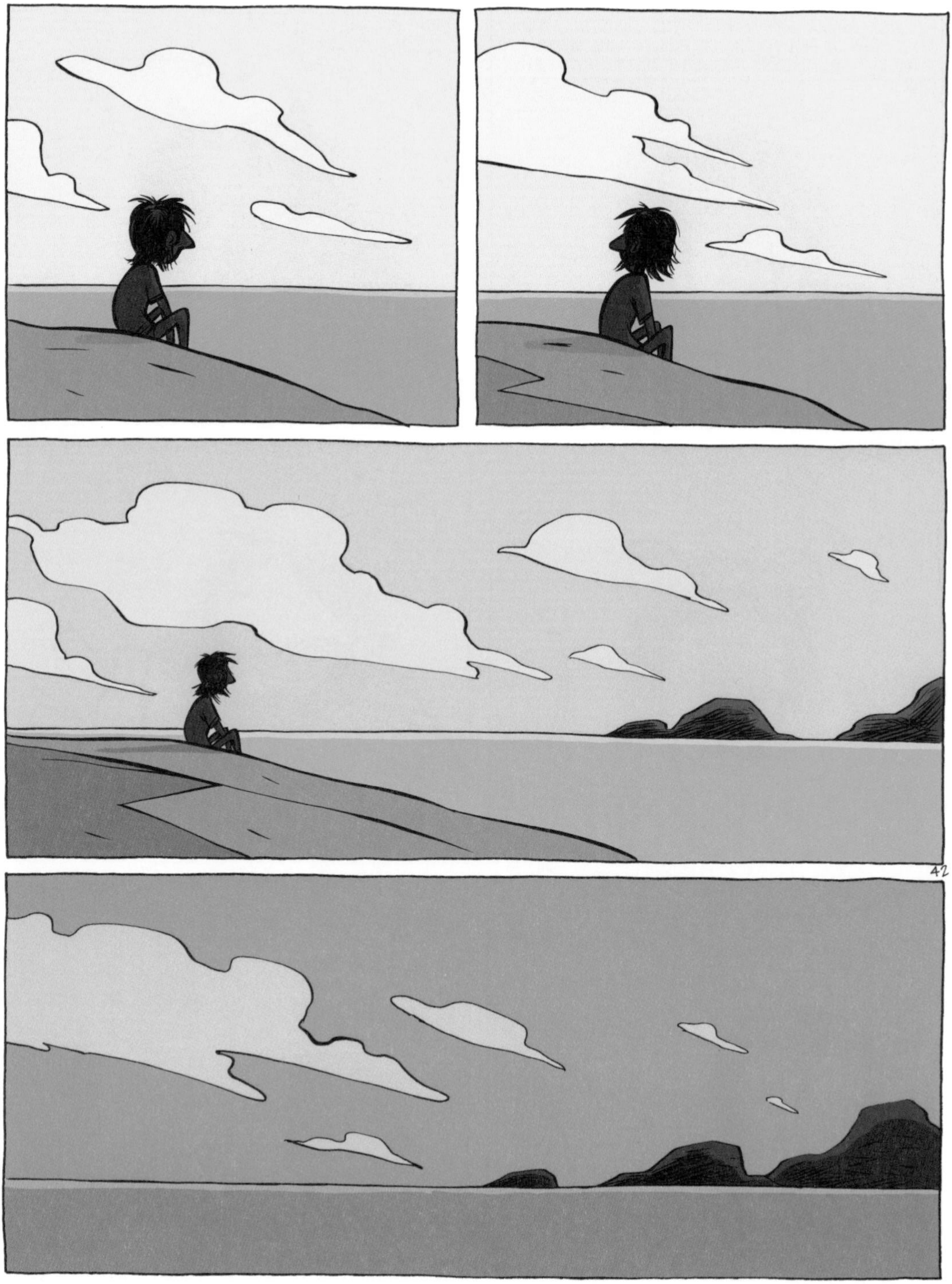
42

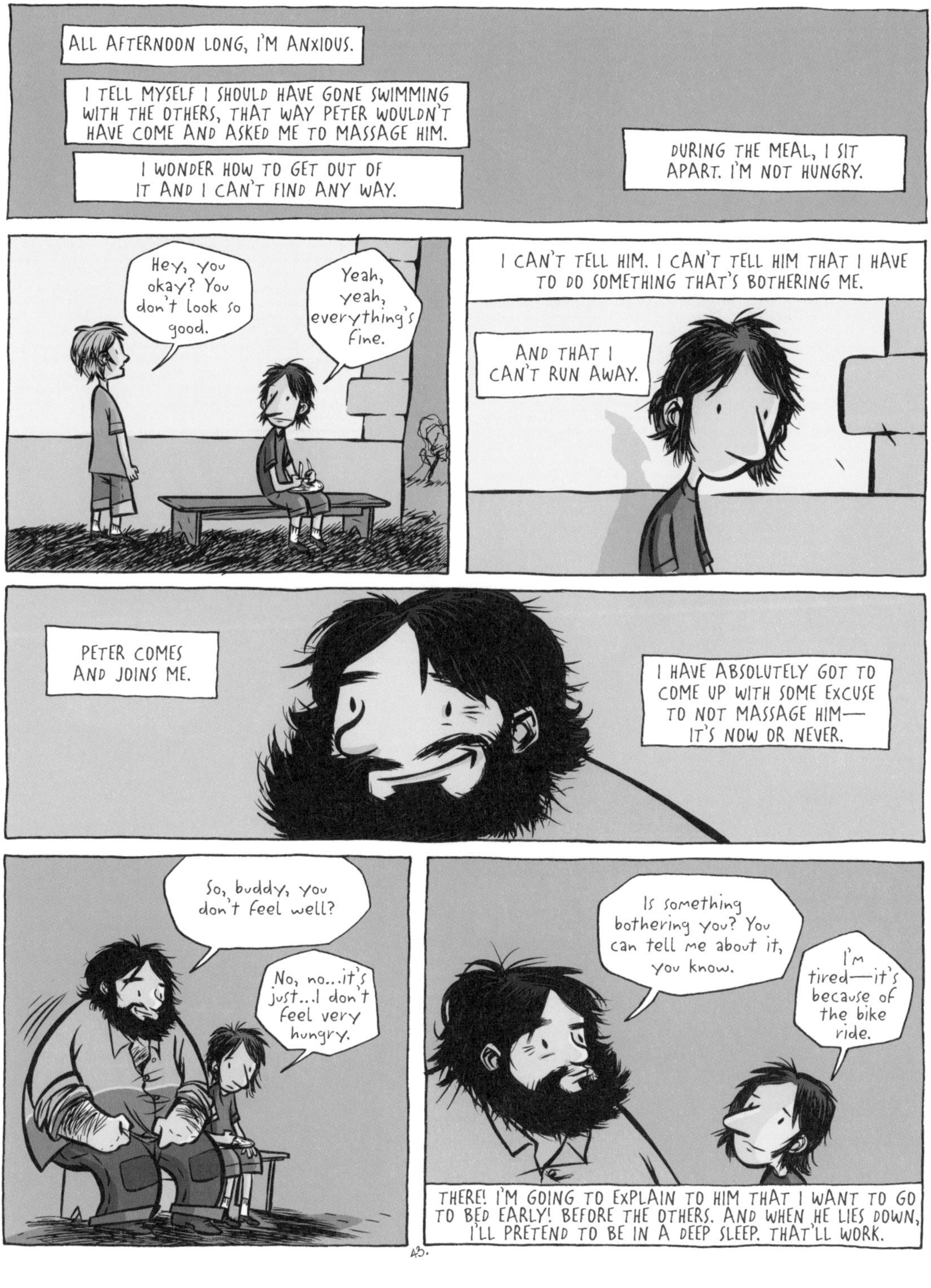
ALL AFTERNOON LONG, I'M ANXIOUS.
I TELL MYSELF I SHOULD HAVE GONE SWIMMING WITH THE OTHERS, THAT WAY PETER WOULDN'T HAVE COME AND ASKED ME TO MASSAGE HIM.
I WONDER HOW TO GET OUT OF IT AND I CAN'T FIND ANY WAY.
DURING THE MEAL, I SIT APART. I'M NOT HUNGRY.
Hey, you okay? You don't look so good.
Yeah, yeah, everything's fine.
I CAN'T TELL HIM. I CAN'T TELL HIM THAT I HAVE TO DO SOMETHING THAT'S BOTHERING ME.
AND THAT I CAN'T RUN AWAY.
PETER COMES AND JOINS ME.
I HAVE ABSOLUTELY GOT TO COME UP WITH SOME EXCUSE TO NOT MASSAGE HIM— IT'S NOW OR NEVER.
So, buddy, you don't feel well?
No, no...it's just...I don't feel very hungry.
Is something bothering you? You can tell me about it, you know.
I'm tired—it's because of the bike ride.
THERE! I'M GOING TO EXPLAIN TO HIM THAT I WANT TO GO TO BED EARLY! BEFORE THE OTHERS. AND WHEN HE LIES DOWN, I'LL PRETEND TO BE IN A DEEP SLEEP. THAT'LL WORK.
43.

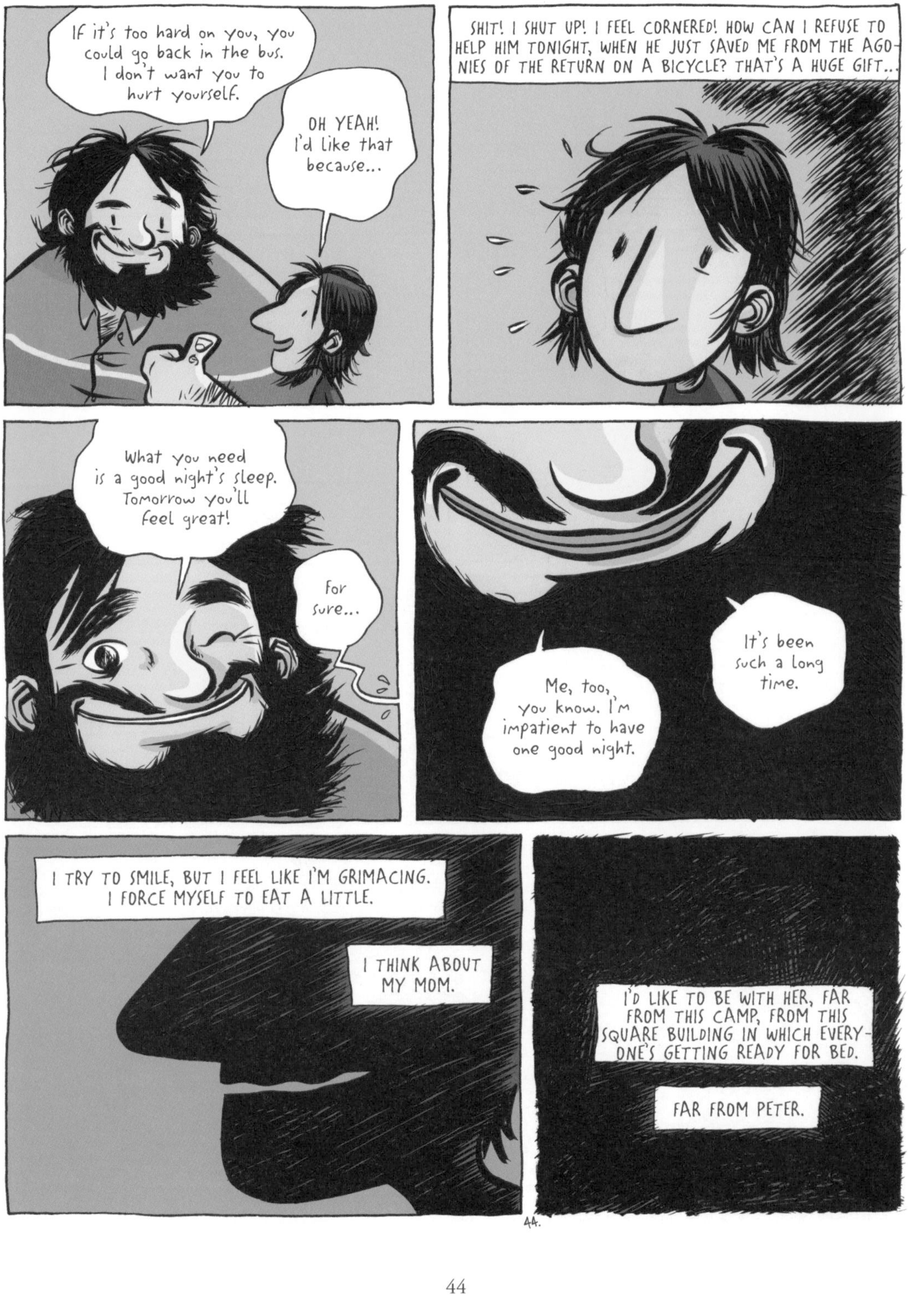
If it's too hard on you, you could go back in the bus. I don't want you to hurt yourself.
OH YEAH! I'd like that because...
SHIT! I SHUT UP! I FEEL CORNERED! HOW CAN I REFUSE TO HELP HIM TONIGHT, WHEN HE JUST SAVED ME FROM THE AGONIES OF THE RETURN ON A BICYCLE? THAT'S A HUGE GIFT...
What you need is a good night's sleep. Tomorrow you'll feel great!
For sure...
It's been such a long time.
Me, too, you know. I'm impatient to have one good night.
I TRY TO SMILE, BUT I FEEL LIKE I'M GRIMACING. I FORCE MYSELF TO EAT A LITTLE.
I THINK ABOUT MY MOM.
I'D LIKE TO BE WITH HER, FAR FROM THIS CAMP, FROM THIS SQUARE BUILDING IN WHICH EVERYONE'S GETTING READY FOR BED.
FAR FROM PETER.
44.

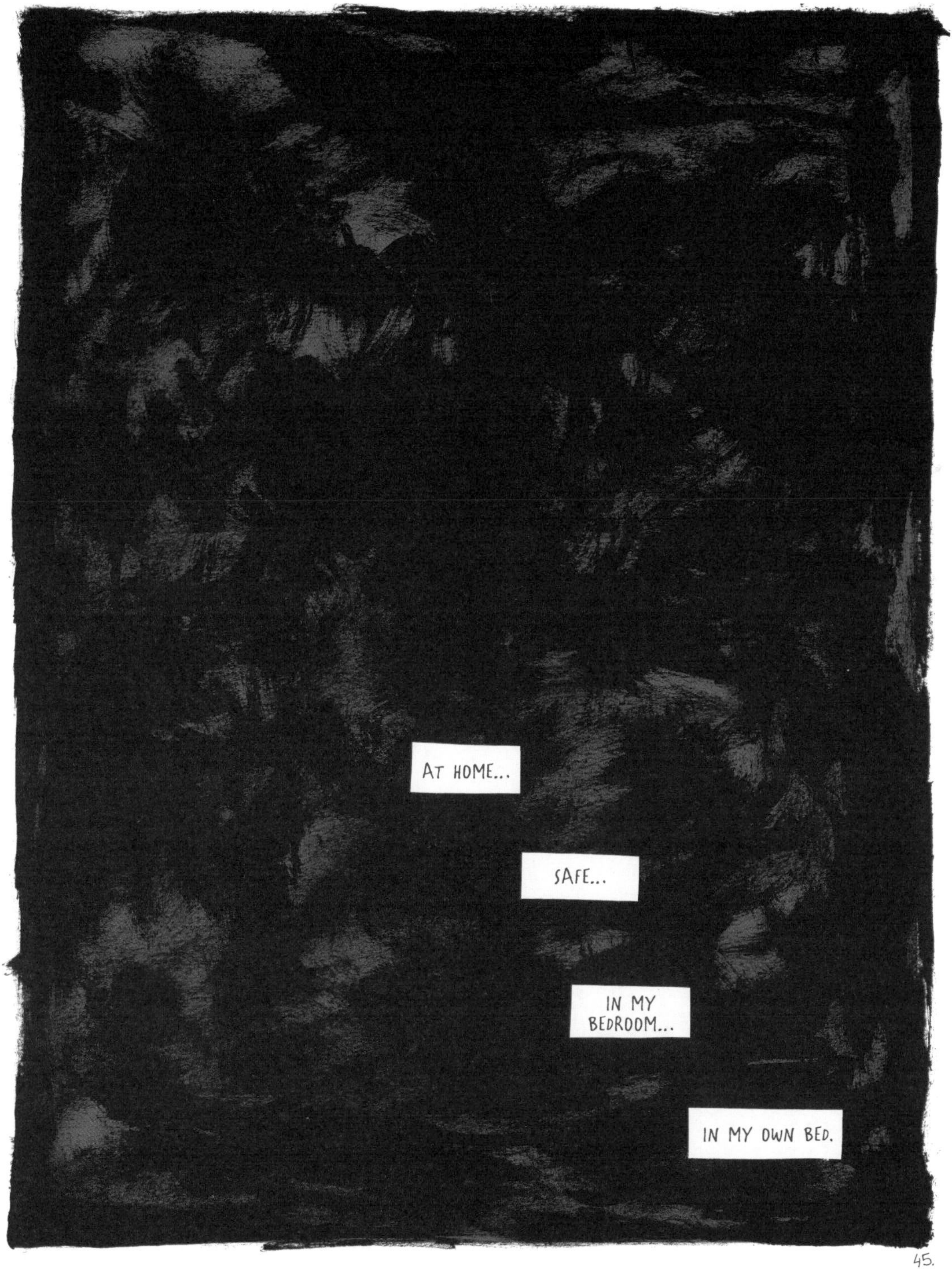
AT HOME...
SAFE...
IN MY BEDROOM...
IN MY OWN BED.

45.

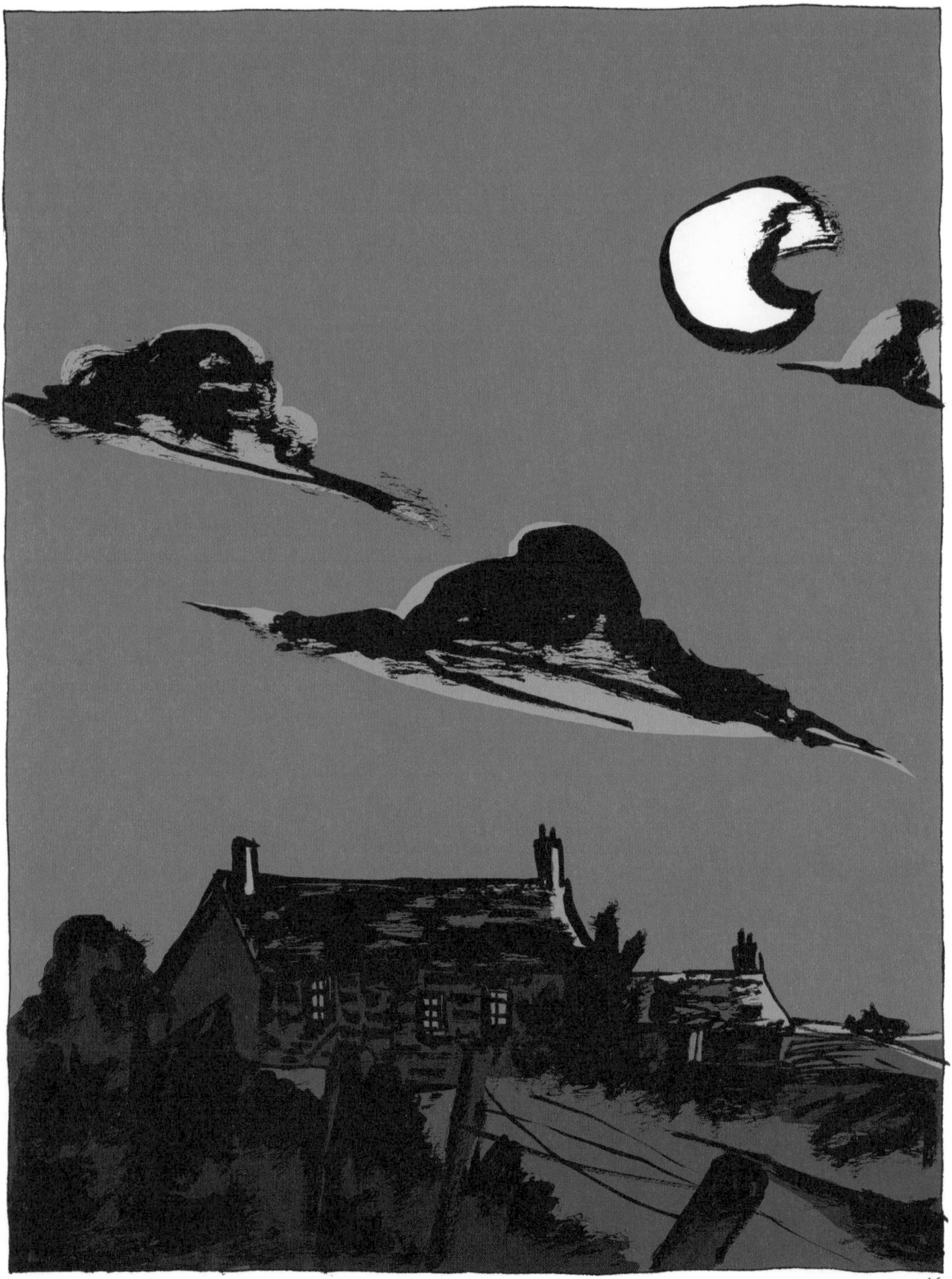
46.

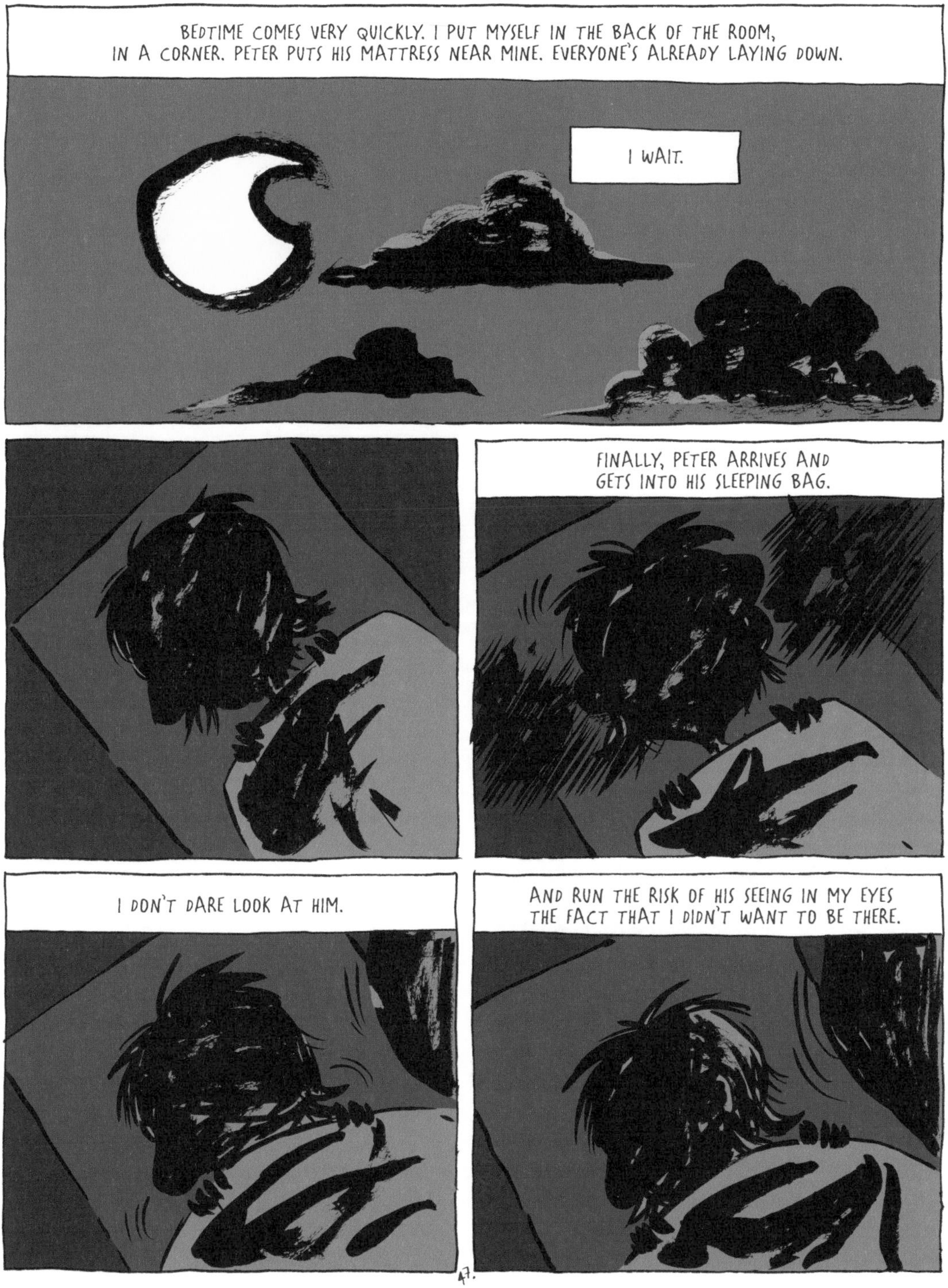
BEDTIME COMES VERY QUICKLY. I PUT MYSELF IN THE BACK OF THE ROOM, IN A CORNER. PETER PUTS HIS MATTRESS NEAR MINE. EVERYONE'S ALREADY LAYING DOWN.
I WAIT.
FINALLY, PETER ARRIVES AND GETS INTO HIS SLEEPING BAG.
I DON'T DARE LOOK AT HIM.
AND RUN THE RISK OF HIS SEEING IN MY EYES THE FACT THAT I DIDN'T WANT TO BE THERE.
47.

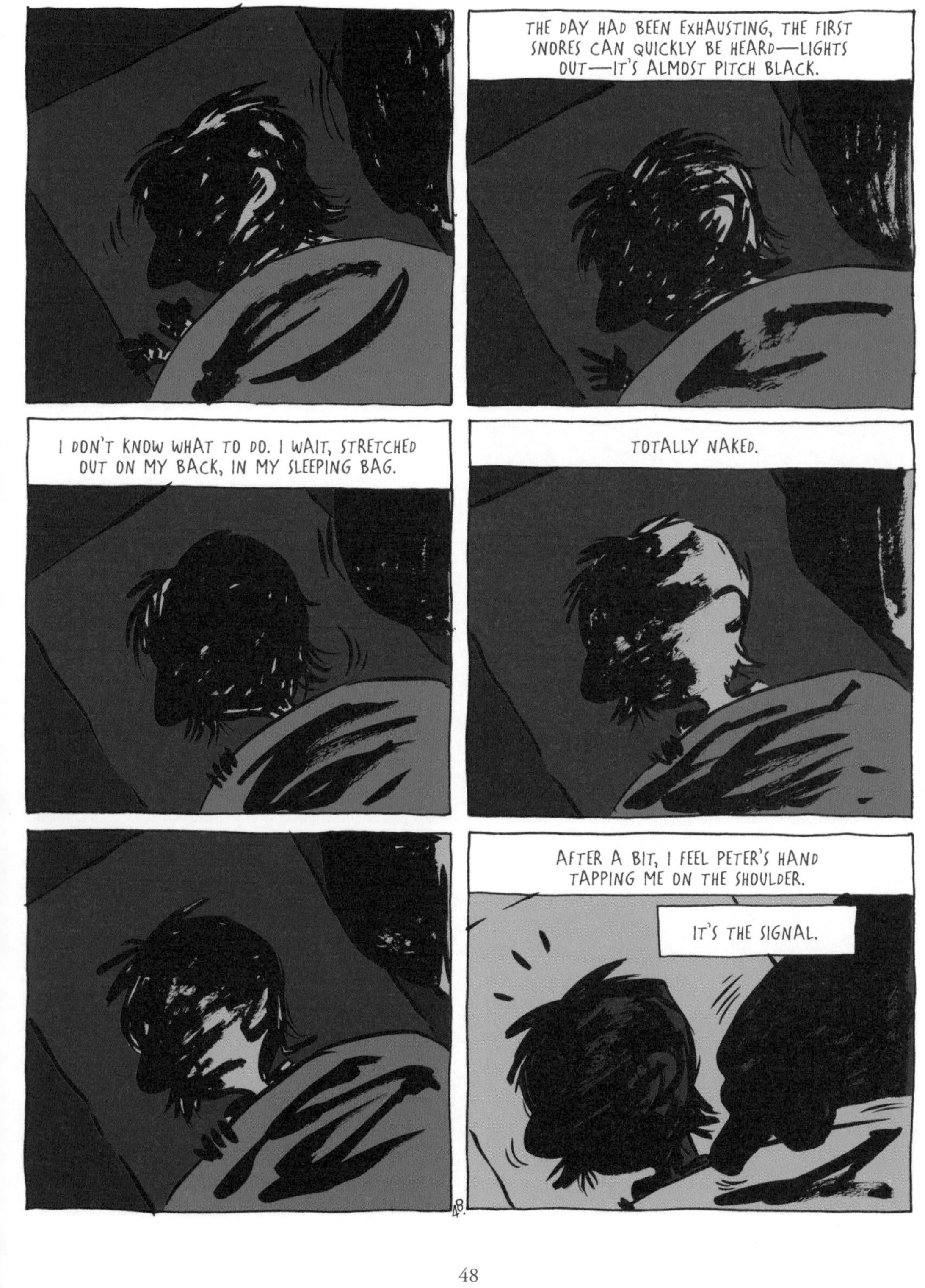
THE DAY HAD BEEN EXHAUSTING, THE FIRST SNORES CAN QUICKLY BE HEARD—LIGHTS OUT—IT'S ALMOST PITCH BLACK.
I DON'T KNOW WHAT TO DO. I WAIT, STRETCHED OUT ON MY BACK, IN MY SLEEPING BAG.
TOTALLY NAKED.
AFTER A BIT, I FEEL PETER'S HAND TAPPING ME ON THE SHOULDER.
IT'S THE SIGNAL.

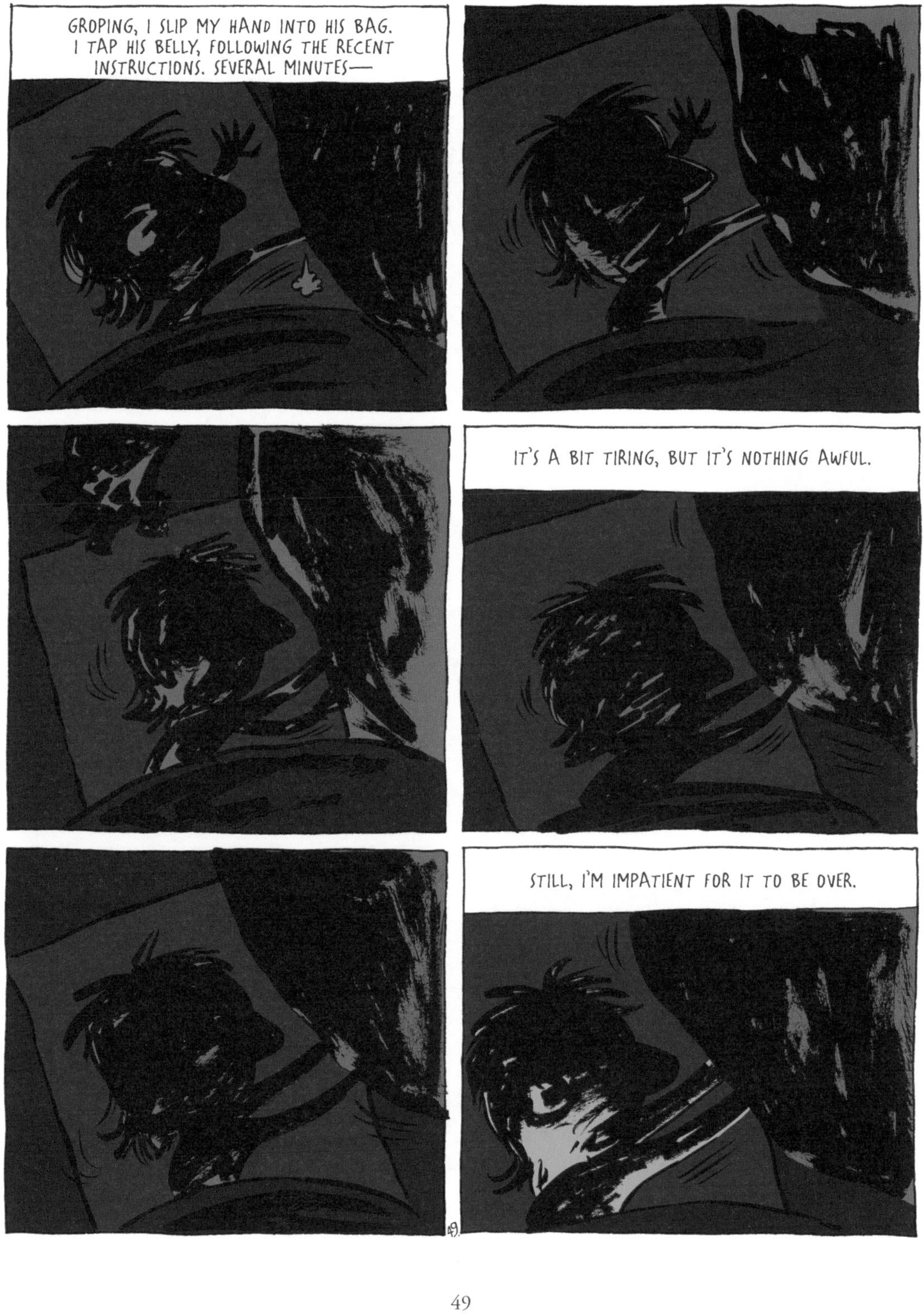
GROPING, I SLIP MY HAND INTO HIS BAG. I TAP HIS BELLY, FOLLOWING THE RECENT INSTRUCTIONS. SEVERAL MINUTES—
IT'S A BIT TIRING, BUT IT'S NOTHING AWFUL.
STILL, I'M IMPATIENT FOR IT TO BE OVER.

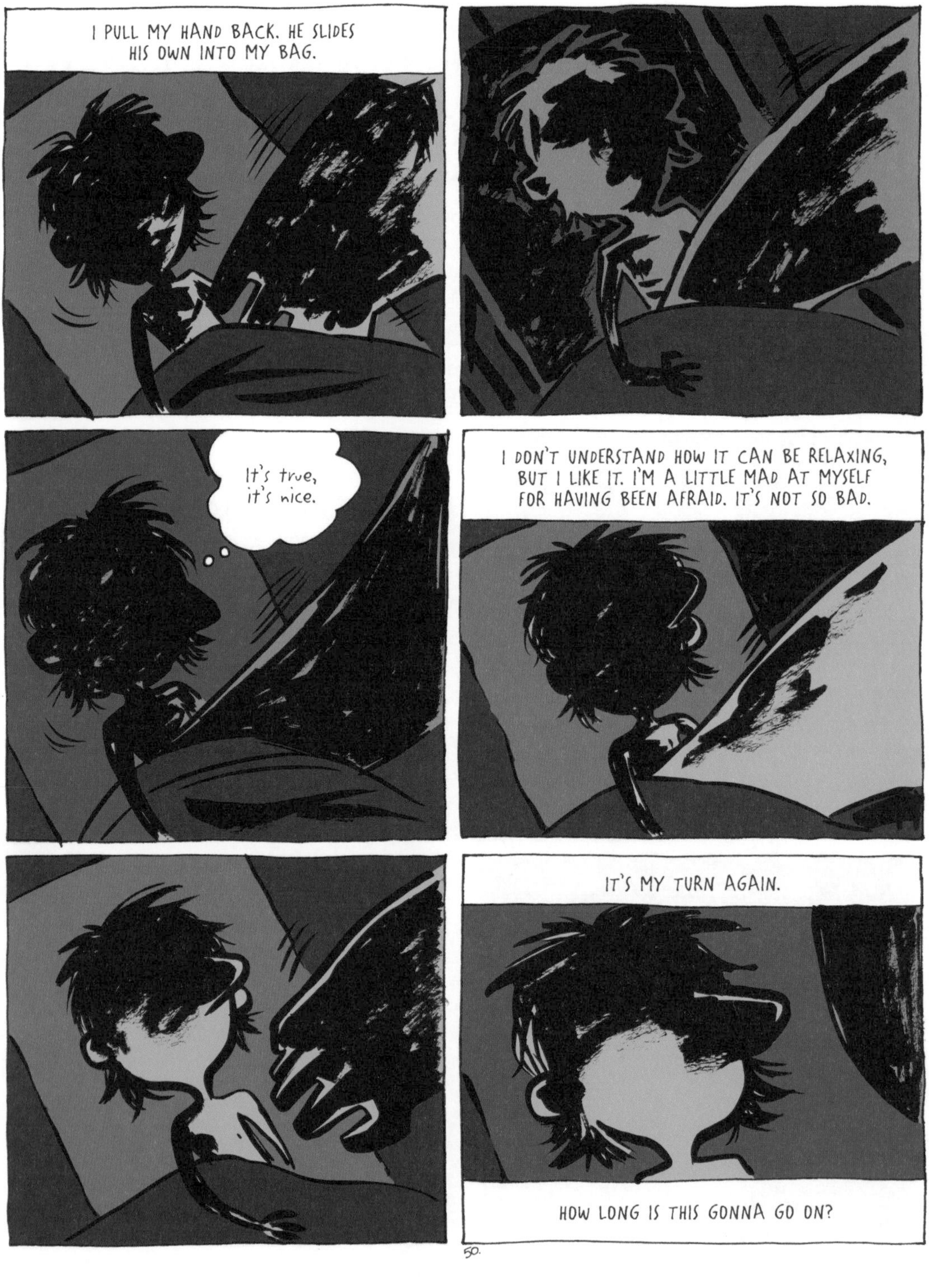
I PULL MY HAND BACK. HE SLIDES HIS OWN INTO MY BAG.
It's true, it's nice.
I DON'T UNDERSTAND HOW IT CAN BE RELAXING, BUT I LIKE IT. I'M A LITTLE MAD AT MYSELF FOR HAVING BEEN AFRAID. IT'S NOT SO BAD.
IT'S MY TURN AGAIN.
HOW LONG IS THIS GONNA GO ON?
50.

I RUB, HE RUBS, I RUB—

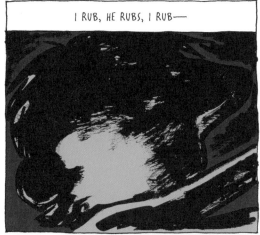

Hey!

SUDDENLY HE PULLS ME TOWARDS HIM, PRESSING MY HAND ONTO SOMETHING LARGE, AS HARD AS WOOD.

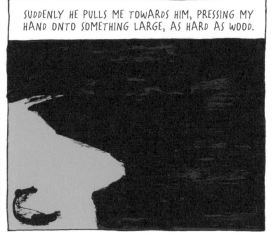

I DON'T UNDERSTAND RIGHT AWAY WHAT I'M TOUCHING.

IT FEELS HOT.

ONCE I UNDERSTAND WHAT'S GOING ON, MY STOMACH KNOTS UP!

SHIT! IT'S HIS DICK!!!

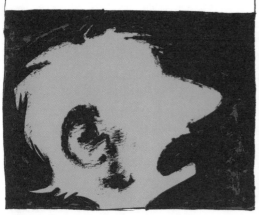

I TRY HARD TO PULL BACK MY HAND, BUT HE HOLDS ONTO IT—

HE HOLDS ME TIGHT AGAINST HIM.

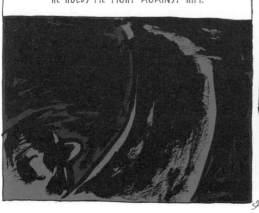

I FEEL HIS BODY, SMELL HIS ODOR—

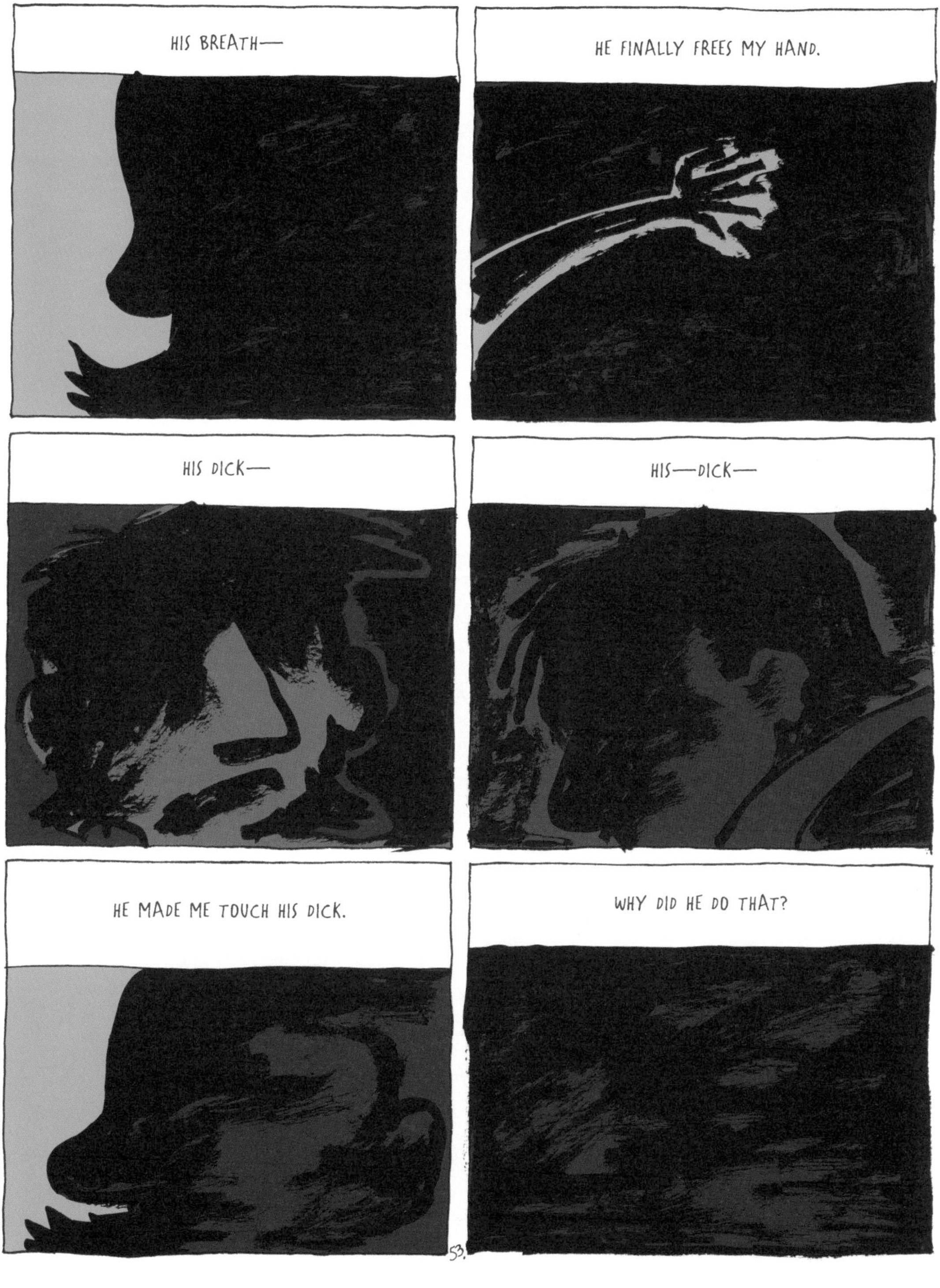
HIS BREATH—
HE FINALLY FREES MY HAND.
HIS DICK—
HIS—DICK—
HE MADE ME TOUCH HIS DICK.
WHY DID HE DO THAT?

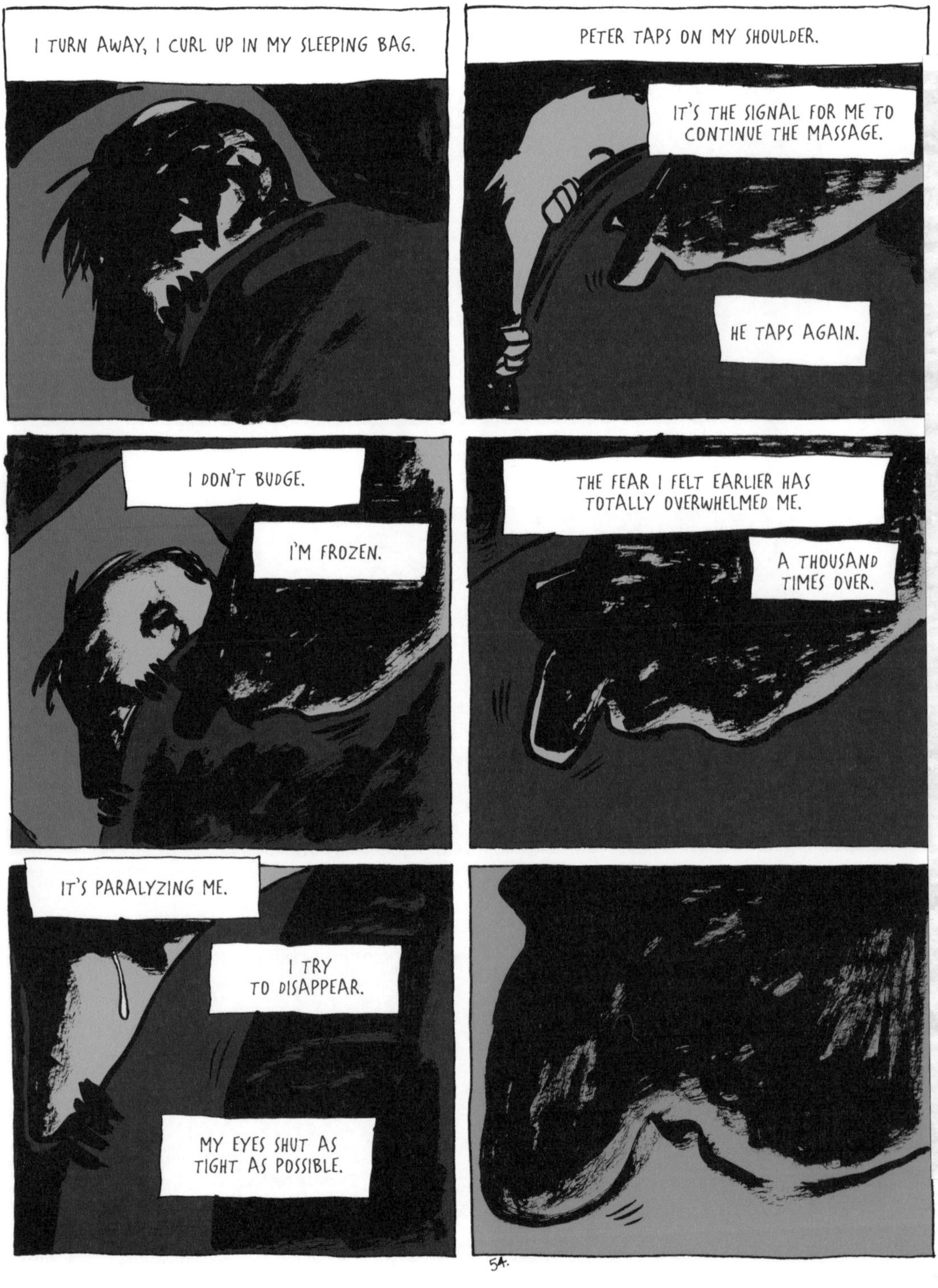
I TURN AWAY, I CURL UP IN MY SLEEPING BAG.
PETER TAPS ON MY SHOULDER.
IT'S THE SIGNAL FOR ME TO CONTINUE THE MASSAGE.
HE TAPS AGAIN.
I DON'T BUDGE.
I'M FROZEN.
THE FEAR I FELT EARLIER HAS TOTALLY OVERWHELMED ME.
A THOUSAND TIMES OVER.
IT'S PARALYZING ME.
I TRY TO DISAPPEAR.
MY EYES SHUT AS TIGHT AS POSSIBLE.
54.

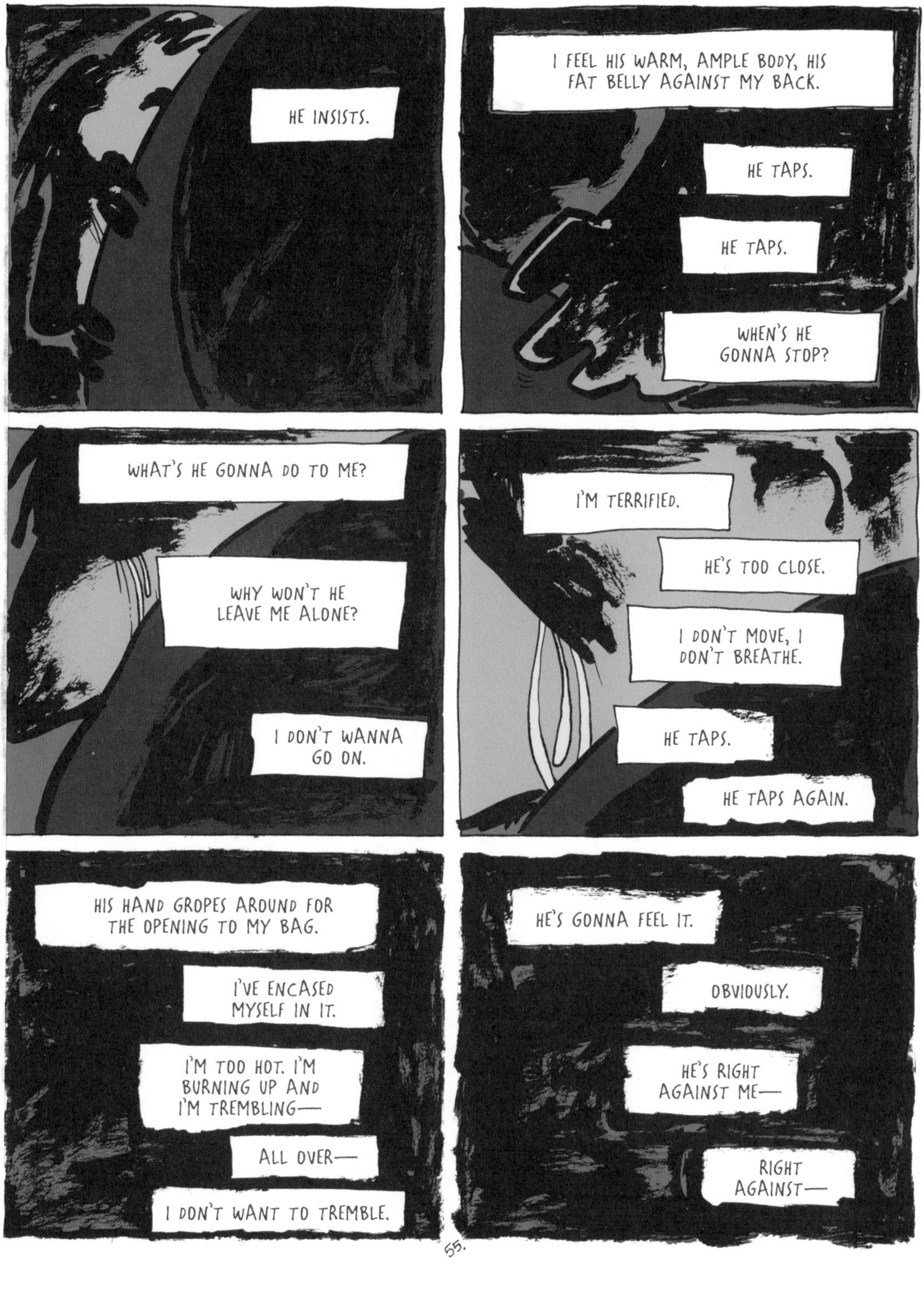
HE INSISTS.
I FEEL HIS WARM, AMPLE BODY, HIS FAT BELLY AGAINST MY BACK.
HE TAPS.
HE TAPS.
WHEN'S HE GONNA STOP?
WHAT'S HE GONNA DO TO ME?
WHY WON'T HE LEAVE ME ALONE?
I DON'T WANNA GO ON.
I'M TERRIFIED.
HE'S TOO CLOSE.
I DON'T MOVE, I DON'T BREATHE.
HE TAPS.
HE TAPS AGAIN.
HIS HAND GROPES AROUND FOR THE OPENING TO MY BAG.
I'VE ENCASED MYSELF IN IT.
I'M TOO HOT. I'M BURNING UP AND I'M TREMBLING—
ALL OVER—
I DON'T WANT TO TREMBLE.
HE'S GONNA FEEL IT.
OBVIOUSLY.
HE'S RIGHT AGAINST ME—
RIGHT AGAINST—
55.

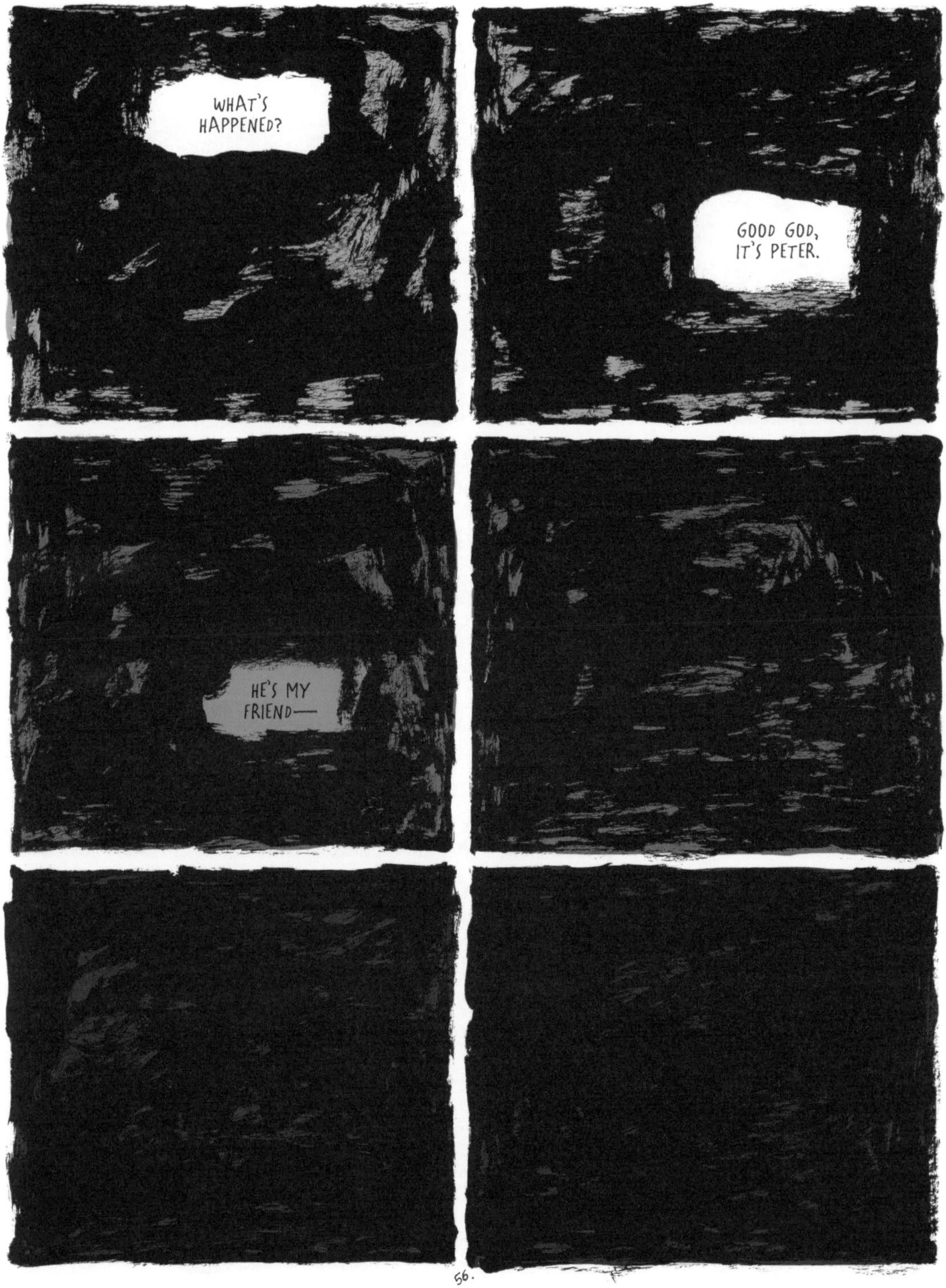
WHAT'S HAPPENED?
GOOD GOD, IT'S PETER.
HE'S MY FRIEND—
56.

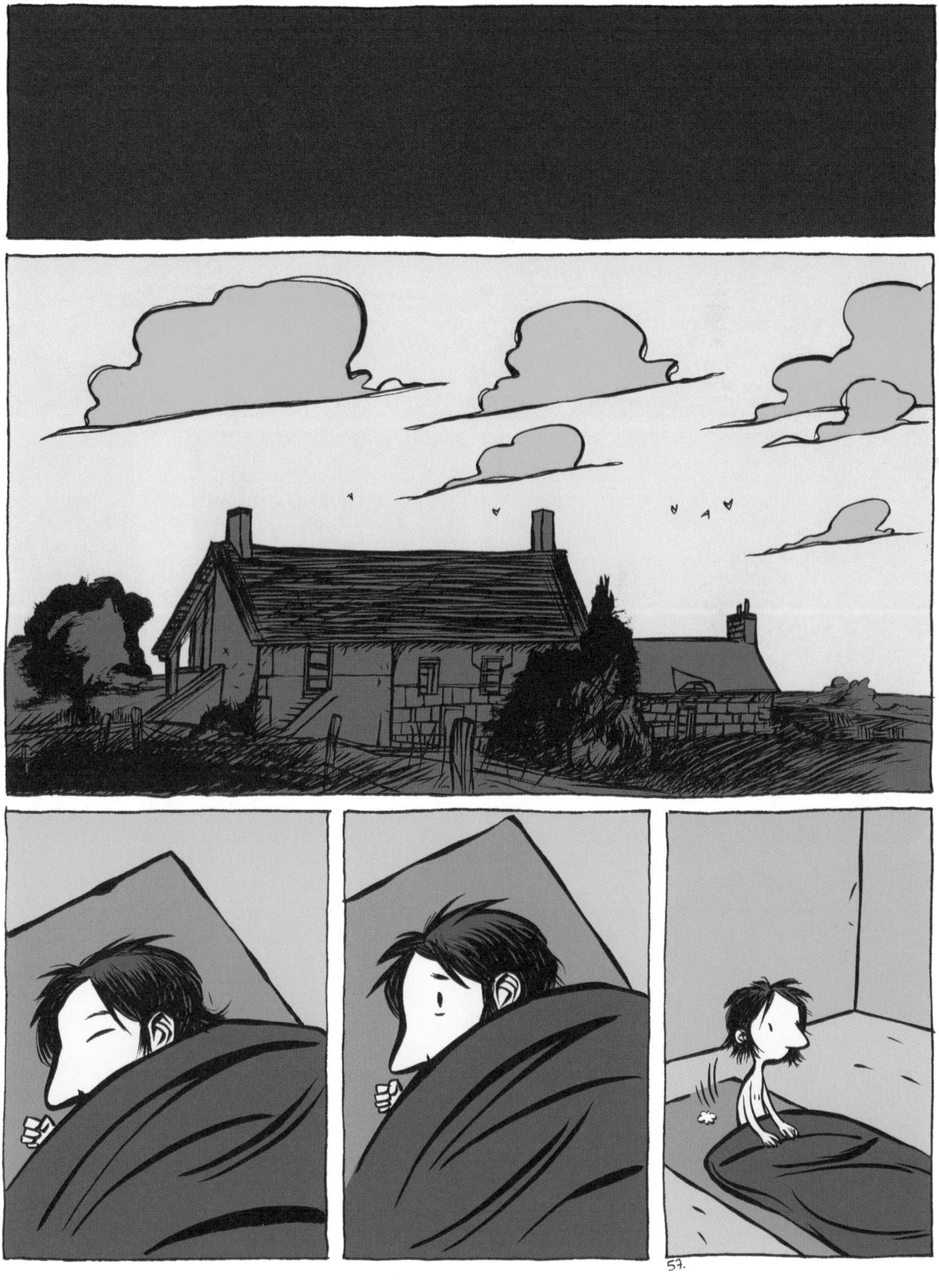
57.

Want to come walk Baloo with me?

So what do you think about last night?

You're an adult—I'm a kid. It won't work.

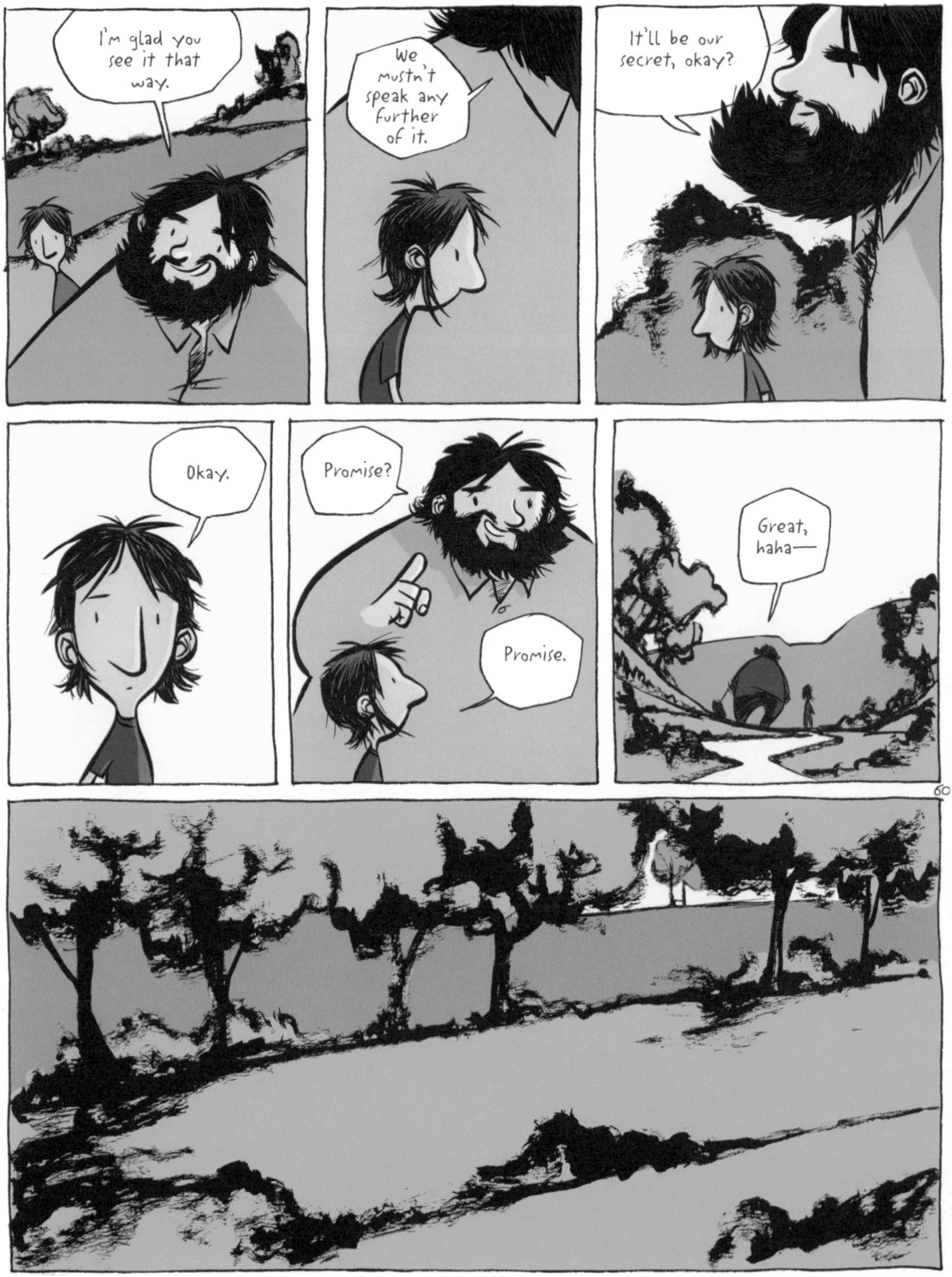
I'm glad you see it that way.
We mustn't speak any further of it.
It'll be our secret, okay?
Okay.
Promise?
Promise.
Great, haha—
60

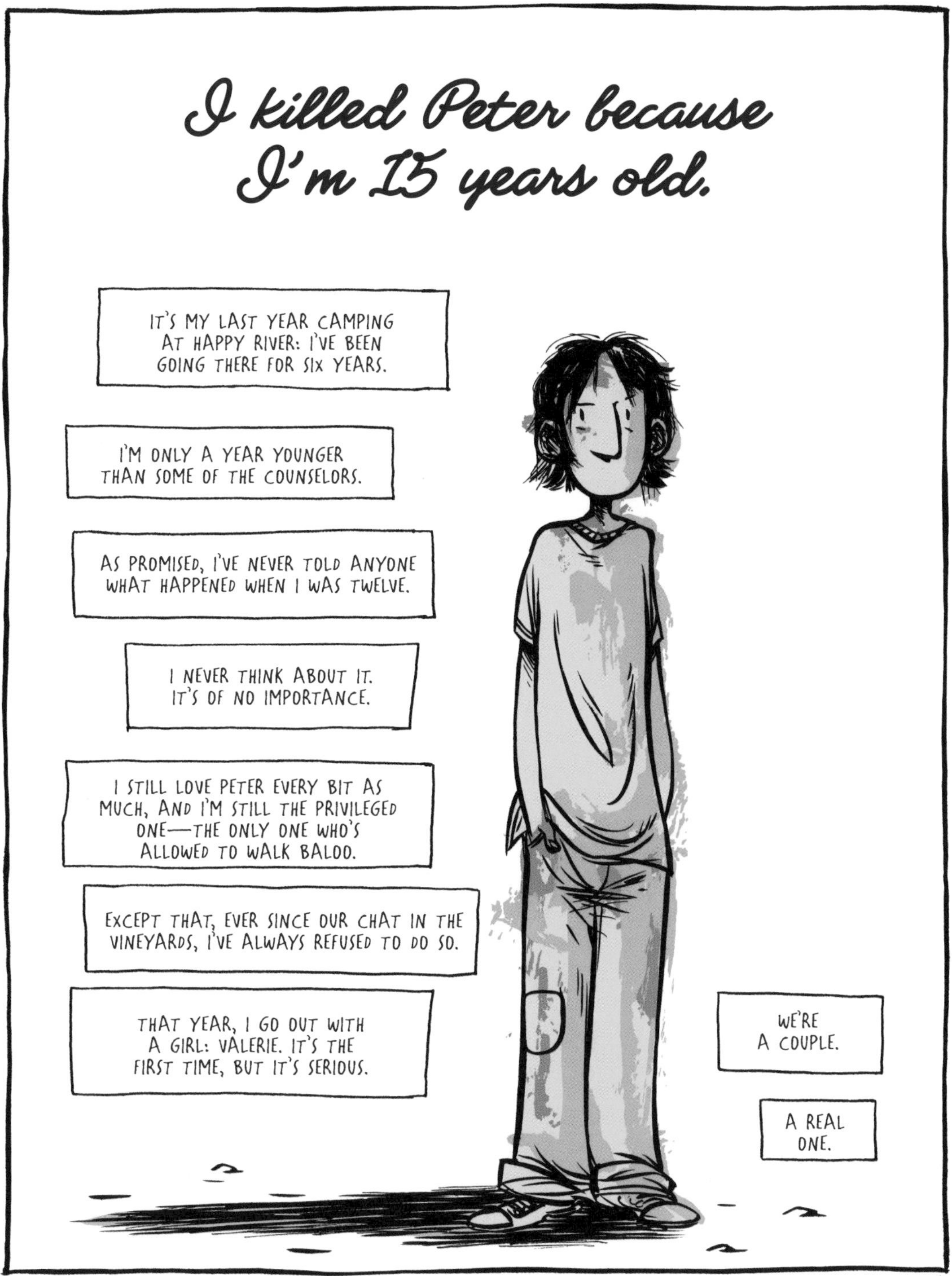
I killed Peter because I'm 15 years old.
IT'S MY LAST YEAR CAMPING AT HAPPY RIVER: I'VE BEEN GOING THERE FOR SIX YEARS.
I'M ONLY A YEAR YOUNGER THAN SOME OF THE COUNSELORS.
AS PROMISED, I'VE NEVER TOLD ANYONE WHAT HAPPENED WHEN I WAS TWELVE.
I NEVER THINK ABOUT IT. IT'S OF NO IMPORTANCE.
I STILL LOVE PETER EVERY BIT AS MUCH, AND I'M STILL THE PRIVILEGED ONE—THE ONLY ONE WHO'S ALLOWED TO WALK BALOO.
EXCEPT THAT, EVER SINCE OUR CHAT IN THE VINEYARDS, I'VE ALWAYS REFUSED TO DO SO.
THAT YEAR, I GO OUT WITH A GIRL: VALERIE. IT'S THE FIRST TIME, BUT IT'S SERIOUS.
WE'RE A COUPLE.
A REAL ONE.

61

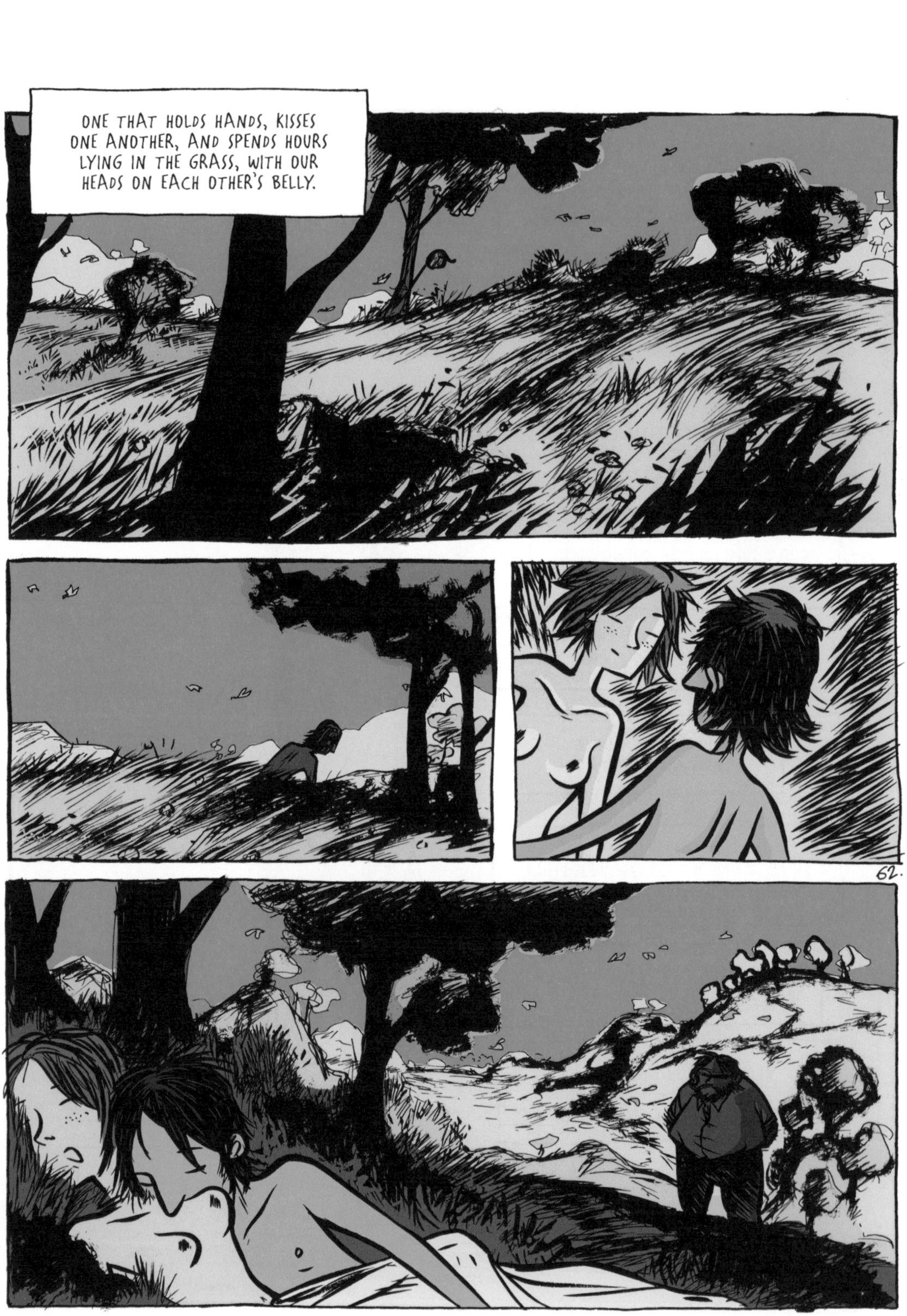
ONE THAT HOLDS HANDS, KISSES ONE ANOTHER, AND SPENDS HOURS LYING IN THE GRASS, WITH OUR HEADS ON EACH OTHER'S BELLY.
62.

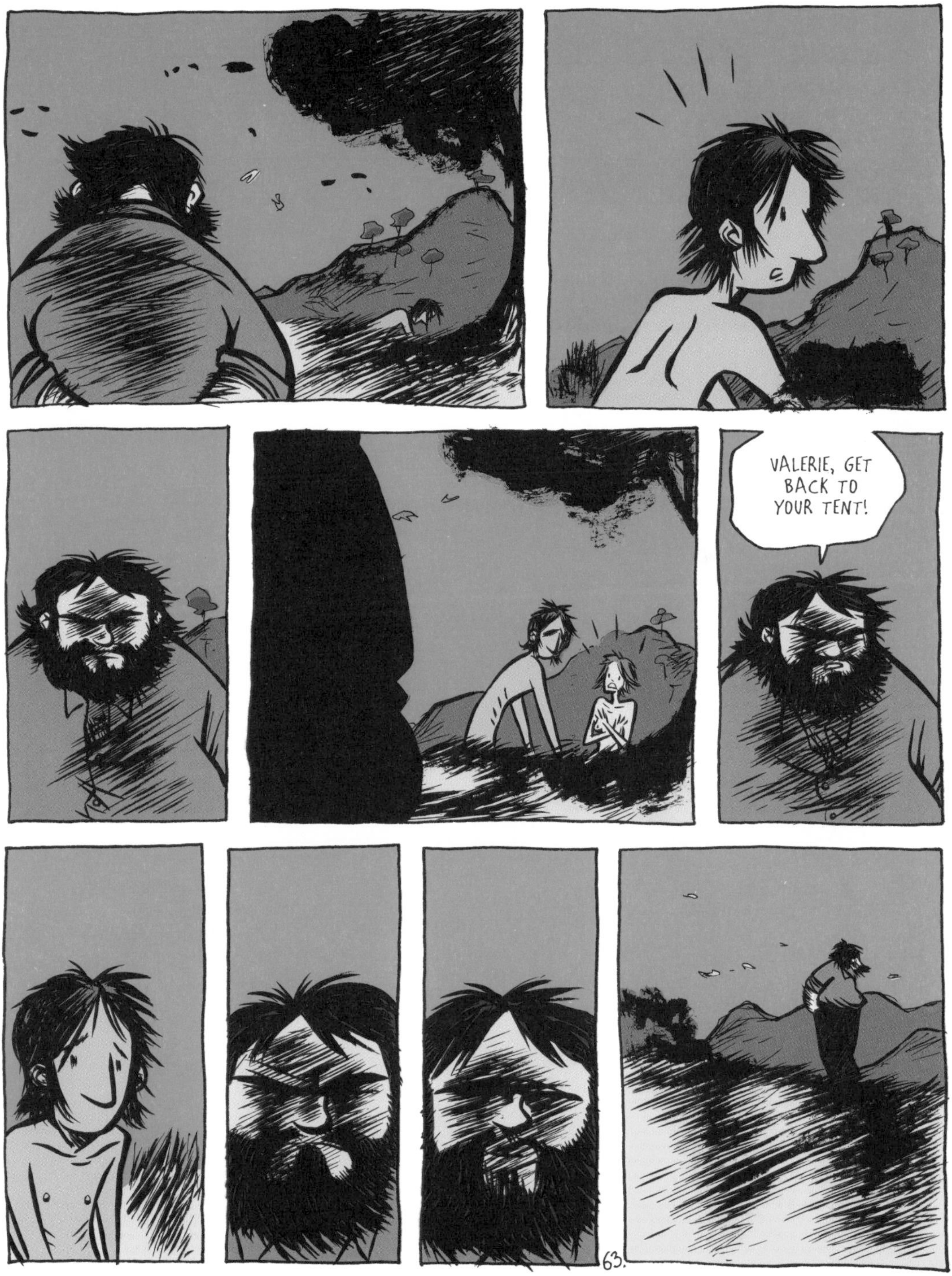
VALERIE, GET BACK TO YOUR TENT!
63.

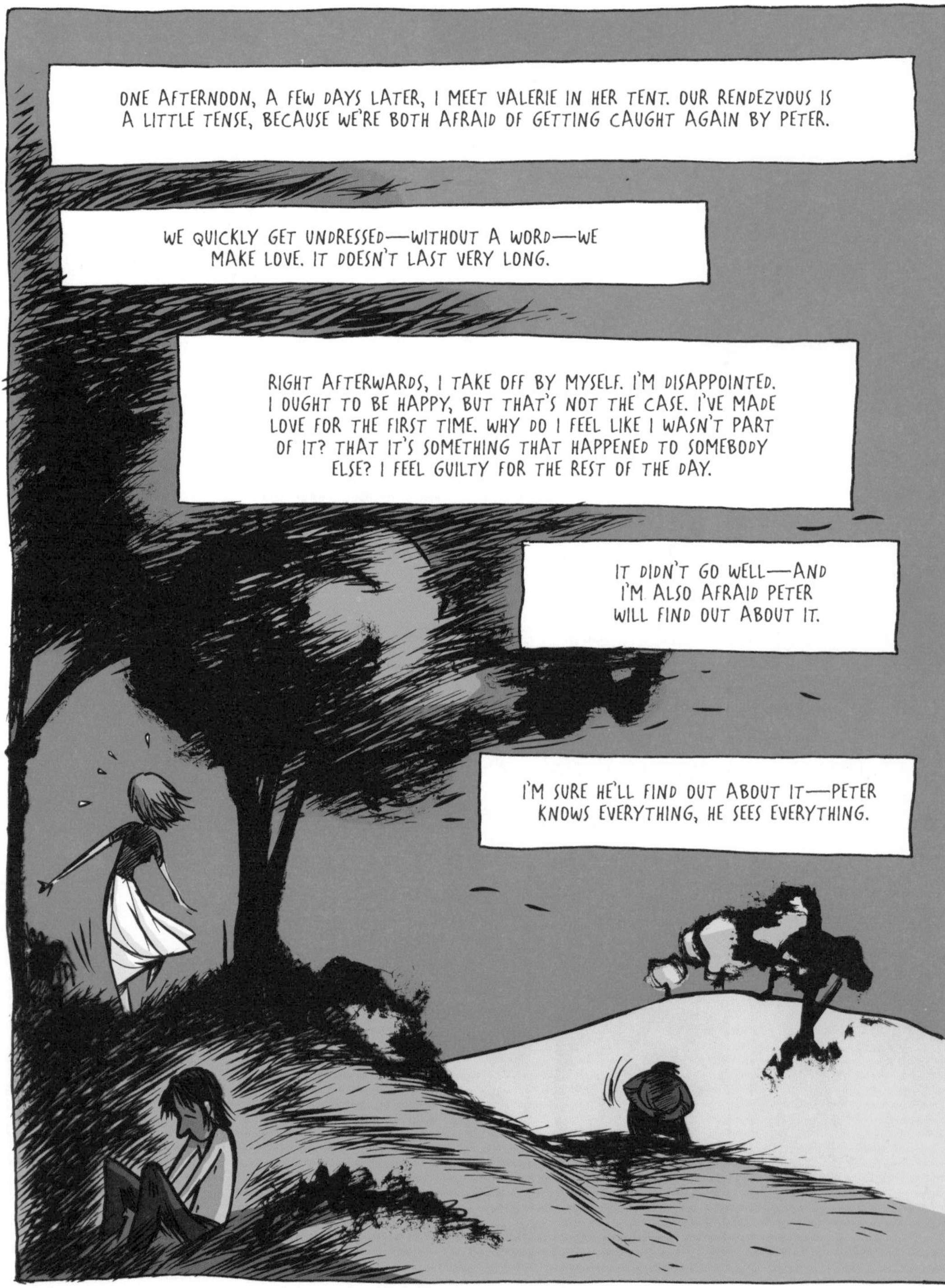
ONE AFTERNOON, A FEW DAYS LATER, I MEET VALERIE IN HER TENT. OUR RENDEZVOUS IS A LITTLE TENSE, BECAUSE WE'RE BOTH AFRAID OF GETTING CAUGHT AGAIN BY PETER.
WE QUICKLY GET UNDRESSED—WITHOUT A WORD—WE MAKE LOVE. IT DOESN'T LAST VERY LONG.
RIGHT AFTERWARDS, I TAKE OFF BY MYSELF. I'M DISAPPOINTED. I OUGHT TO BE HAPPY, BUT THAT'S NOT THE CASE. I'VE MADE LOVE FOR THE FIRST TIME. WHY DO I FEEL LIKE I WASN'T PART OF IT? THAT IT'S SOMETHING THAT HAPPENED TO SOMEBODY ELSE? I FEEL GUILTY FOR THE REST OF THE DAY.
IT DIDN'T GO WELL—AND I'M ALSO AFRAID PETER WILL FIND OUT ABOUT IT.
I'M SURE HE'LL FIND OUT ABOUT IT—PETER KNOWS EVERYTHING, HE SEES EVERYTHING.

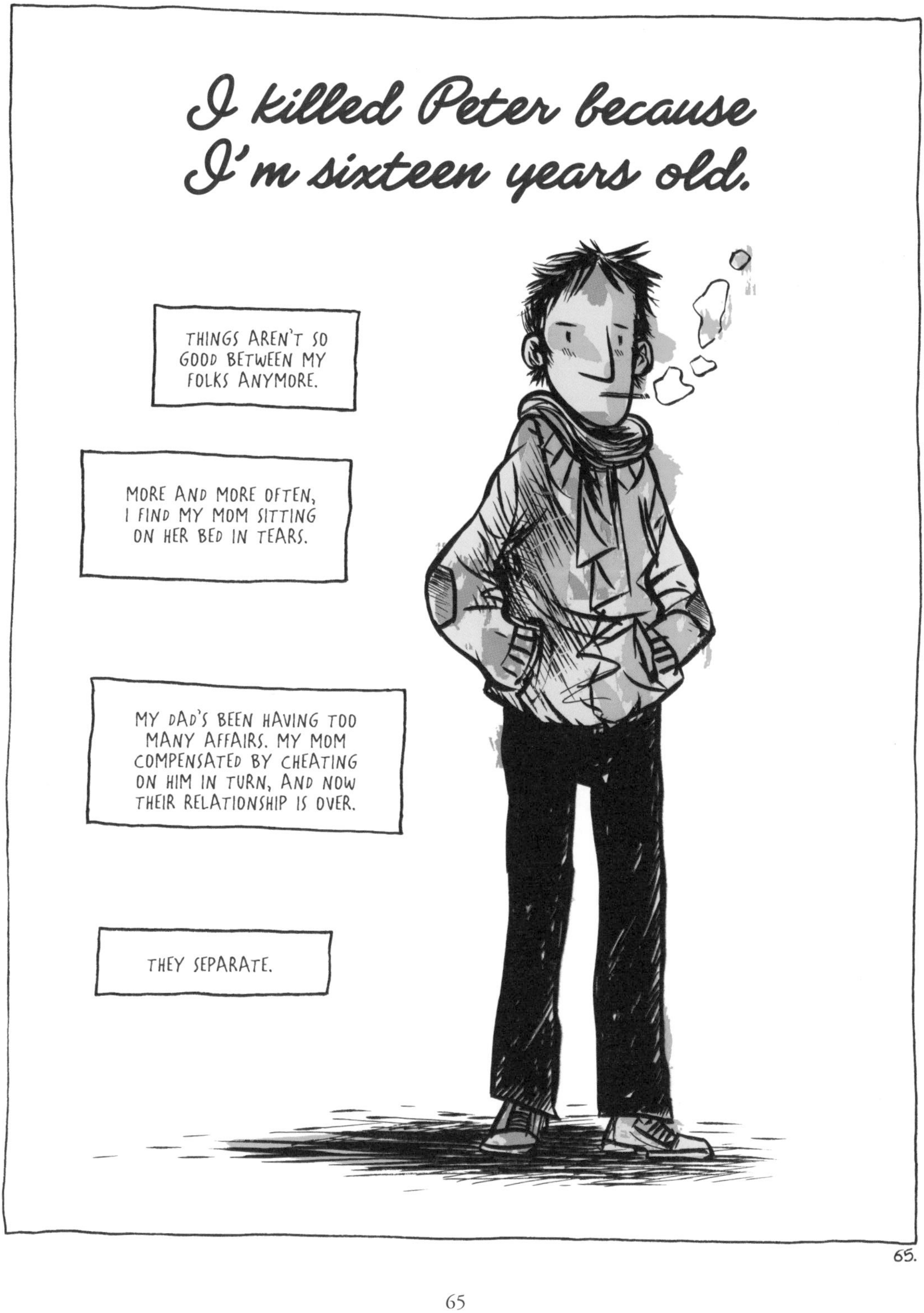
I killed Peter because I'm sixteen years old.
THINGS AREN'T SO GOOD BETWEEN MY FOLKS ANYMORE.
MORE AND MORE OFTEN, I FIND MY MOM SITTING ON HER BED IN TEARS.
MY DAD'S BEEN HAVING TOO MANY AFFAIRS. MY MOM COMPENSATED BY CHEATING ON HIM IN TURN, AND NOW THEIR RELATIONSHIP IS OVER.
THEY SEPARATE.
65.

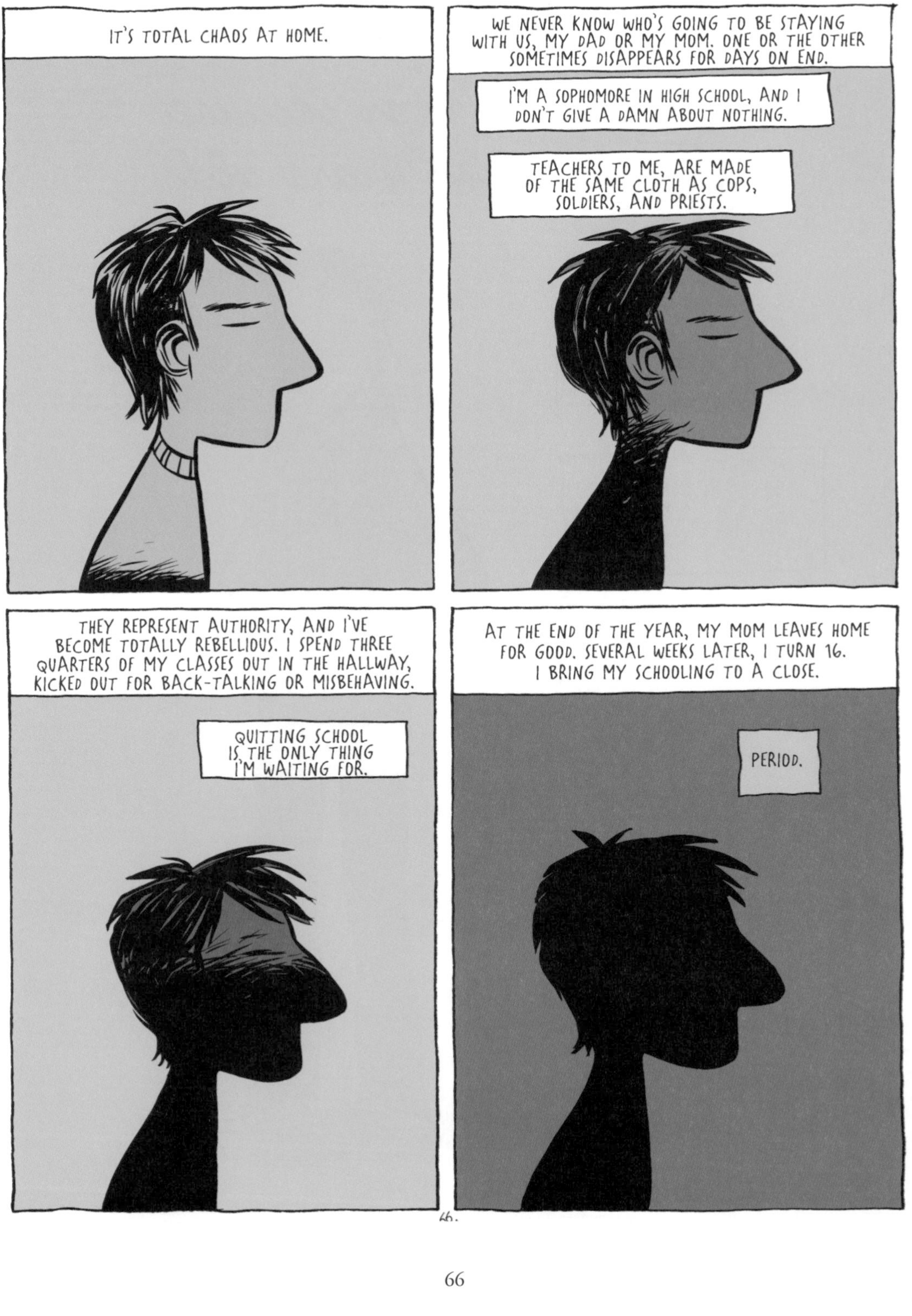
IT'S TOTAL CHAOS AT HOME.
WE NEVER KNOW WHO'S GOING TO BE STAYING WITH US, MY DAD OR MY MOM. ONE OR THE OTHER SOMETIMES DISAPPEARS FOR DAYS ON END.
I'M A SOPHOMORE IN HIGH SCHOOL, AND I DON'T GIVE A DAMN ABOUT NOTHING.
TEACHERS TO ME, ARE MADE OF THE SAME CLOTH AS COPS, SOLDIERS, AND PRIESTS.
THEY REPRESENT AUTHORITY, AND I'VE BECOME TOTALLY REBELLIOUS. I SPEND THREE QUARTERS OF MY CLASSES OUT IN THE HALLWAY, KICKED OUT FOR BACK-TALKING OR MISBEHAVING.
QUITTING SCHOOL IS THE ONLY THING I'M WAITING FOR.
AT THE END OF THE YEAR, MY MOM LEAVES HOME FOR GOOD. SEVERAL WEEKS LATER, I TURN 16. I BRING MY SCHOOLING TO A CLOSE.
PERIOD.
66.

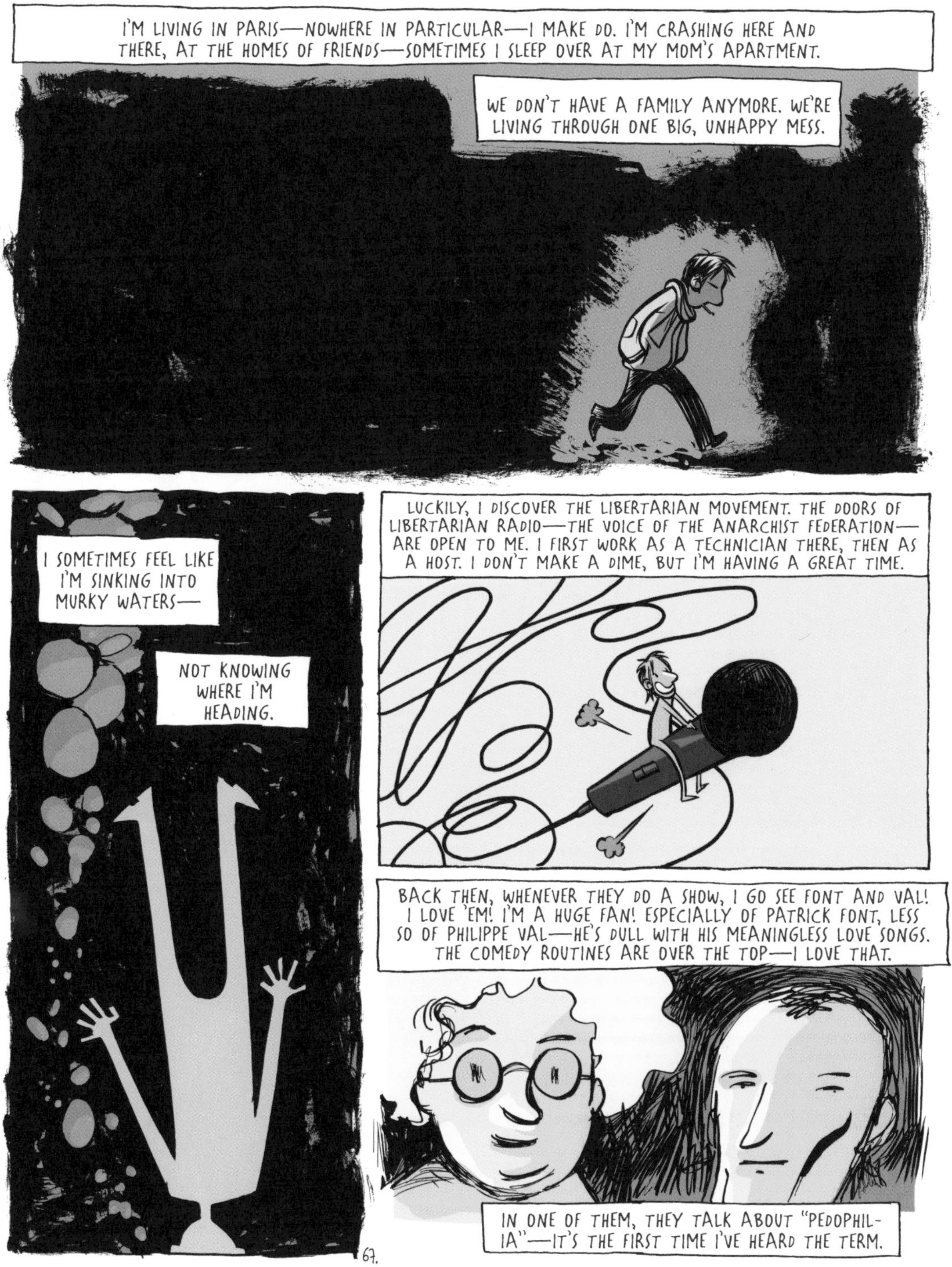
I'M LIVING IN PARIS—NOWHERE IN PARTICULAR—I MAKE DO. I'M CRASHING HERE AND THERE, AT THE HOMES OF FRIENDS—SOMETIMES I SLEEP OVER AT MY MOM'S APARTMENT.
WE DON'T HAVE A FAMILY ANYMORE. WE'RE LIVING THROUGH ONE BIG, UNHAPPY MESS.
I SOMETIMES FEEL LIKE I'M SINKING INTO MURKY WATERS—
NOT KNOWING WHERE I'M HEADING.
LUCKILY, I DISCOVER THE LIBERTARIAN MOVEMENT. THE DOORS OF LIBERTARIAN RADIO—THE VOICE OF THE ANARCHIST FEDERATION—ARE OPEN TO ME. I FIRST WORK AS A TECHNICIAN THERE, THEN AS A HOST. I DON'T MAKE A DIME, BUT I'M HAVING A GREAT TIME.
BACK THEN, WHENEVER THEY DO A SHOW, I GO SEE FONT AND VAL! I LOVE 'EM! I'M A HUGE FAN! ESPECIALLY OF PATRICK FONT, LESS SO OF PHILIPPE VAL—HE'S DULL WITH HIS MEANINGLESS LOVE SONGS. THE COMEDY ROUTINES ARE OVER THE TOP—I LOVE THAT.
IN ONE OF THEM, THEY TALK ABOUT "PEDOPHILIA"—IT'S THE FIRST TIME I'VE HEARD THE TERM.
67.

I BREAK THE SECRET. ONE NIGHT, I TELL MY MOM EVERYTHING. IN DETAIL. SHE CAN'T GET OVER IT.

I ALSO DESCRIBE THE NEXT DAY'S WALK AND MY ANSWER TO PETER'S QUESTION.

You really said that?

It's incredible how mature you already were.

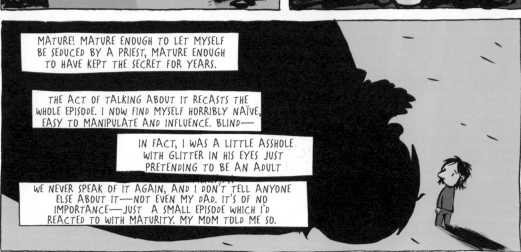

MATURE! MATURE ENOUGH TO LET MYSELF BE SEDUCED BY A PRIEST, MATURE ENOUGH TO HAVE KEPT THE SECRET FOR YEARS.

THE ACT OF TALKING ABOUT IT RECASTS THE WHOLE EPISODE. I NOW FIND MYSELF HORRIBLY NAÏVE, EASY TO MANIPULATE AND INFLUENCE. BLIND—

IN FACT, I WAS A LITTLE ASSHOLE WITH GLITTER IN HIS EYES JUST PRETENDING TO BE AN ADULT

WE NEVER SPEAK OF IT AGAIN, AND I DON'T TELL ANYONE ELSE ABOUT IT—NOT EVEN MY DAD. IT'S OF NO IMPORTANCE—JUST A SMALL EPISODE WHICH I'D REACTED TO WITH MATURITY. MY MOM TOLD ME SO.

68.

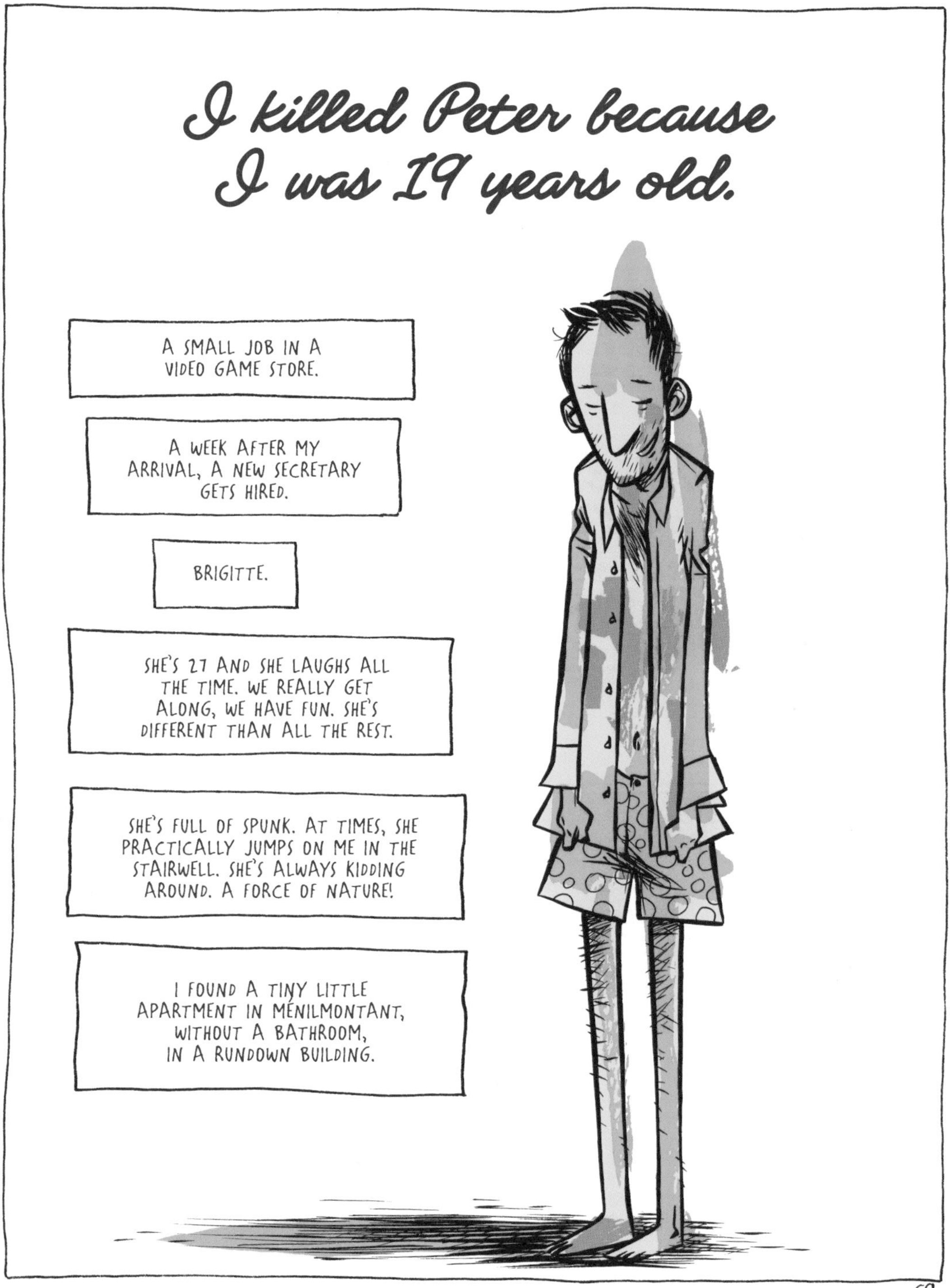
I killed Peter because I was 19 years old.
A SMALL JOB IN A VIDEO GAME STORE.
A WEEK AFTER MY ARRIVAL, A NEW SECRETARY GETS HIRED.
BRIGITTE.
SHE'S 27 AND SHE LAUGHS ALL THE TIME. WE REALLY GET ALONG, WE HAVE FUN. SHE'S DIFFERENT THAN ALL THE REST.
SHE'S FULL OF SPUNK. AT TIMES, SHE PRACTICALLY JUMPS ON ME IN THE STAIRWELL. SHE'S ALWAYS KIDDING AROUND. A FORCE OF NATURE!
I FOUND A TINY LITTLE APARTMENT IN MÉNILMONTANT, WITHOUT A BATHROOM, IN A RUNDOWN BUILDING.
69.

ONE NIGHT, BRIGITTE COMES OVER FOR DINNER. I'VE GOT NOTHING TO EAT, SO WE DRINK A LITTLE.

AND SHE SLEEPS OVER.

WE MAKE LOVE—AND WE MAKE LOVE AGAIN—IT'S WONDERFUL—SHE'S RADIANT! IT'S LIKE THERE'S A SUN IN HER BELLY.

A FEW WEEKS LATER, THE STORE CLOSES, AND WE GET LAID OFF.

WE DON'T CARE. WE DECIDE TO HAVE A BABY. SHE ALREADY HAS A LITTLE GIRL—THAT DOESN'T SCARE ME OFF.

TWO MONTHS LATER, SHE'S PREGNANT—AND I'M ON CLOUD NINE.

IT'S LIFE HOW I WANT TO LIVE IT, WITH SURPRISES POPPING UP RIGHT BEFORE MY VERY EYES.

70.

70

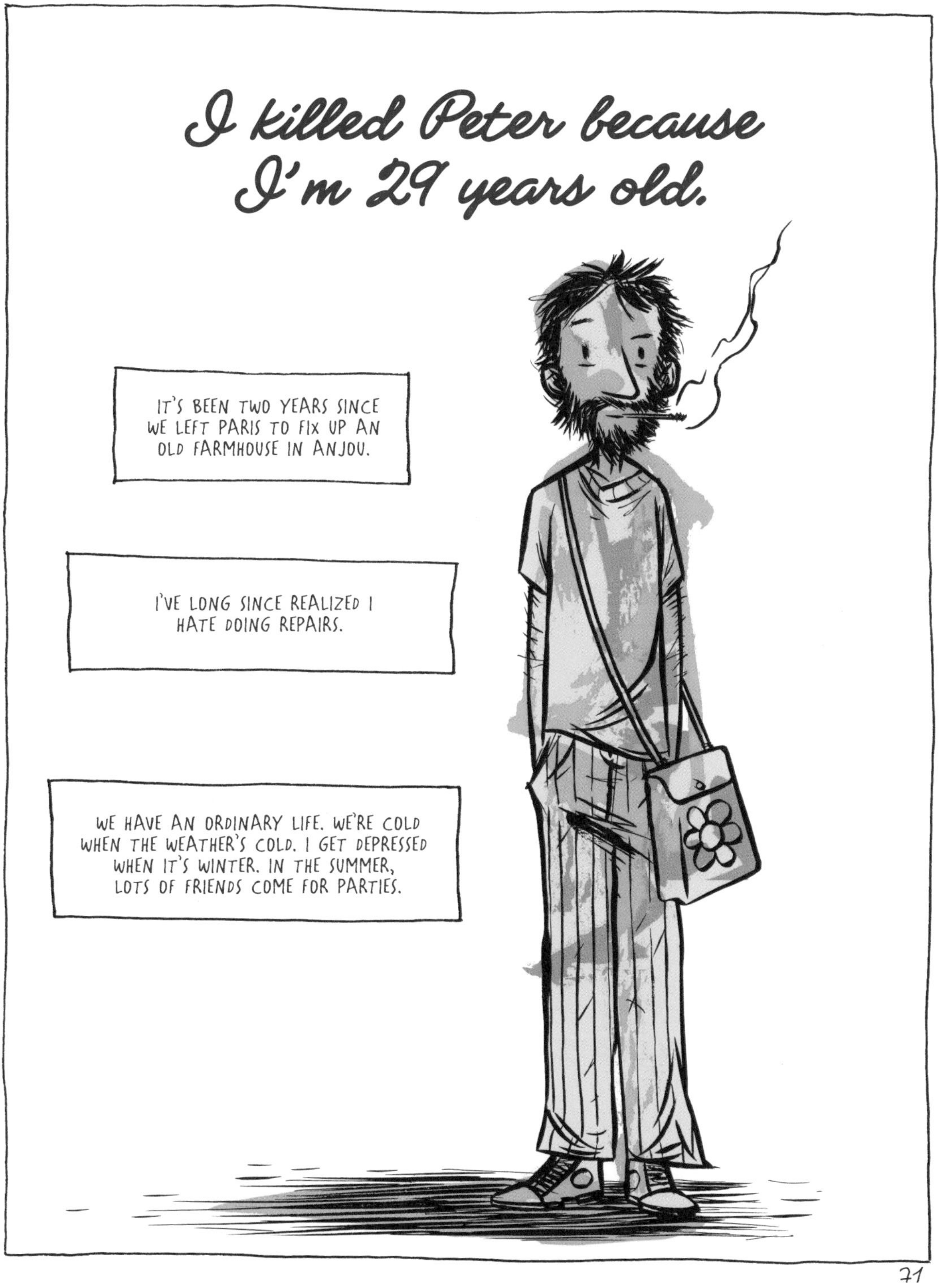
I killed Peter because I'm 29 years old.
IT'S BEEN TWO YEARS SINCE WE LEFT PARIS TO FIX UP AN OLD FARMHOUSE IN ANJOU.
I'VE LONG SINCE REALIZED I HATE DOING REPAIRS.
WE HAVE AN ORDINARY LIFE. WE'RE COLD WHEN THE WEATHER'S COLD. I GET DEPRESSED WHEN IT'S WINTER. IN THE SUMMER, LOTS OF FRIENDS COME FOR PARTIES.

71

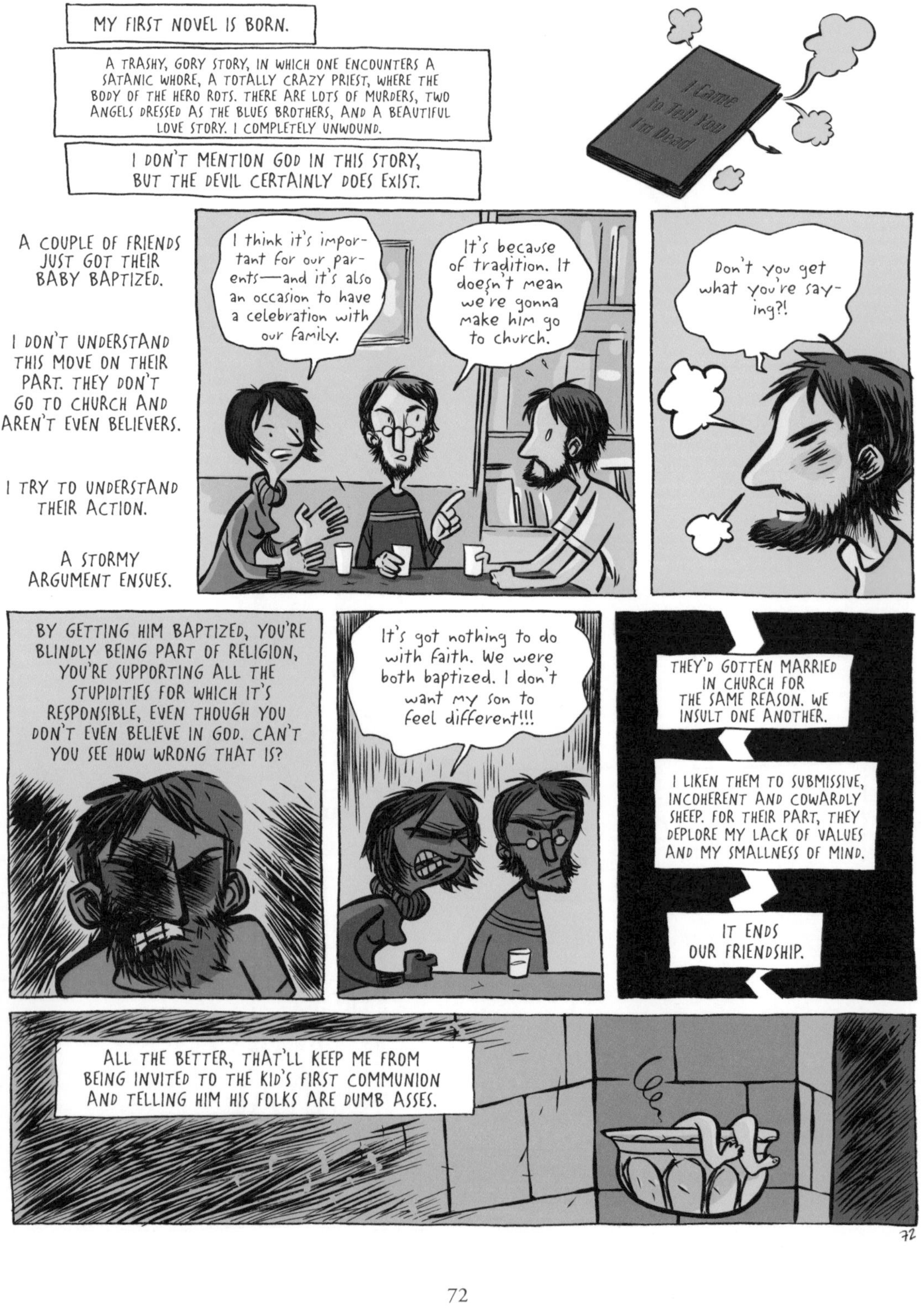
MY FIRST NOVEL IS BORN.
A TRASHY, GORY STORY, IN WHICH ONE ENCOUNTERS A SATANIC WHORE, A TOTALLY CRAZY PRIEST, WHERE THE BODY OF THE HERO ROTS. THERE ARE LOTS OF MURDERS, TWO ANGELS DRESSED AS THE BLUES BROTHERS, AND A BEAUTIFUL LOVE STORY. I COMPLETELY UNWOUND.
I DON'T MENTION GOD IN THIS STORY, BUT THE DEVIL CERTAINLY DOES EXIST.
I Came to Tell You I'm Dead
A COUPLE OF FRIENDS JUST GOT THEIR BABY BAPTIZED.
I DON'T UNDERSTAND THIS MOVE ON THEIR PART. THEY DON'T GO TO CHURCH AND AREN'T EVEN BELIEVERS.
I TRY TO UNDERSTAND THEIR ACTION.
A STORMY ARGUMENT ENSUES.
I think it's important for our parents—and it's also an occasion to have a celebration with our family.
It's because of tradition. It doesn't mean we're gonna make him go to church.
Don't you get what you're saying?!
BY GETTING HIM BAPTIZED, YOU'RE BLINDLY BEING PART OF RELIGION, YOU'RE SUPPORTING ALL THE STUPIDITIES FOR WHICH IT'S RESPONSIBLE, EVEN THOUGH YOU DON'T EVEN BELIEVE IN GOD. CAN'T YOU SEE HOW WRONG THAT IS?
It's got nothing to do with faith. We were both baptized. I don't want my son to feel different!!!
THEY'D GOTTEN MARRIED IN CHURCH FOR THE SAME REASON. WE INSULT ONE ANOTHER.
I LIKEN THEM TO SUBMISSIVE, INCOHERENT AND COWARDLY SHEEP. FOR THEIR PART, THEY DEPLORE MY LACK OF VALUES AND MY SMALLNESS OF MIND.
IT ENDS OUR FRIENDSHIP.
ALL THE BETTER, THAT'LL KEEP ME FROM BEING INVITED TO THE KID'S FIRST COMMUNION AND TELLING HIM HIS FOLKS ARE DUMB ASSES.
72

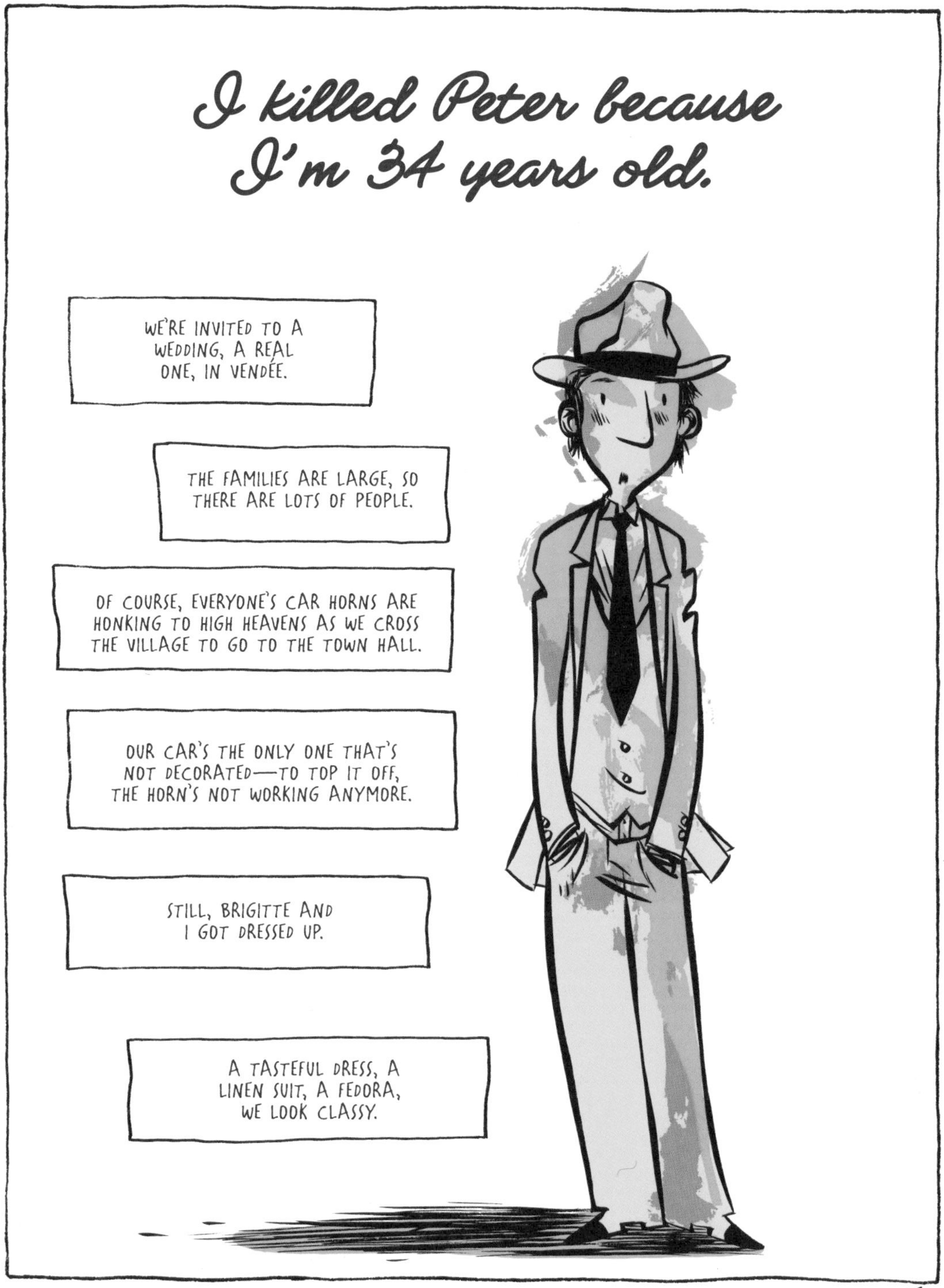
I killed Peter because I'm 34 years old.
WE'RE INVITED TO A WEDDING, A REAL ONE, IN VENDÉE.
THE FAMILIES ARE LARGE, SO THERE ARE LOTS OF PEOPLE.
OF COURSE, EVERYONE'S CAR HORNS ARE HONKING TO HIGH HEAVENS AS WE CROSS THE VILLAGE TO GO TO THE TOWN HALL.
OUR CAR'S THE ONLY ONE THAT'S NOT DECORATED—TO TOP IT OFF, THE HORN'S NOT WORKING ANYMORE.
STILL, BRIGITTE AND I GOT DRESSED UP.
A TASTEFUL DRESS, A LINEN SUIT, A FEDORA, WE LOOK CLASSY.

73.

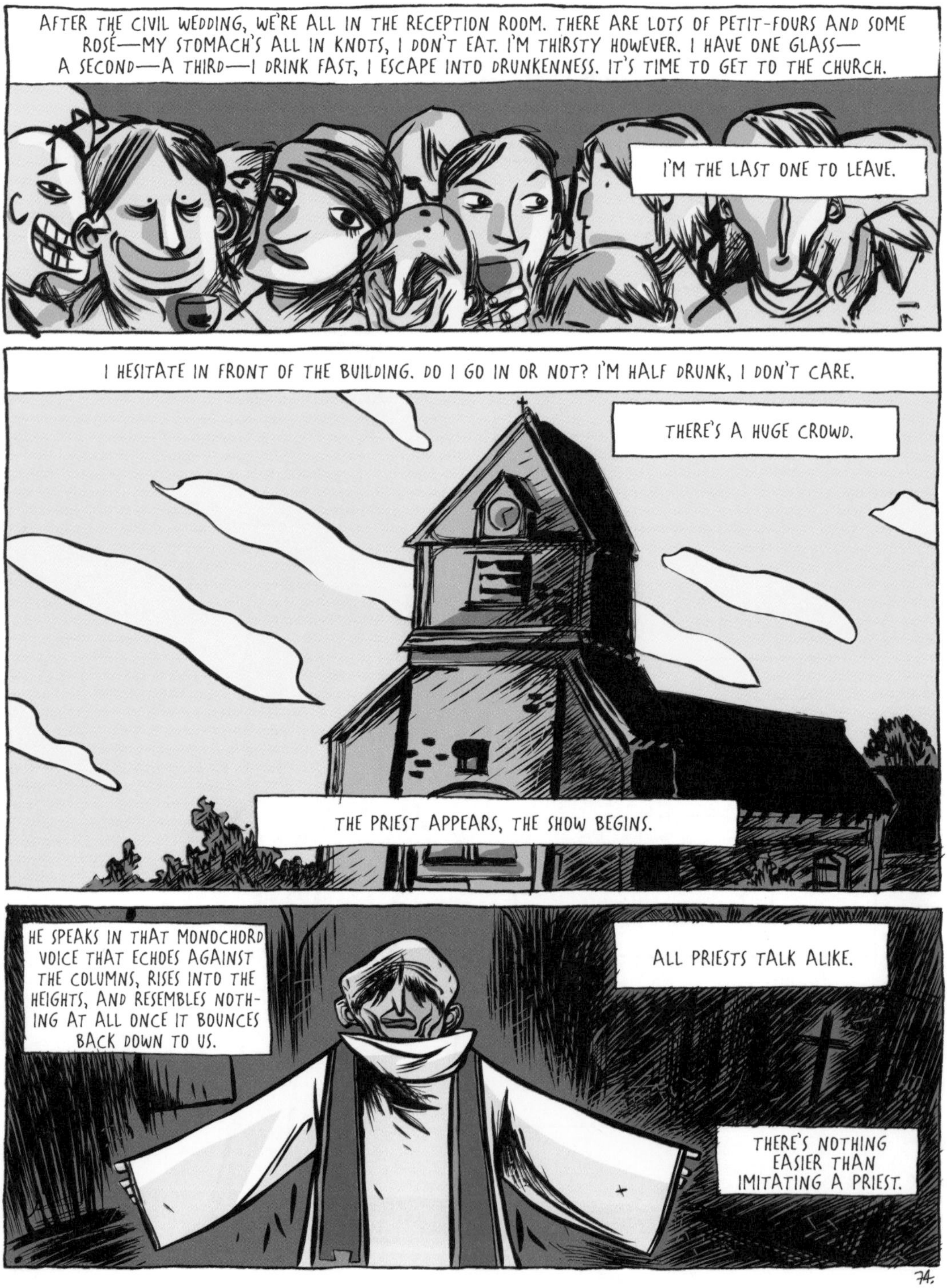
AFTER THE CIVIL WEDDING, WE'RE ALL IN THE RECEPTION ROOM. THERE ARE LOTS OF PETIT-FOURS AND SOME ROSÉ—MY STOMACH'S ALL IN KNOTS, I DON'T EAT. I'M THIRSTY HOWEVER. I HAVE ONE GLASS—A SECOND—A THIRD—I DRINK FAST, I ESCAPE INTO DRUNKENNESS. IT'S TIME TO GET TO THE CHURCH.
I'M THE LAST ONE TO LEAVE.
I HESITATE IN FRONT OF THE BUILDING. DO I GO IN OR NOT? I'M HALF DRUNK, I DON'T CARE.
THERE'S A HUGE CROWD.
THE PRIEST APPEARS, THE SHOW BEGINS.
HE SPEAKS IN THAT MONOCHORD VOICE THAT ECHOES AGAINST THE COLUMNS, RISES INTO THE HEIGHTS, AND RESEMBLES NOTHING AT ALL ONCE IT BOUNCES BACK DOWN TO US.
ALL PRIESTS TALK ALIKE.
THERE'S NOTHING EASIER THAN IMITATING A PRIEST.
74.

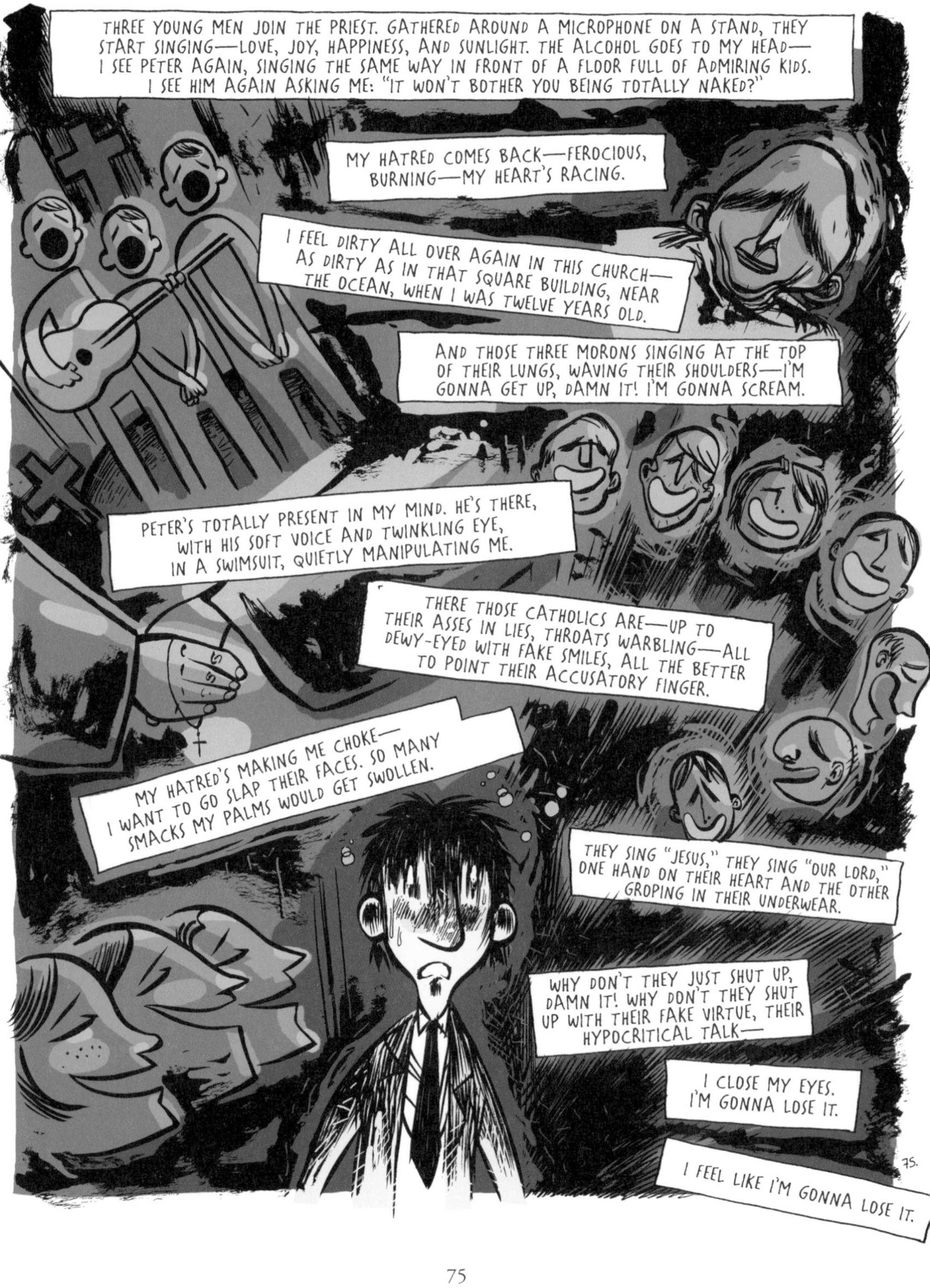
THREE YOUNG MEN JOIN THE PRIEST. GATHERED AROUND A MICROPHONE ON A STAND, THEY START SINGING—LOVE, JOY, HAPPINESS, AND SUNLIGHT. THE ALCOHOL GOES TO MY HEAD—I SEE PETER AGAIN, SINGING THE SAME WAY IN FRONT OF A FLOOR FULL OF ADMIRING KIDS. I SEE HIM AGAIN ASKING ME: "IT WON'T BOTHER YOU BEING TOTALLY NAKED?"
MY HATRED COMES BACK—FEROCIOUS, BURNING—MY HEART'S RACING.
I FEEL DIRTY ALL OVER AGAIN IN THIS CHURCH—AS DIRTY AS IN THAT SQUARE BUILDING, NEAR THE OCEAN, WHEN I WAS TWELVE YEARS OLD.
AND THOSE THREE MORONS SINGING AT THE TOP OF THEIR LUNGS, WAVING THEIR SHOULDERS—I'M GONNA GET UP, DAMN IT! I'M GONNA SCREAM.
PETER'S TOTALLY PRESENT IN MY MIND. HE'S THERE, WITH HIS SOFT VOICE AND TWINKLING EYE, IN A SWIMSUIT, QUIETLY MANIPULATING ME.
THERE THOSE CATHOLICS ARE—UP TO THEIR ASSES IN LIES, THROATS WARBLING—ALL DEWY-EYED WITH FAKE SMILES, ALL THE BETTER TO POINT THEIR ACCUSATORY FINGER.
MY HATRED'S MAKING ME CHOKE—I WANT TO GO SLAP THEIR FACES. SO MANY SMACKS MY PALMS WOULD GET SWOLLEN.
THEY SING "JESUS," THEY SING "OUR LORD," ONE HAND ON THEIR HEART AND THE OTHER GROPING IN THEIR UNDERWEAR.
WHY DON'T THEY JUST SHUT UP, DAMN IT! WHY DON'T THEY SHUT UP WITH THEIR FAKE VIRTUE, THEIR HYPOCRITICAL TALK—
I CLOSE MY EYES. I'M GONNA LOSE IT.
75.
I FEEL LIKE I'M GONNA LOSE IT.

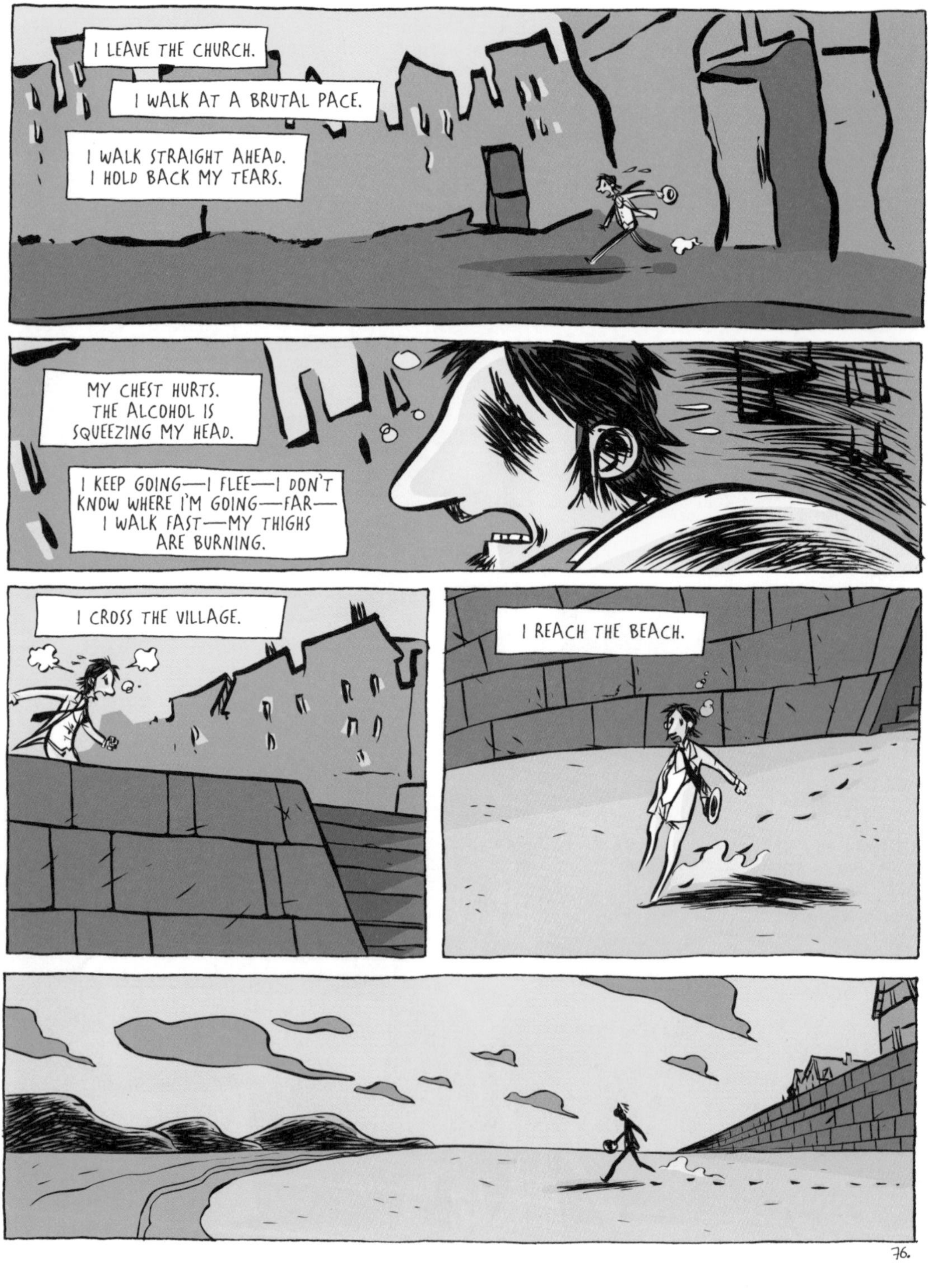

I LEAVE THE CHURCH.
I WALK AT A BRUTAL PACE.
I WALK STRAIGHT AHEAD. I HOLD BACK MY TEARS.
MY CHEST HURTS. THE ALCOHOL IS SQUEEZING MY HEAD.
I KEEP GOING—I FLEE—I DON'T KNOW WHERE I'M GOING—FAR—I WALK FAST—MY THIGHS ARE BURNING.
I CROSS THE VILLAGE.
I REACH THE BEACH.
76.

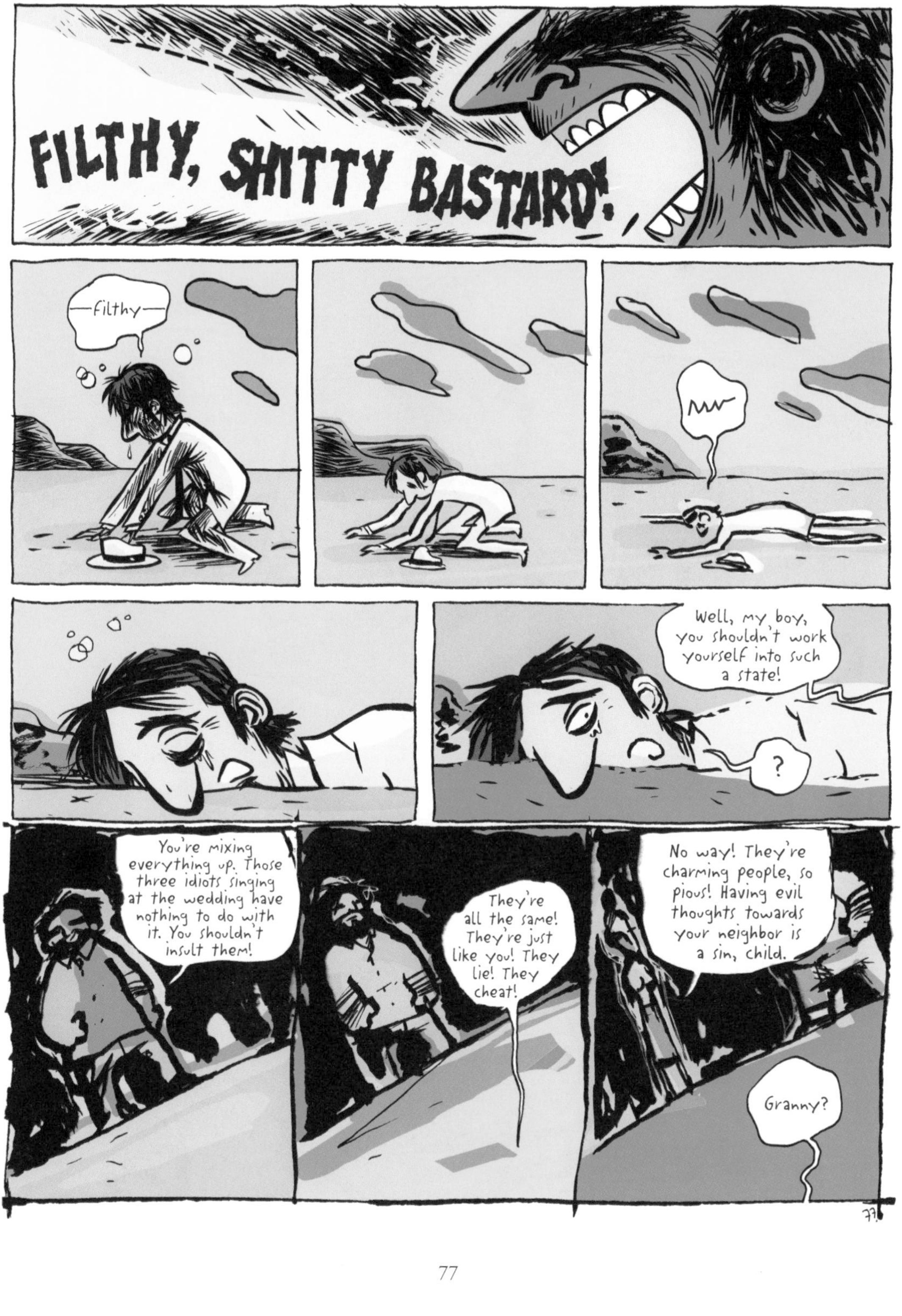
FILTHY, SHITTY BASTARD!
filthy
MM
Well, my boy, you shouldn't work yourself into such a state!
?
You're mixing everything up. Those three idiots singing at the wedding have nothing to do with it. You shouldn't insult them!
They're all the same! They're just like you! They lie! They cheat!
No way! They're charming people, so pious! Having evil thoughts towards your neighbor is a sin, child.
Granny?
77

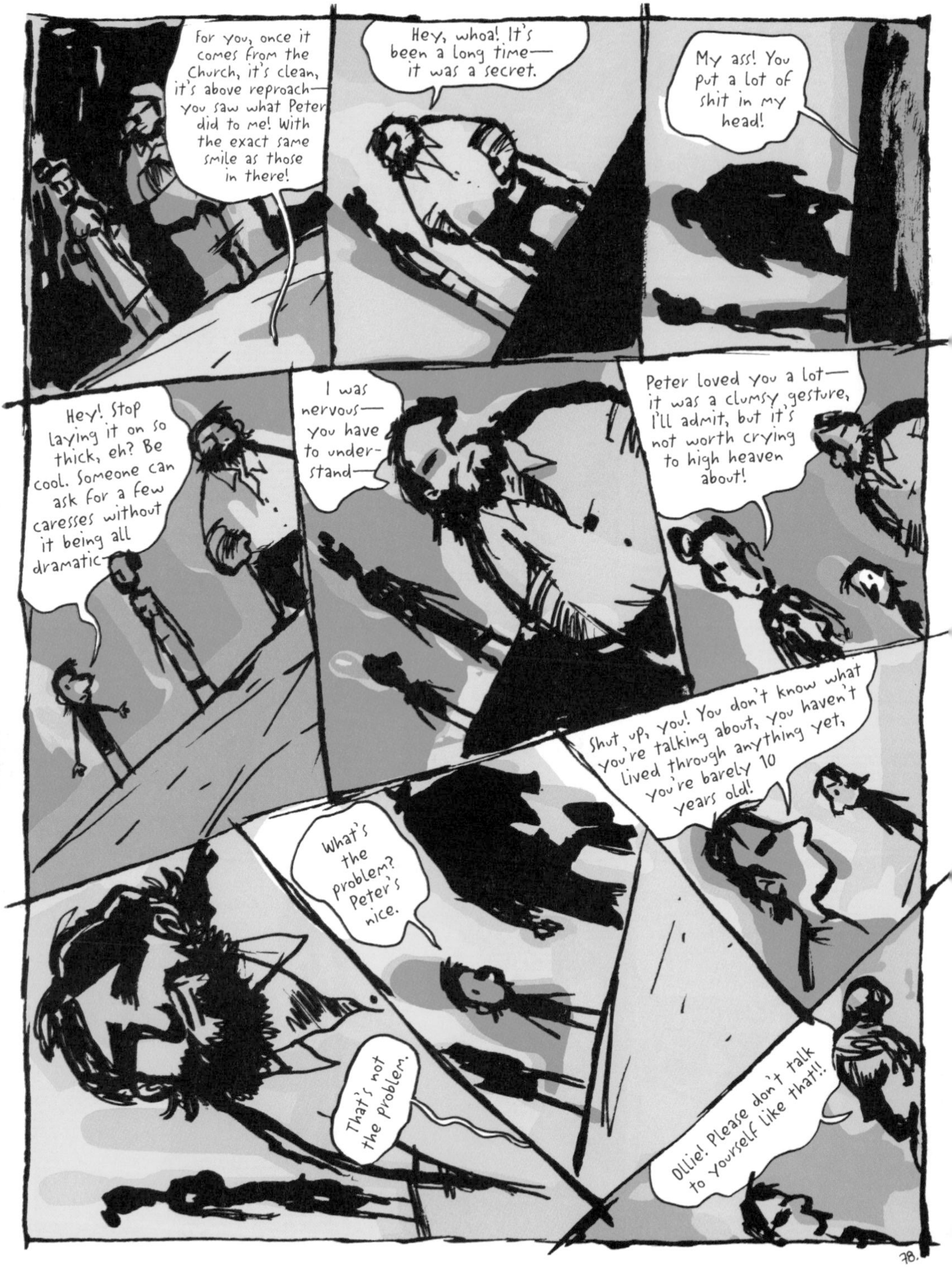
For you, once it comes from the Church, it's clean, it's above reproach— you saw what Peter did to me! With the exact same smile as those in there!
Hey, whoa! It's been a long time— it was a secret.
My ass! You put a lot of shit in my head!
Hey! Stop laying it on so thick, eh? Be cool. Someone can ask for a few caresses without it being all dramatic—
I was nervous— you have to under-stand—
Peter loved you a lot— it was a clumsy gesture, I'll admit, but it's not worth crying to high heaven about!
Shut up, you! You don't know what you're talking about, you haven't lived through anything yet, you're barely 10 years old!
What's the problem? Peter's nice.
That's not the problem.
Ollie! Please don't talk to yourself like that!!
78.

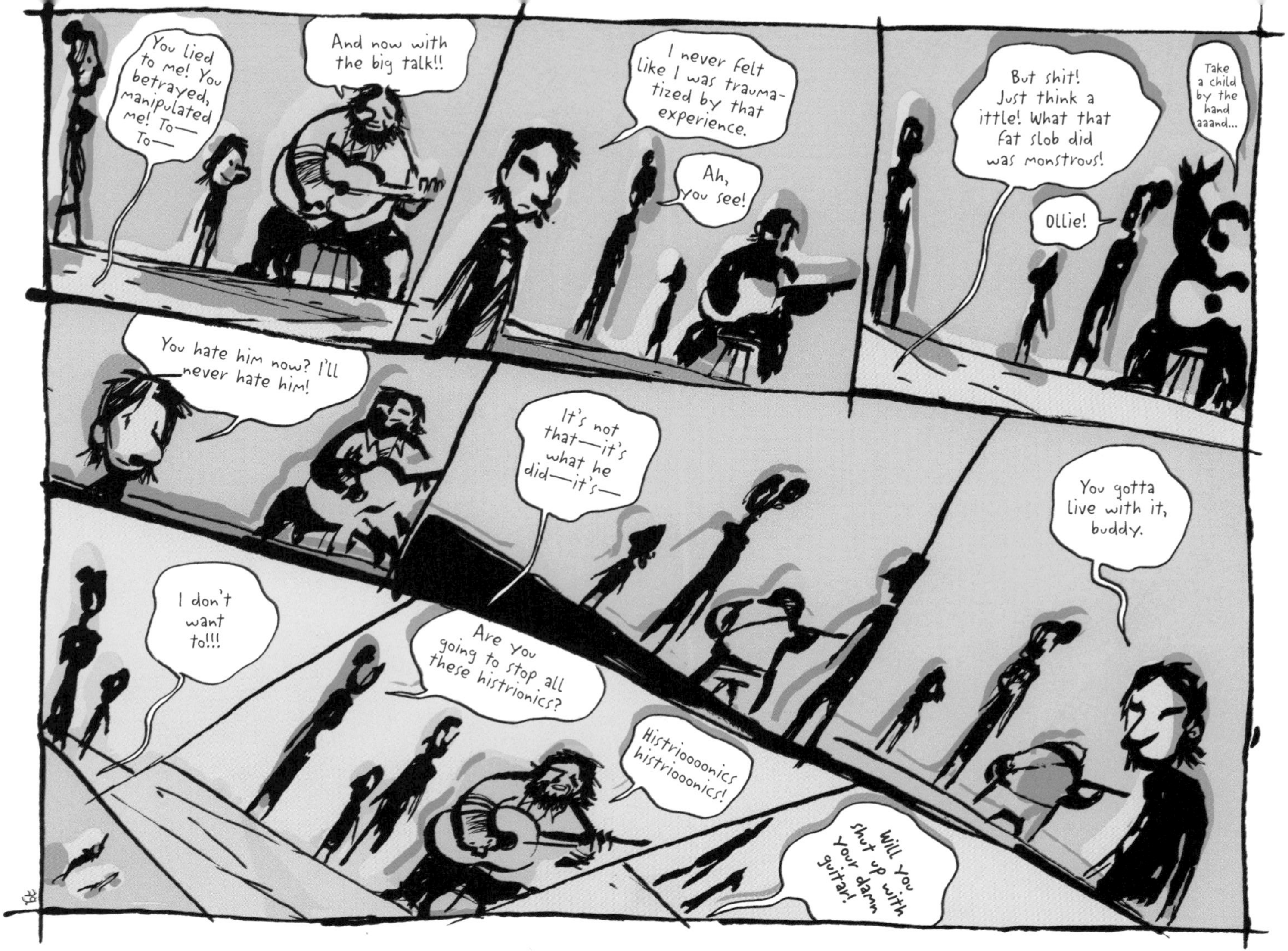
You lied to me! You betrayed, manipulated me! To— To—
And now with the big talk!!
I never felt like I was traumatized by that experience.
Ah, you see!
But shit! Just think a ittle! What that fat slob did was monstrous!
Ollie!
Take a child by the hand aaand...
You hate him now? I'll never hate him!
It's not that—it's what he did—it's—
You gotta live with it, buddy.
I don't want to!!!
Are you going to stop all these histrionics?
Histrioooonics histrioooonics!
Will you shut up with your damn guitar!

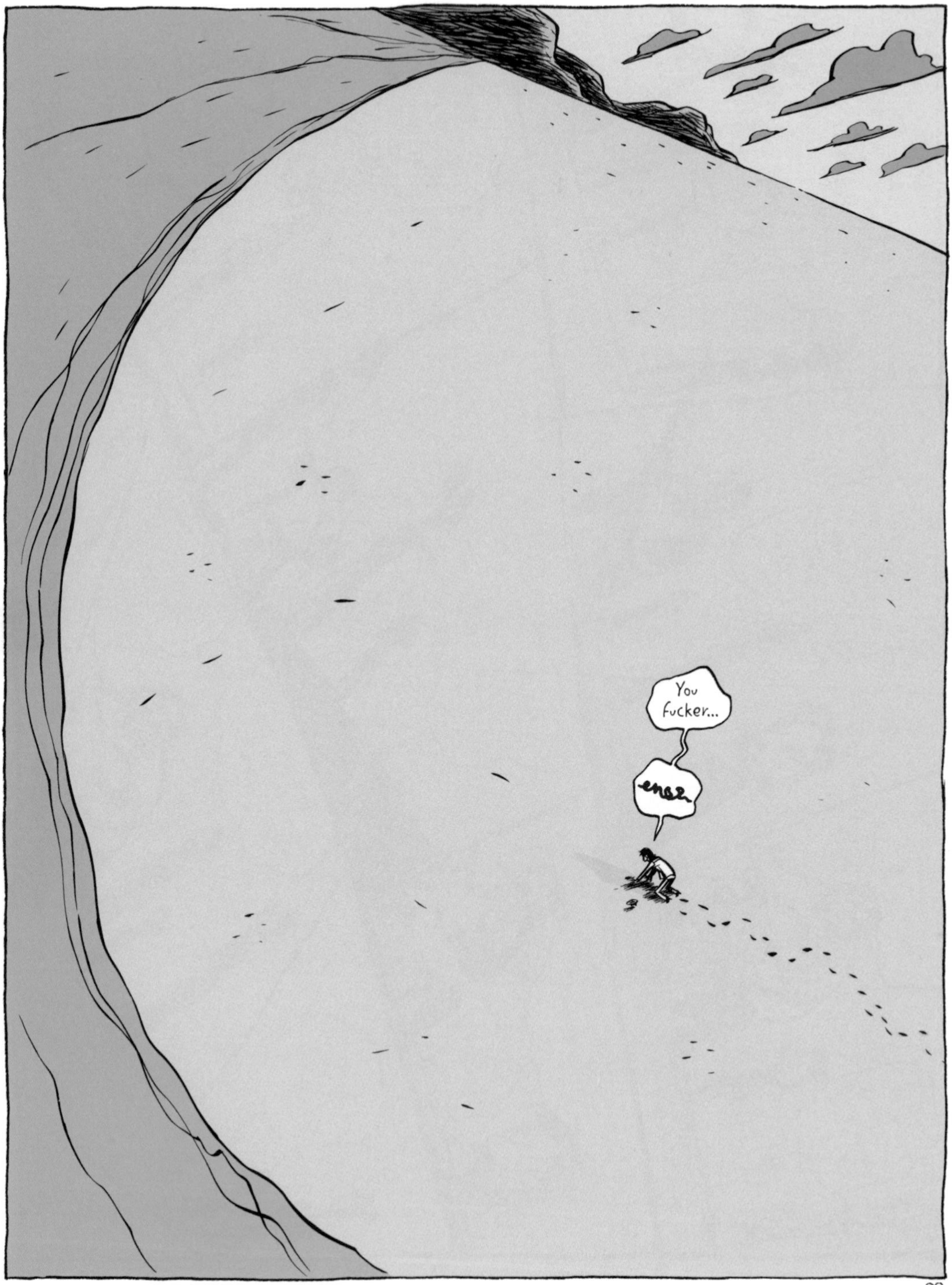
You fucker...

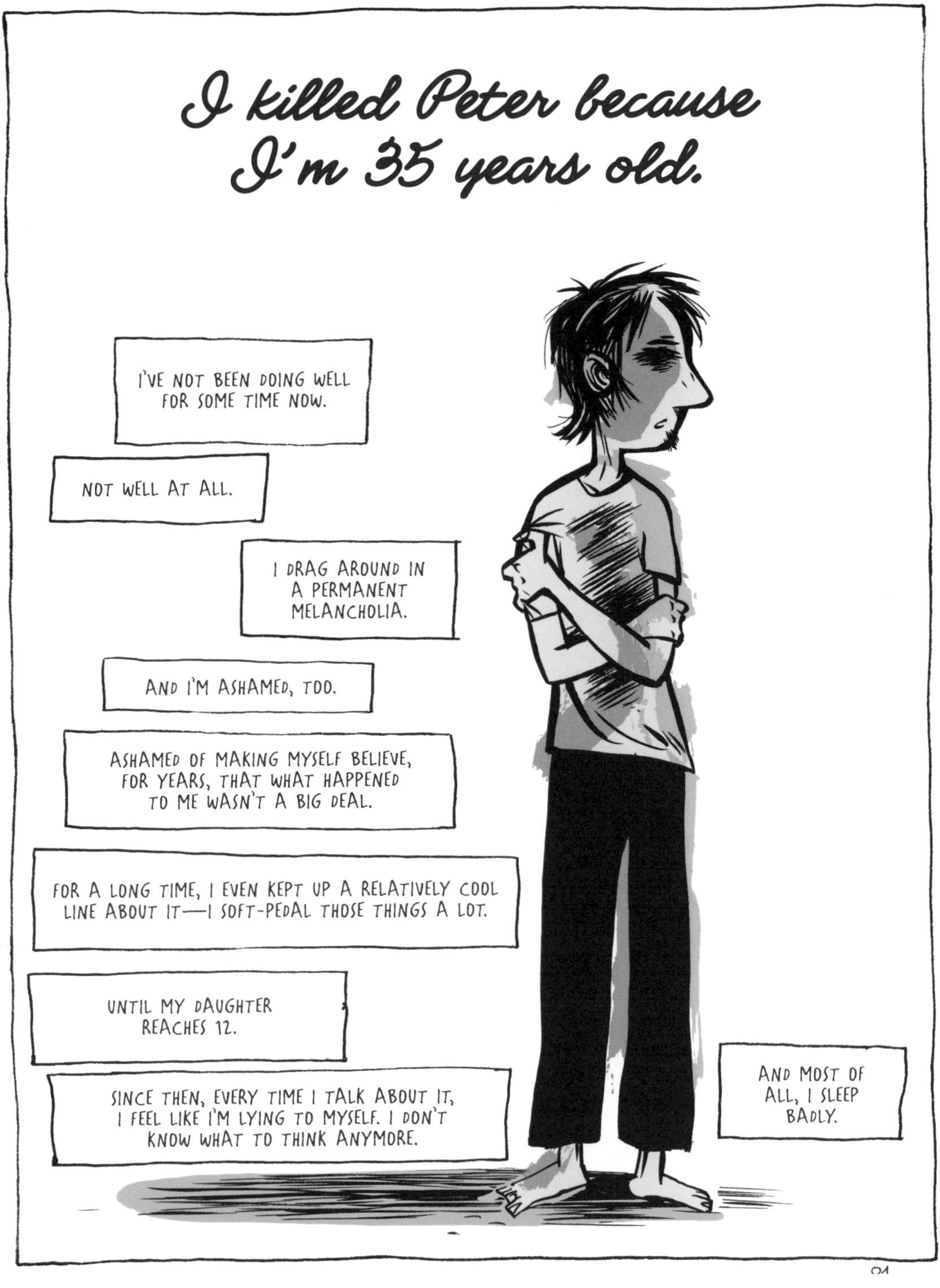
I killed Peter because I'm 35 years old.
I'VE NOT BEEN DOING WELL FOR SOME TIME NOW.
NOT WELL AT ALL.
I DRAG AROUND IN A PERMANENT MELANCHOLIA.
AND I'M ASHAMED, TOO.
ASHAMED OF MAKING MYSELF BELIEVE, FOR YEARS, THAT WHAT HAPPENED TO ME WASN'T A BIG DEAL.
FOR A LONG TIME, I EVEN KEPT UP A RELATIVELY COOL LINE ABOUT IT—I SOFT-PEDAL THOSE THINGS A LOT.
UNTIL MY DAUGHTER REACHES 12.
SINCE THEN, EVERY TIME I TALK ABOUT IT, I FEEL LIKE I'M LYING TO MYSELF. I DON'T KNOW WHAT TO THINK ANYMORE.
AND MOST OF ALL, I SLEEP BADLY.

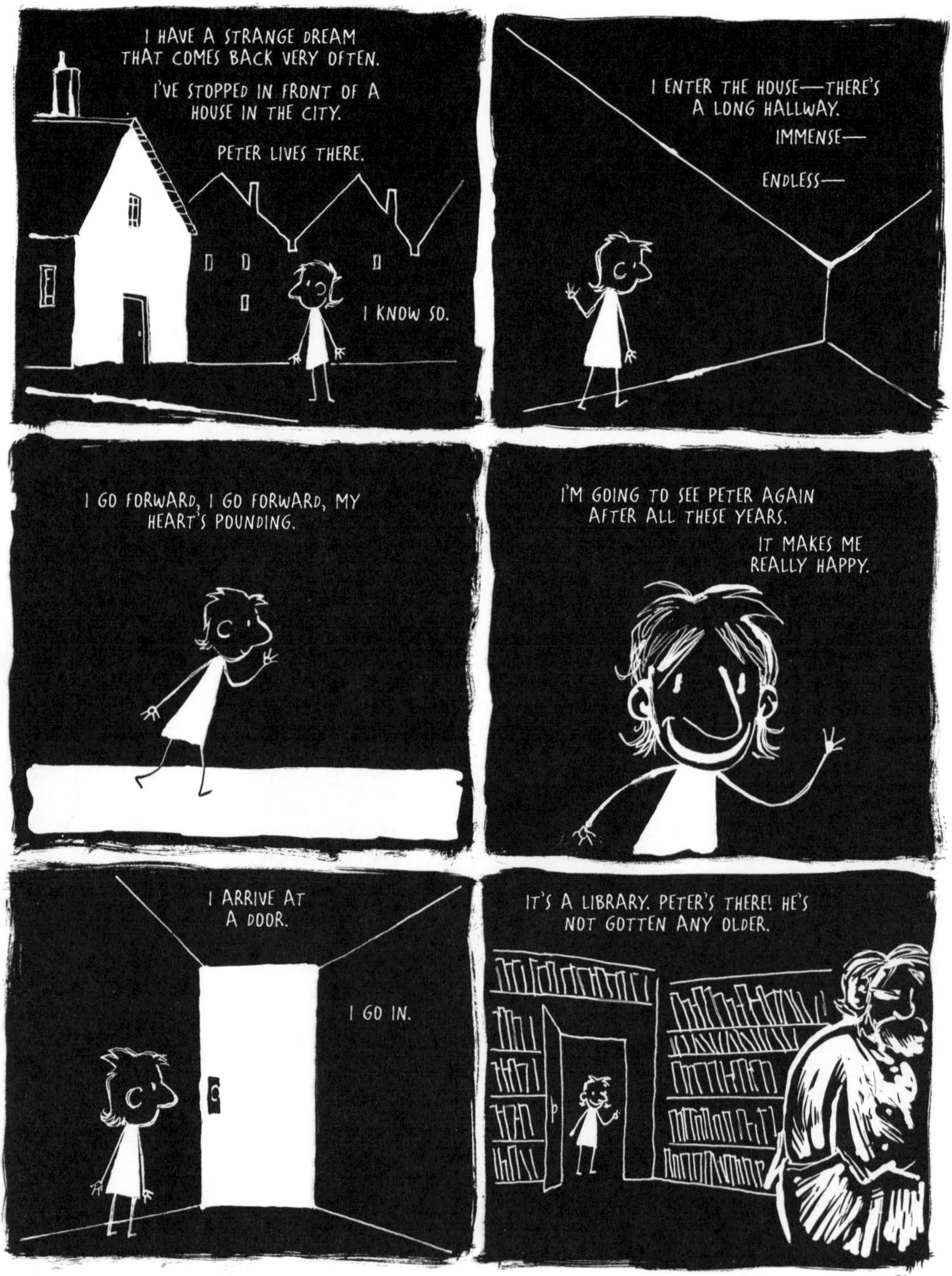
I HAVE A STRANGE DREAM THAT COMES BACK VERY OFTEN.
I'VE STOPPED IN FRONT OF A HOUSE IN THE CITY.
PETER LIVES THERE.
I KNOW SO.
I ENTER THE HOUSE—THERE'S A LONG HALLWAY.
IMMENSE—
ENDLESS—
I GO FORWARD, I GO FORWARD, MY HEART'S POUNDING.
I'M GOING TO SEE PETER AGAIN AFTER ALL THESE YEARS.
IT MAKES ME REALLY HAPPY.
I ARRIVE AT A DOOR.
I GO IN.
IT'S A LIBRARY. PETER'S THERE! HE'S NOT GOTTEN ANY OLDER.
82.

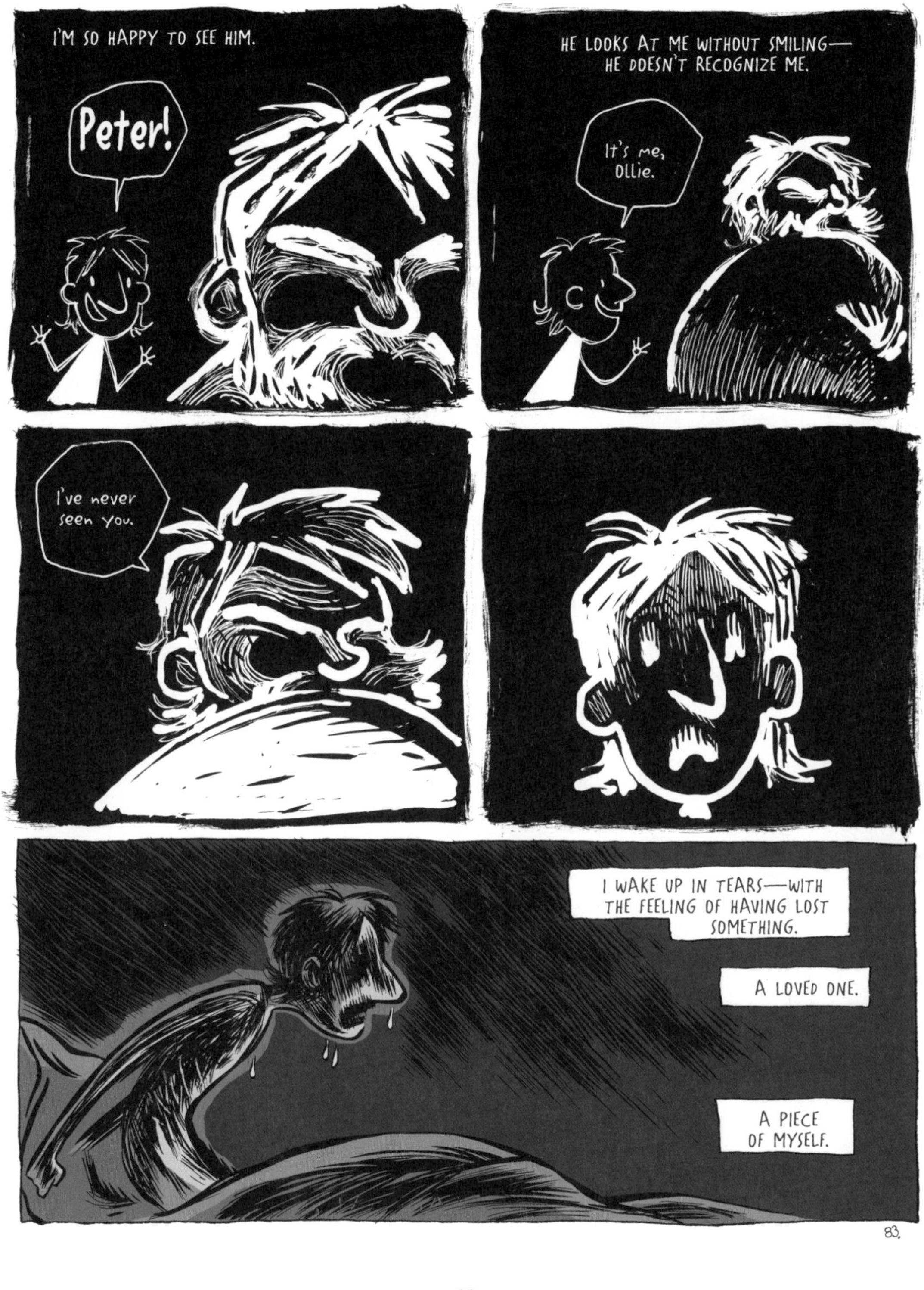
I'M SO HAPPY TO SEE HIM.
Peter!
HE LOOKS AT ME WITHOUT SMILING—
HE DOESN'T RECOGNIZE ME.
It's me, Ollie.
I've never seen you.
I WAKE UP IN TEARS—WITH THE FEELING OF HAVING LOST SOMETHING.
A LOVED ONE.
A PIECE OF MYSELF.
83.

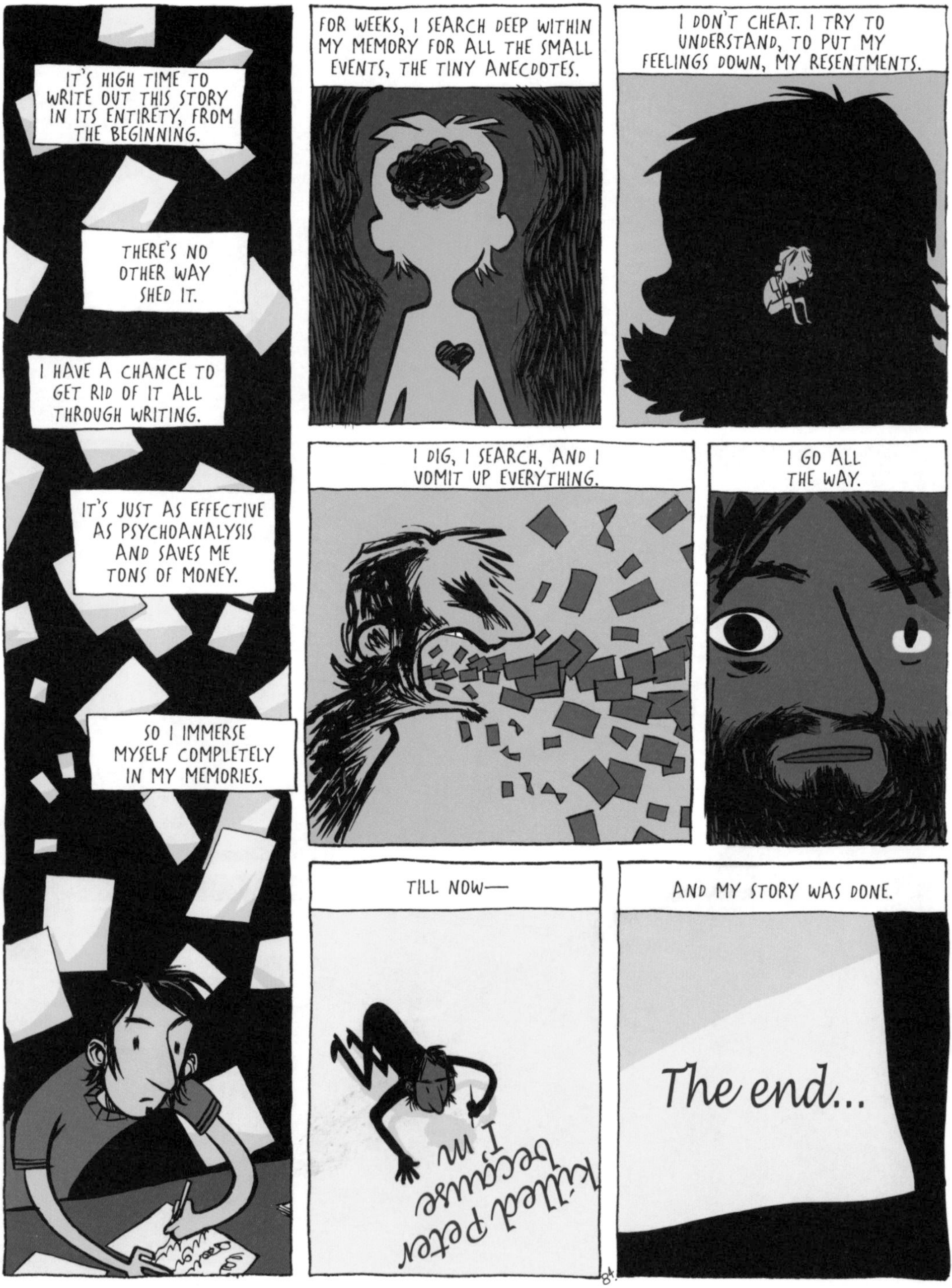
IT'S HIGH TIME TO WRITE OUT THIS STORY IN ITS ENTIRETY, FROM THE BEGINNING.
THERE'S NO OTHER WAY SHED IT.
I HAVE A CHANCE TO GET RID OF IT ALL THROUGH WRITING.
IT'S JUST AS EFFECTIVE AS PSYCHOANALYSIS AND SAVES ME TONS OF MONEY.
SO I IMMERSE MYSELF COMPLETELY IN MY MEMORIES.
FOR WEEKS, I SEARCH DEEP WITHIN MY MEMORY FOR ALL THE SMALL EVENTS, THE TINY ANECDOTES.
I DON'T CHEAT. I TRY TO UNDERSTAND, TO PUT MY FEELINGS DOWN, MY RESENTMENTS.
I DIG, I SEARCH, AND I VOMIT UP EVERYTHING.
I GO ALL THE WAY.
TILL NOW—
killed Peter
because
AND MY STORY WAS DONE.
The end...

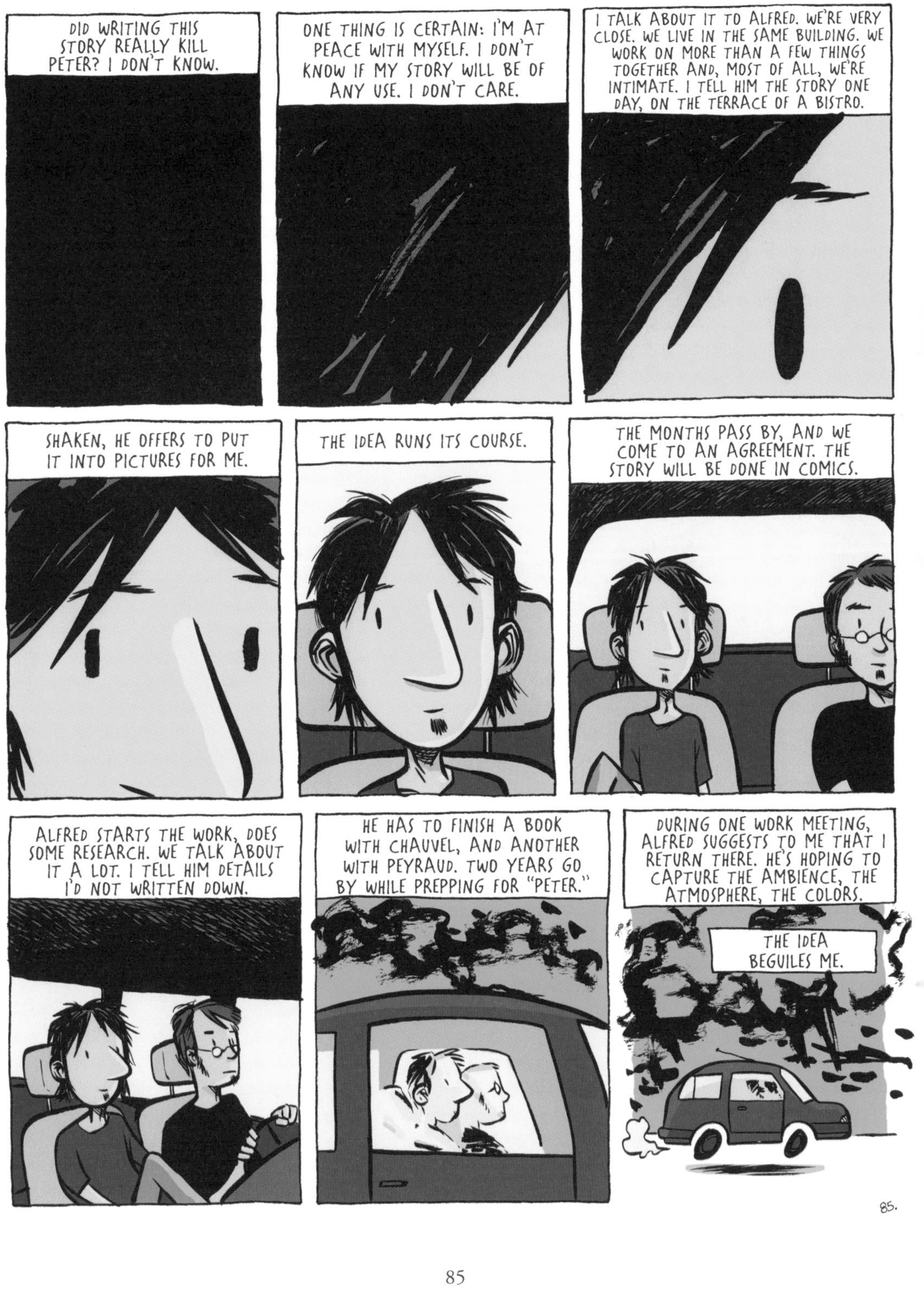

DID WRITING THIS STORY REALLY KILL PETER? I DON'T KNOW.
ONE THING IS CERTAIN: I'M AT PEACE WITH MYSELF. I DON'T KNOW IF MY STORY WILL BE OF ANY USE. I DON'T CARE.
I TALK ABOUT IT TO ALFRED. WE'RE VERY CLOSE. WE LIVE IN THE SAME BUILDING. WE WORK ON MORE THAN A FEW THINGS TOGETHER AND, MOST OF ALL, WE'RE INTIMATE. I TELL HIM THE STORY ONE DAY, ON THE TERRACE OF A BISTRO.
SHAKEN, HE OFFERS TO PUT IT INTO PICTURES FOR ME.
THE IDEA RUNS ITS COURSE.
THE MONTHS PASS BY, AND WE COME TO AN AGREEMENT. THE STORY WILL BE DONE IN COMICS.
ALFRED STARTS THE WORK, DOES SOME RESEARCH. WE TALK ABOUT IT A LOT. I TELL HIM DETAILS I'D NOT WRITTEN DOWN.
HE HAS TO FINISH A BOOK WITH CHAUVEL, AND ANOTHER WITH PEYRAUD. TWO YEARS GO BY WHILE PREPPING FOR "PETER."
DURING ONE WORK MEETING, ALFRED SUGGESTS TO ME THAT I RETURN THERE. HE'S HOPING TO CAPTURE THE AMBIENCE, THE ATMOSPHERE, THE COLORS.
THE IDEA BEGUILES ME.
85.

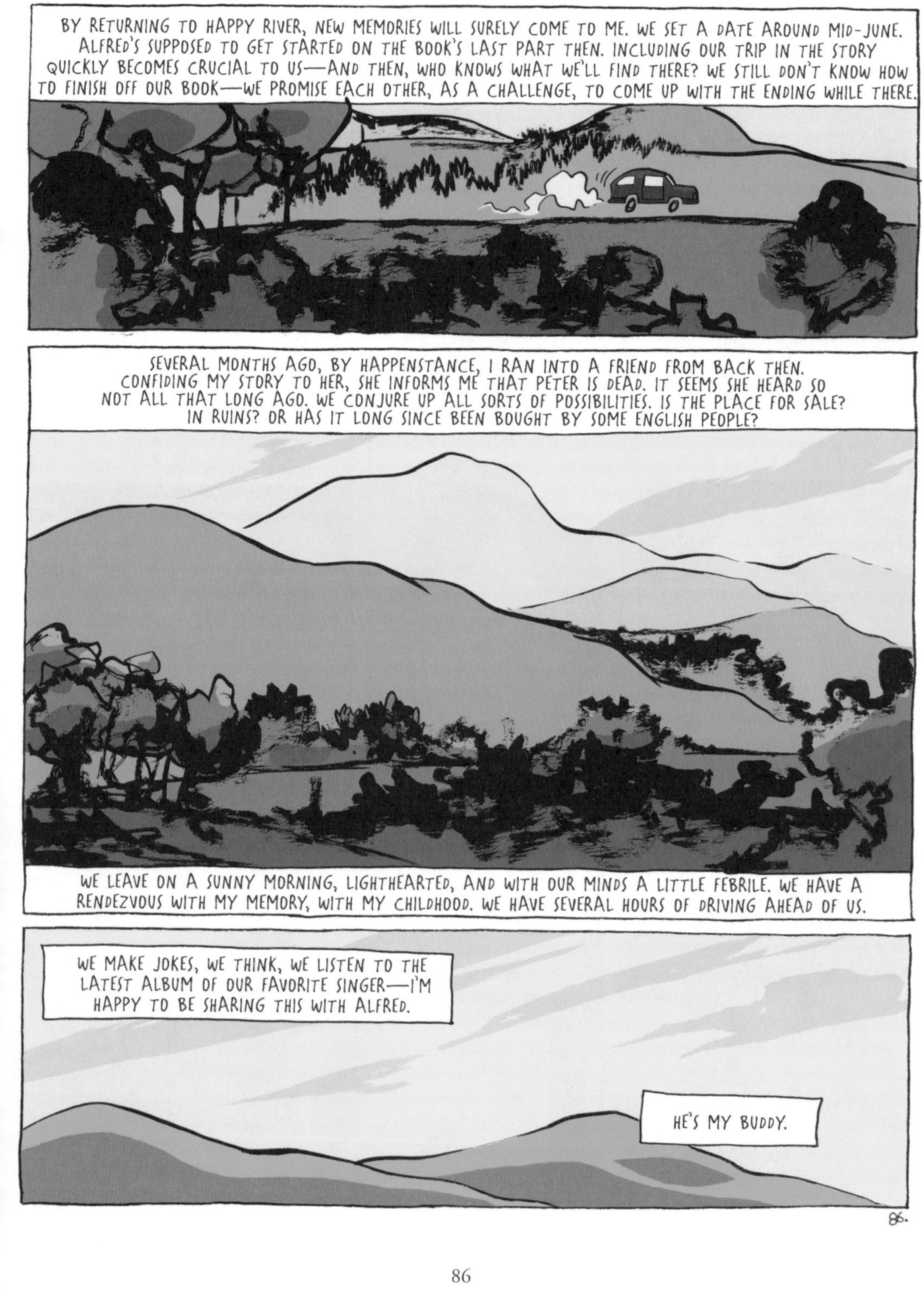
BY RETURNING TO HAPPY RIVER, NEW MEMORIES WILL SURELY COME TO ME. WE SET A DATE AROUND MID-JUNE. ALFRED'S SUPPOSED TO GET STARTED ON THE BOOK'S LAST PART THEN. INCLUDING OUR TRIP IN THE STORY QUICKLY BECOMES CRUCIAL TO US—AND THEN, WHO KNOWS WHAT WE'LL FIND THERE? WE STILL DON'T KNOW HOW TO FINISH OFF OUR BOOK—WE PROMISE EACH OTHER, AS A CHALLENGE, TO COME UP WITH THE ENDING WHILE THERE.
SEVERAL MONTHS AGO, BY HAPPENSTANCE, I RAN INTO A FRIEND FROM BACK THEN. CONFIDING MY STORY TO HER, SHE INFORMS ME THAT PETER IS DEAD. IT SEEMS SHE HEARD SO NOT ALL THAT LONG AGO. WE CONJURE UP ALL SORTS OF POSSIBILITIES. IS THE PLACE FOR SALE? IN RUINS? OR HAS IT LONG SINCE BEEN BOUGHT BY SOME ENGLISH PEOPLE?
WE LEAVE ON A SUNNY MORNING, LIGHTHEARTED, AND WITH OUR MINDS A LITTLE FEBRILE. WE HAVE A RENDEZVOUS WITH MY MEMORY, WITH MY CHILDHOOD. WE HAVE SEVERAL HOURS OF DRIVING AHEAD OF US.
WE MAKE JOKES, WE THINK, WE LISTEN TO THE LATEST ALBUM OF OUR FAVORITE SINGER—I'M HAPPY TO BE SHARING THIS WITH ALFRED.
HE'S MY BUDDY.
86.

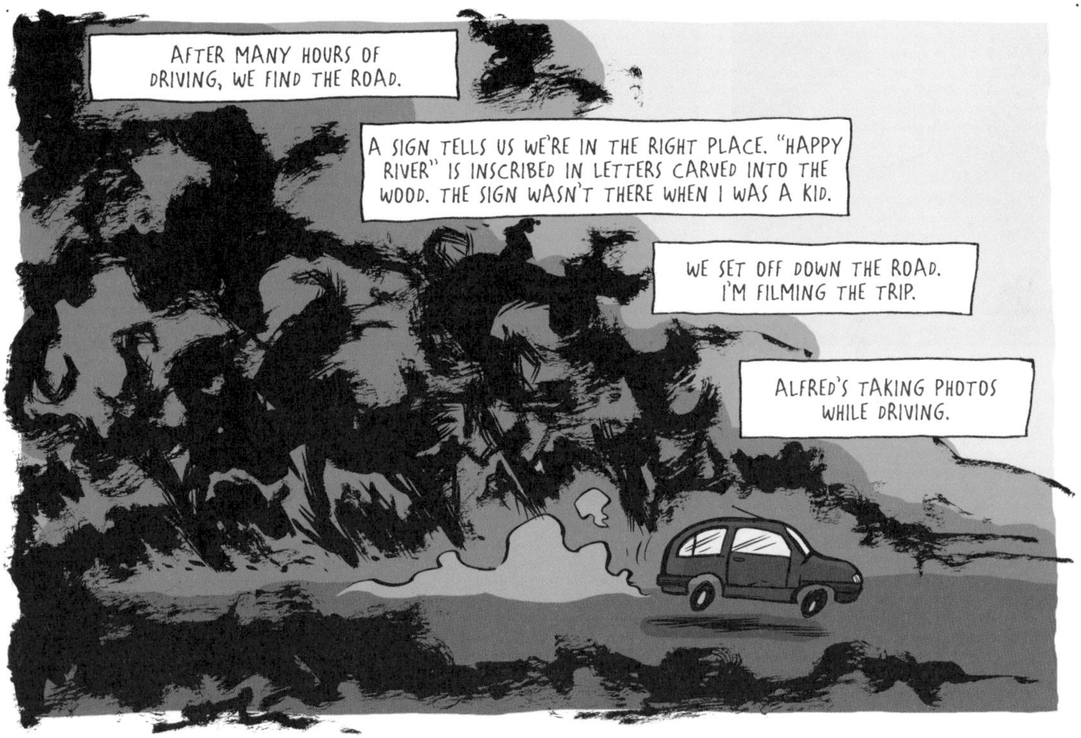
AFTER MANY HOURS OF DRIVING, WE FIND THE ROAD.
A SIGN TELLS US WE'RE IN THE RIGHT PLACE. "HAPPY RIVER" IS INSCRIBED IN LETTERS CARVED INTO THE WOOD. THE SIGN WASN'T THERE WHEN I WAS A KID.
WE SET OFF DOWN THE ROAD. I'M FILMING THE TRIP.
ALFRED'S TAKING PHOTOS WHILE DRIVING.

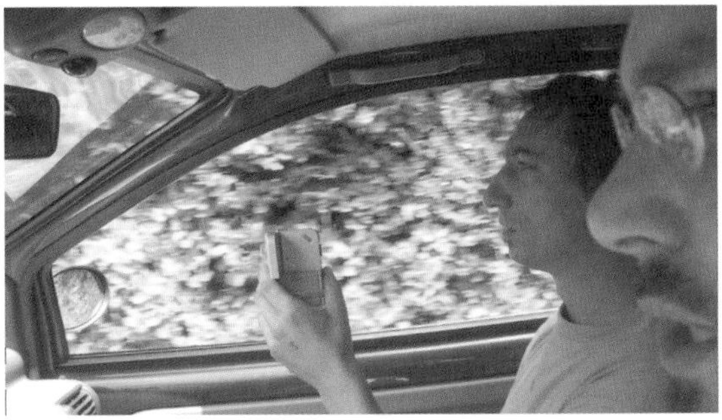

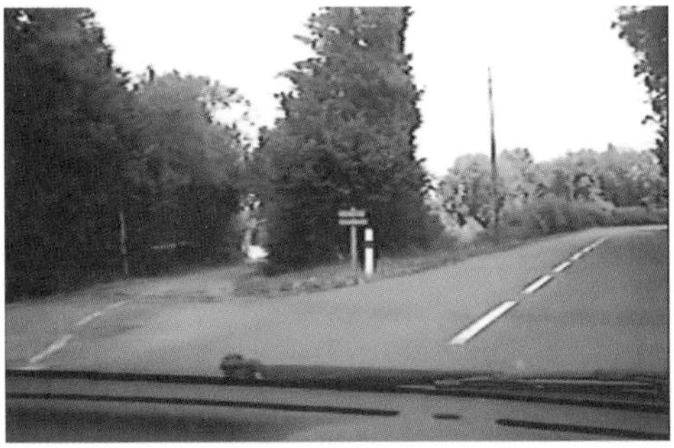

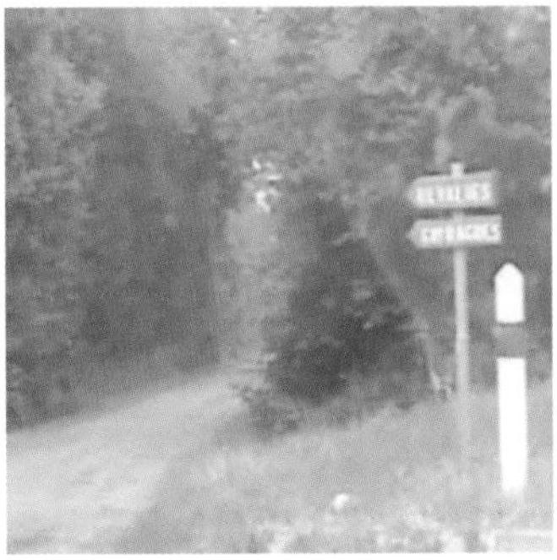

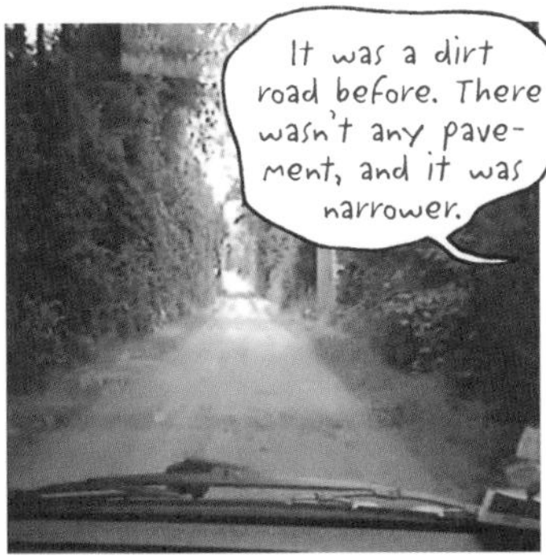
It was a dirt road before. There wasn't any pavement, and it was narrower.

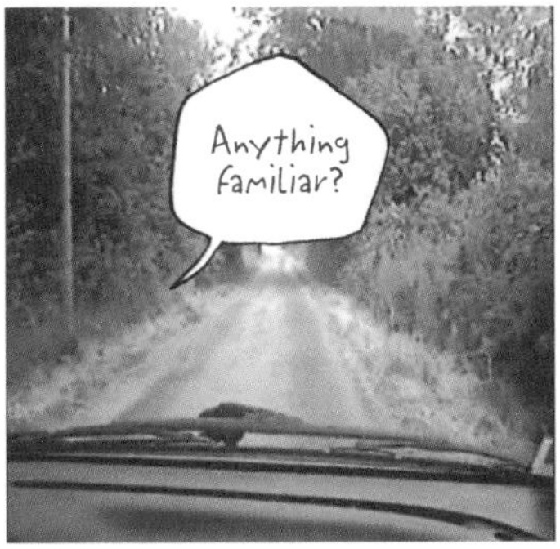
Anything familiar?

87

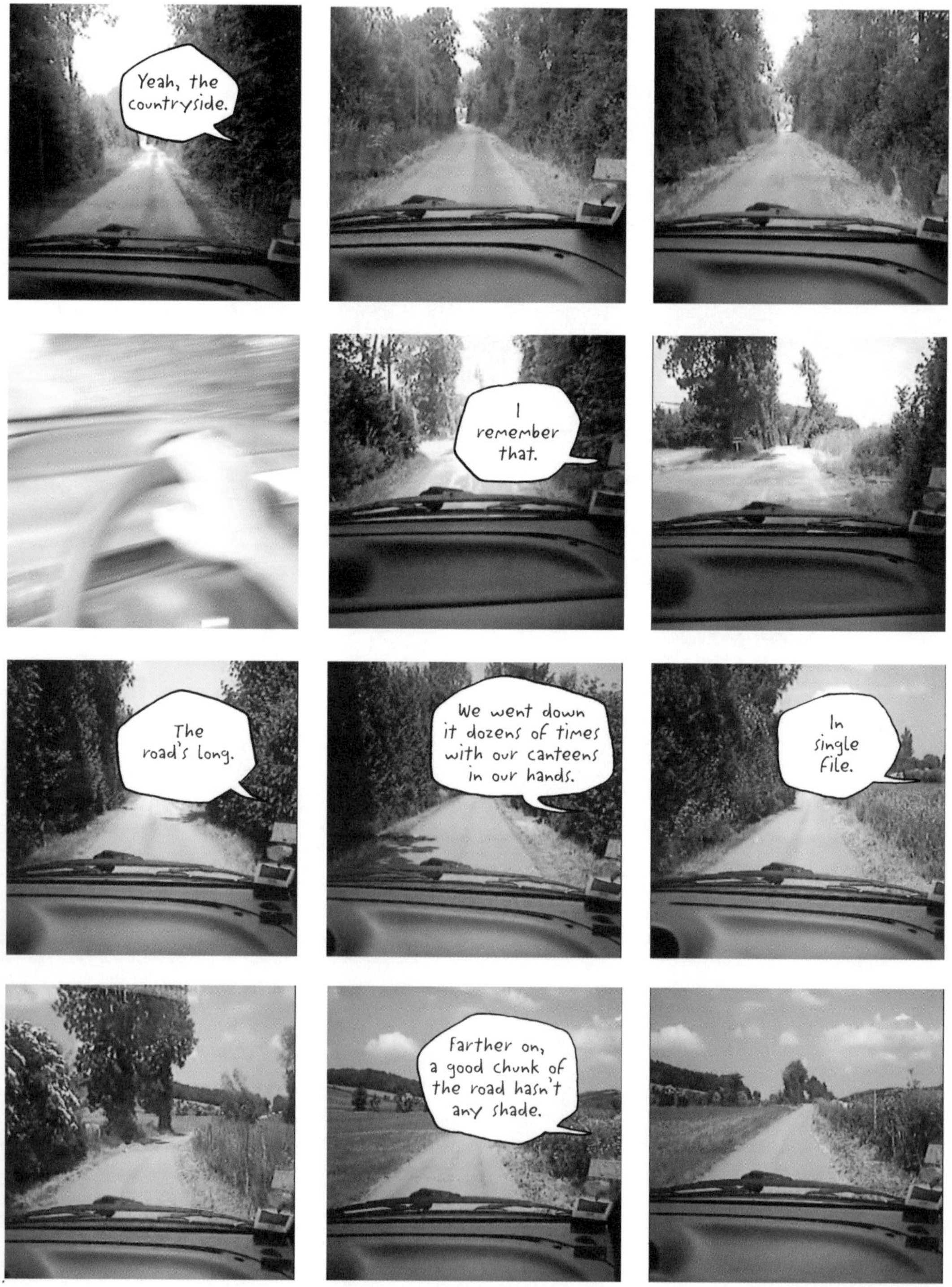
Yeah, the countryside.
I remember that.
The road's long.
We went down it dozens of times with our canteens in our hands.
In single file.
Farther on, a good chunk of the road hasn't any shade.

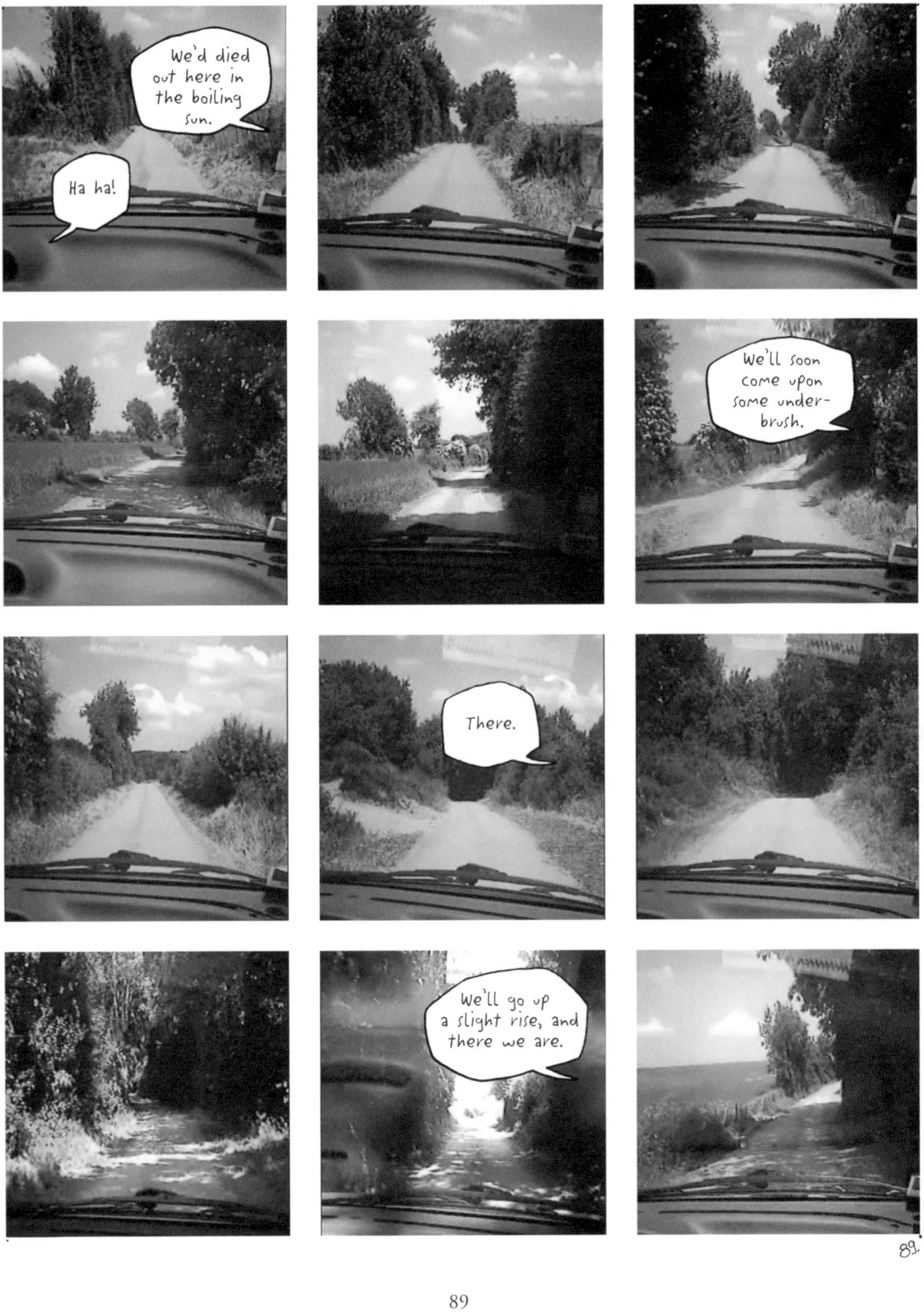
We'd died out here in the boiling sun.
Ha ha!
We'll soon come upon some under-brush.
There.
We'll go up a slight rise, and there we are.
89.

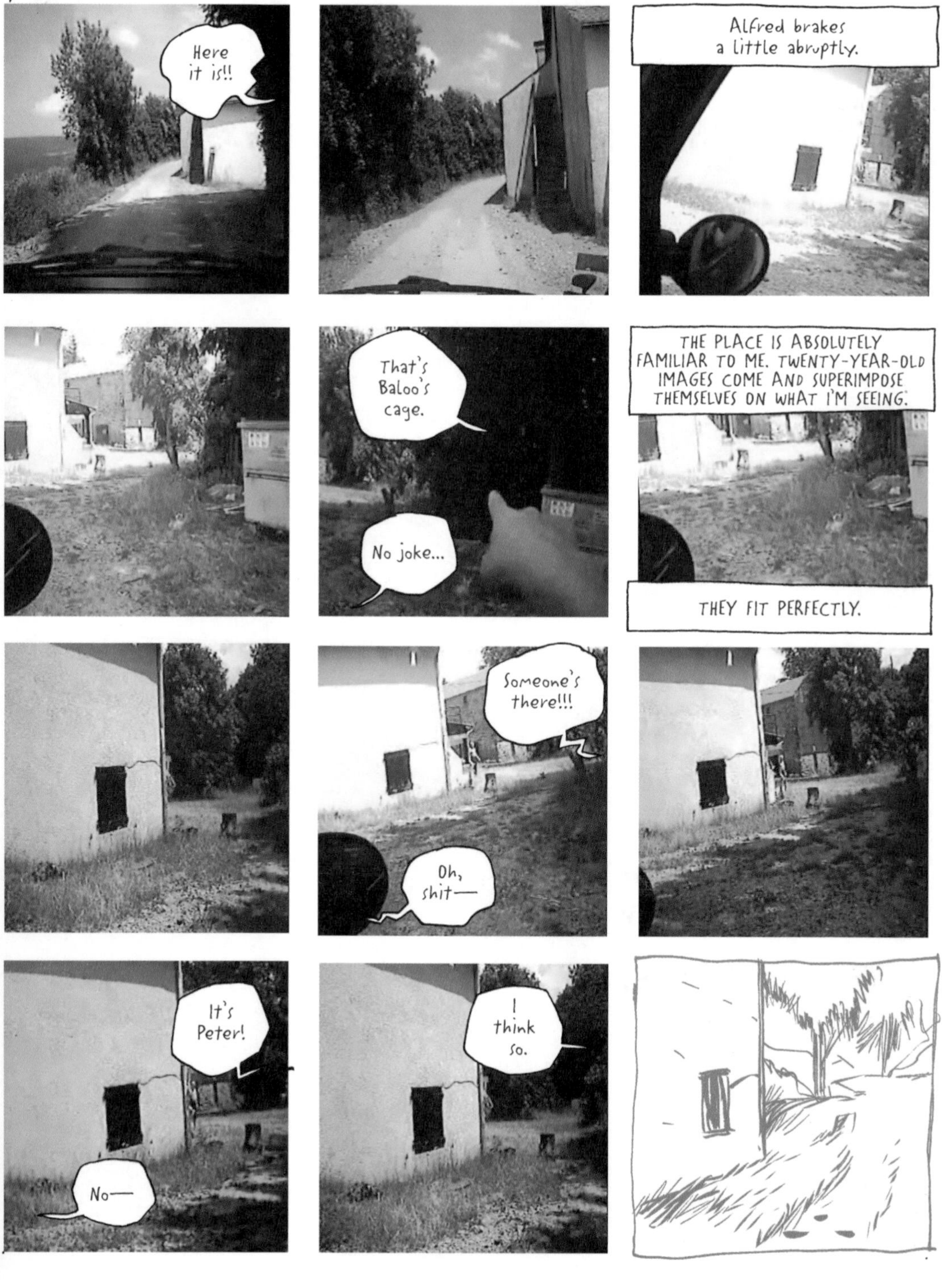
Here it is!!
Alfred brakes a little abruptly.
That's Baloo's cage.
No joke...
THE PLACE IS ABSOLUTELY FAMILIAR TO ME. TWENTY-YEAR-OLD IMAGES COME AND SUPERIMPOSE THEMSELVES ON WHAT I'M SEEING.
THEY FIT PERFECTLY.
Someone's there!!!
Oh, shit—
It's Peter!
No—
I think so.

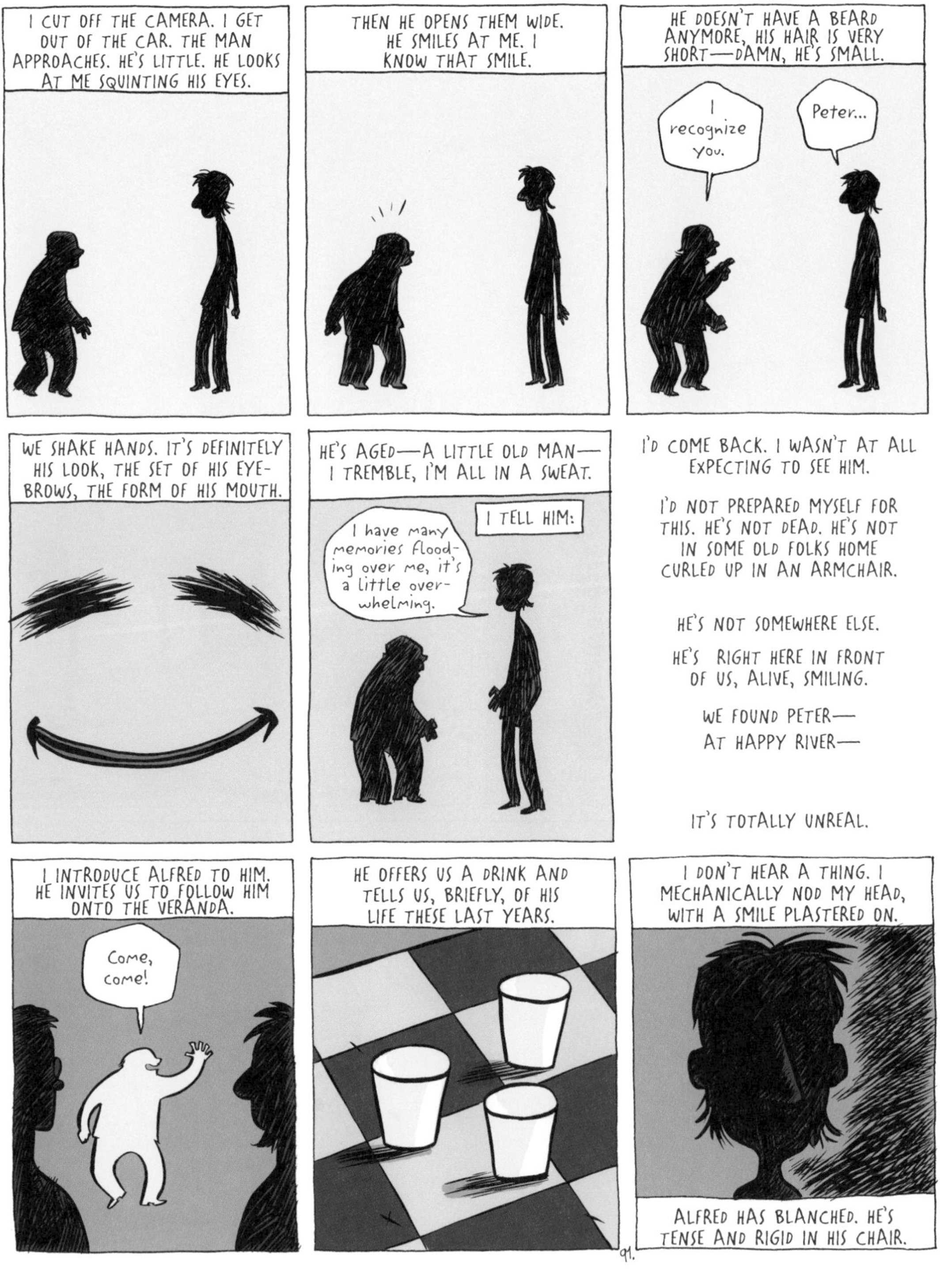
I CUT OFF THE CAMERA. I GET OUT OF THE CAR. THE MAN APPROACHES. HE'S LITTLE. HE LOOKS AT ME SQUINTING HIS EYES.
THEN HE OPENS THEM WIDE. HE SMILES AT ME. I KNOW THAT SMILE.
HE DOESN'T HAVE A BEARD ANYMORE, HIS HAIR IS VERY SHORT—DAMN, HE'S SMALL.
I recognize you.
Peter...
WE SHAKE HANDS. IT'S DEFINITELY HIS LOOK, THE SET OF HIS EYEBROWS, THE FORM OF HIS MOUTH.
HE'S AGED—A LITTLE OLD MAN—I TREMBLE, I'M ALL IN A SWEAT.
I TELL HIM:
I have many memories flooding over me, it's a little overwhelming.
I'D COME BACK. I WASN'T AT ALL EXPECTING TO SEE HIM.
I'D NOT PREPARED MYSELF FOR THIS. HE'S NOT DEAD. HE'S NOT IN SOME OLD FOLKS HOME CURLED UP IN AN ARMCHAIR.
HE'S NOT SOMEWHERE ELSE.
HE'S RIGHT HERE IN FRONT OF US, ALIVE, SMILING.
WE FOUND PETER—
AT HAPPY RIVER—
IT'S TOTALLY UNREAL.
I INTRODUCE ALFRED TO HIM. HE INVITES US TO FOLLOW HIM ONTO THE VERANDA.
Come, come!
HE OFFERS US A DRINK AND TELLS US, BRIEFLY, OF HIS LIFE THESE LAST YEARS.
I DON'T HEAR A THING. I MECHANICALLY NOD MY HEAD, WITH A SMILE PLASTERED ON.
ALFRED HAS BLANCHED. HE'S TENSE AND RIGID IN HIS CHAIR.

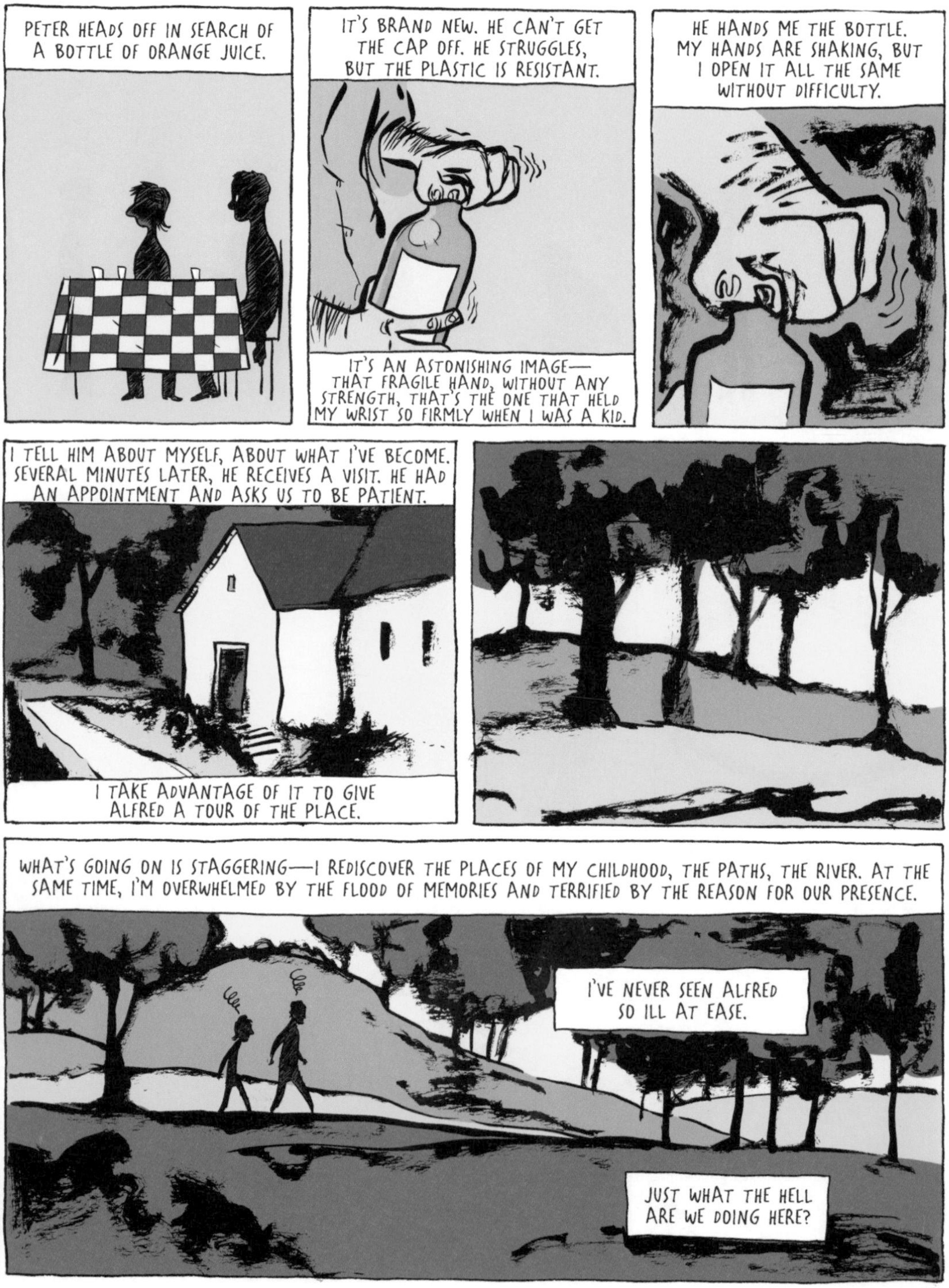
PETER HEADS OFF IN SEARCH OF A BOTTLE OF ORANGE JUICE.
IT'S BRAND NEW. HE CAN'T GET THE CAP OFF. HE STRUGGLES, BUT THE PLASTIC IS RESISTANT.
IT'S AN ASTONISHING IMAGE— THAT FRAGILE HAND, WITHOUT ANY STRENGTH, THAT'S THE ONE THAT HELD MY WRIST SO FIRMLY WHEN I WAS A KID.
HE HANDS ME THE BOTTLE. MY HANDS ARE SHAKING, BUT I OPEN IT ALL THE SAME WITHOUT DIFFICULTY.
I TELL HIM ABOUT MYSELF, ABOUT WHAT I'VE BECOME. SEVERAL MINUTES LATER, HE RECEIVES A VISIT. HE HAD AN APPOINTMENT AND ASKS US TO BE PATIENT.
I TAKE ADVANTAGE OF IT TO GIVE ALFRED A TOUR OF THE PLACE.
WHAT'S GOING ON IS STAGGERING—I REDISCOVER THE PLACES OF MY CHILDHOOD, THE PATHS, THE RIVER. AT THE SAME TIME, I'M OVERWHELMED BY THE FLOOD OF MEMORIES AND TERRIFIED BY THE REASON FOR OUR PRESENCE.
I'VE NEVER SEEN ALFRED SO ILL AT EASE.
JUST WHAT THE HELL ARE WE DOING HERE?
92.

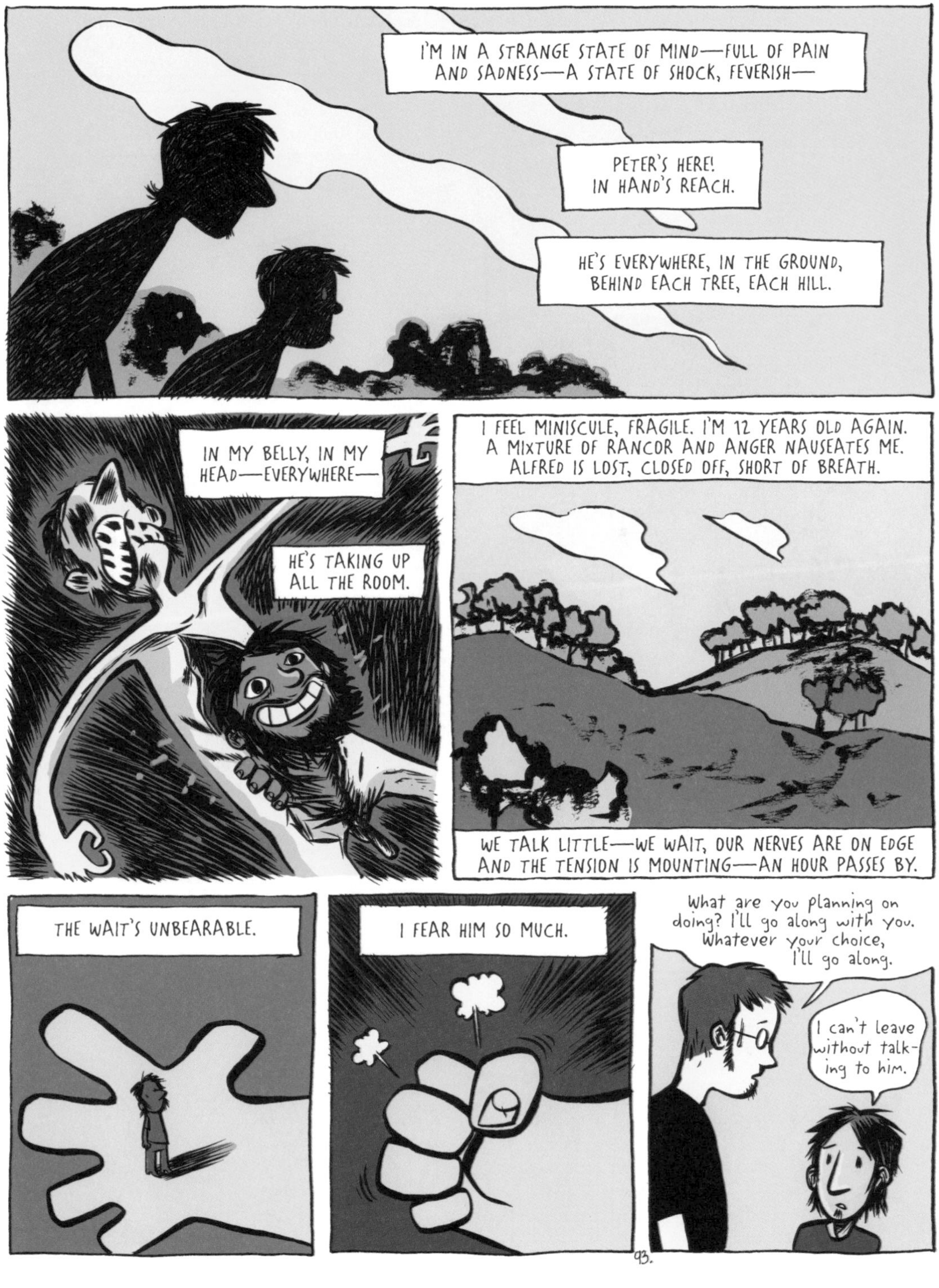
I'M IN A STRANGE STATE OF MIND—FULL OF PAIN AND SADNESS—A STATE OF SHOCK, FEVERISH—
PETER'S HERE! IN HAND'S REACH.
HE'S EVERYWHERE, IN THE GROUND, BEHIND EACH TREE, EACH HILL.
IN MY BELLY, IN MY HEAD—EVERYWHERE—
HE'S TAKING UP ALL THE ROOM.
I FEEL MINISCULE, FRAGILE. I'M 12 YEARS OLD AGAIN. A MIXTURE OF RANCOR AND ANGER NAUSEATES ME. ALFRED IS LOST, CLOSED OFF, SHORT OF BREATH.
WE TALK LITTLE—WE WAIT, OUR NERVES ARE ON EDGE AND THE TENSION IS MOUNTING—AN HOUR PASSES BY.
THE WAIT'S UNBEARABLE.
I FEAR HIM SO MUCH.
What are you planning on doing? I'll go along with you. Whatever your choice, I'll go along.
I can't leave without talking to him.
93.

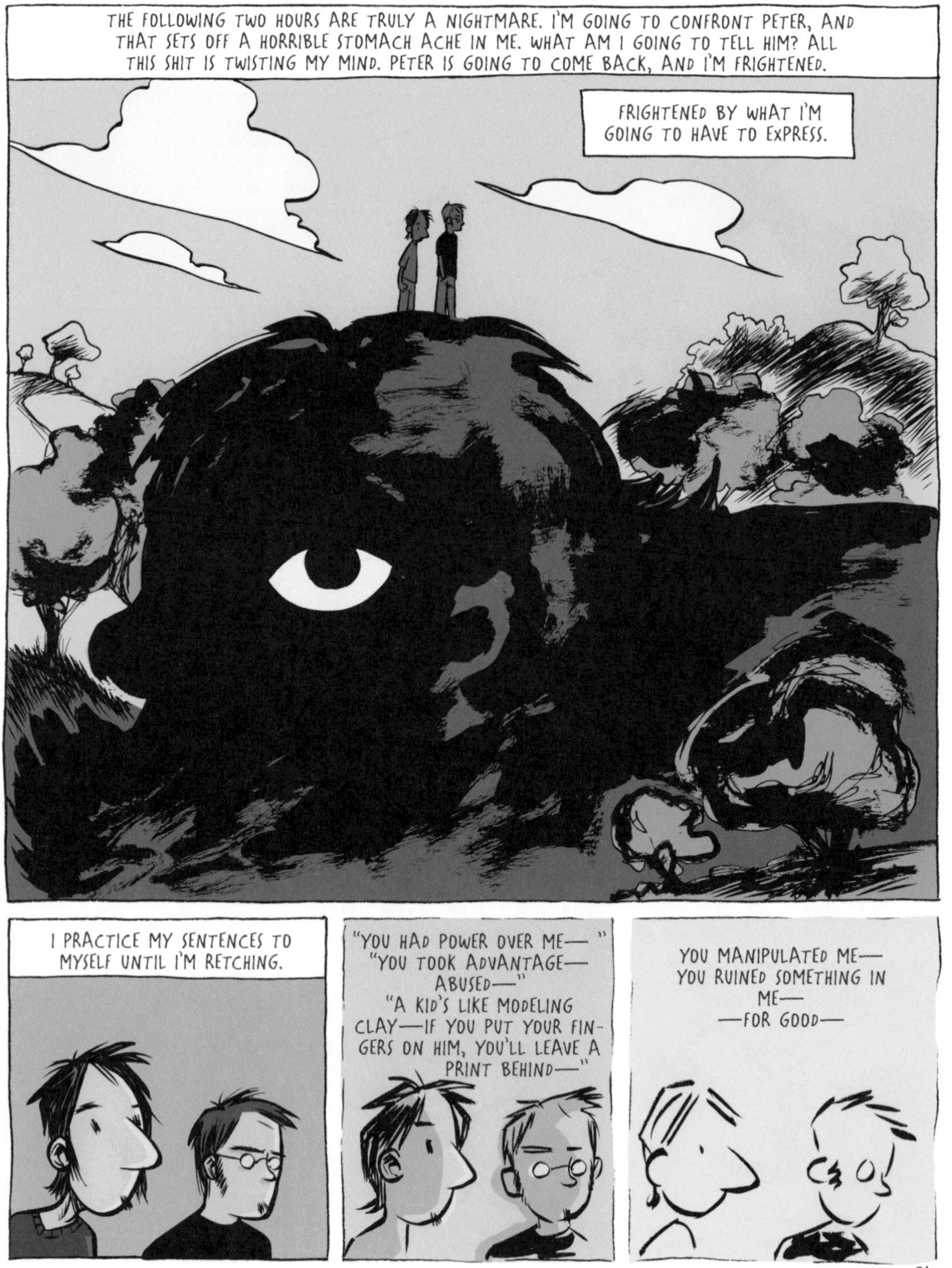
THE FOLLOWING TWO HOURS ARE TRULY A NIGHTMARE. I'M GOING TO CONFRONT PETER, AND THAT SETS OFF A HORRIBLE STOMACH ACHE IN ME. WHAT AM I GOING TO TELL HIM? ALL THIS SHIT IS TWISTING MY MIND. PETER IS GOING TO COME BACK, AND I'M FRIGHTENED.
FRIGHTENED BY WHAT I'M GOING TO HAVE TO EXPRESS.
I PRACTICE MY SENTENCES TO MYSELF UNTIL I'M RETCHING.
"YOU HAD POWER OVER ME— " "YOU TOOK ADVANTAGE— ABUSED—" "A KID'S LIKE MODELING CLAY—IF YOU PUT YOUR FINGERS ON HIM, YOU'LL LEAVE A PRINT BEHIND—"
YOU MANIPULATED ME— YOU RUINED SOMETHING IN ME— —FOR GOOD—

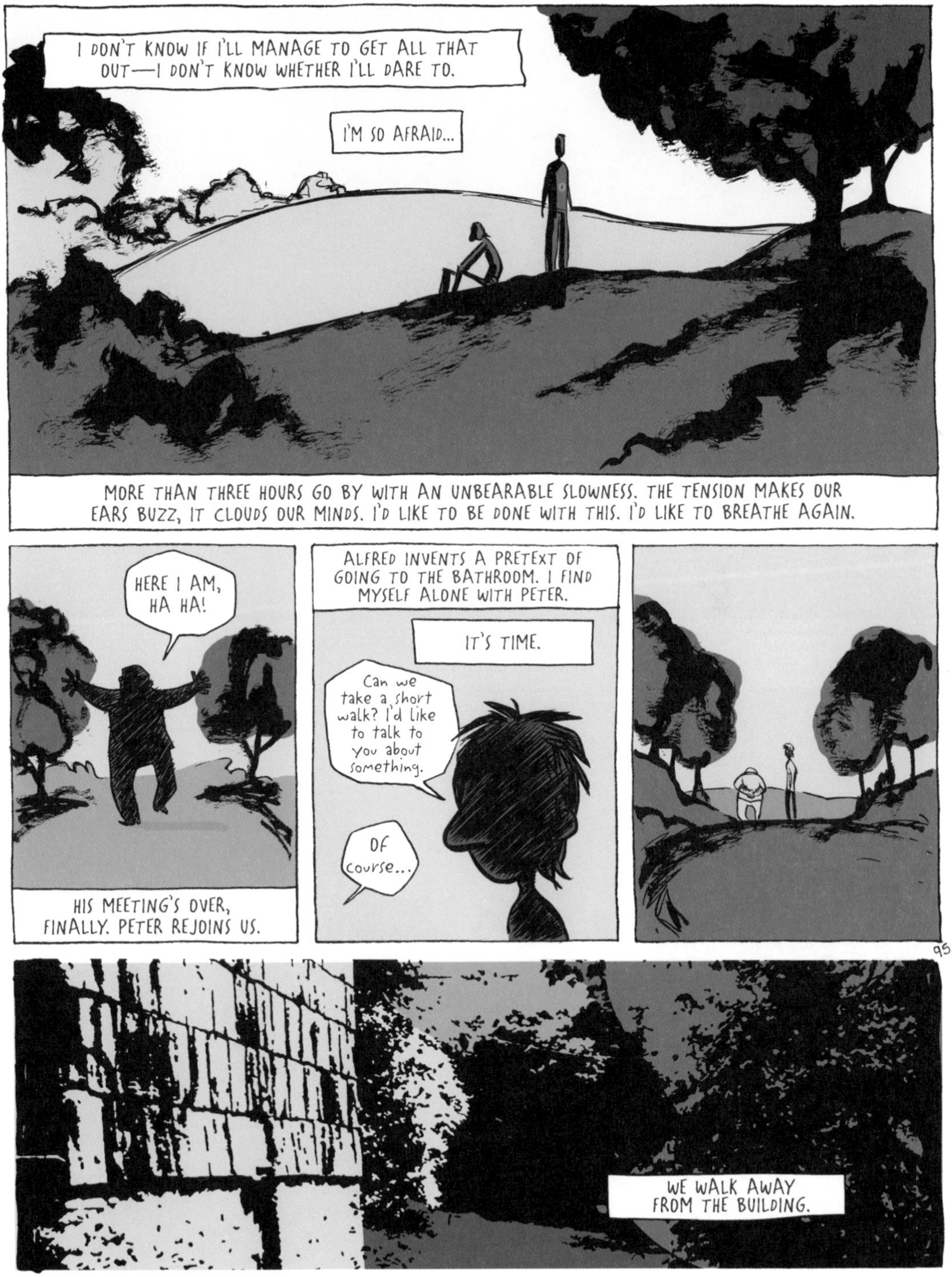
I DON'T KNOW IF I'LL MANAGE TO GET ALL THAT OUT—I DON'T KNOW WHETHER I'LL DARE TO.
I'M SO AFRAID...
MORE THAN THREE HOURS GO BY WITH AN UNBEARABLE SLOWNESS. THE TENSION MAKES OUR EARS BUZZ, IT CLOUDS OUR MINDS. I'D LIKE TO BE DONE WITH THIS. I'D LIKE TO BREATHE AGAIN.
HERE I AM, HA HA!
HIS MEETING'S OVER, FINALLY. PETER REJOINS US.
ALFRED INVENTS A PRETEXT OF GOING TO THE BATHROOM. I FIND MYSELF ALONE WITH PETER.
IT'S TIME.
Can we take a short walk? I'd like to talk to you about something.
Of course...
95.
WE WALK AWAY FROM THE BUILDING.

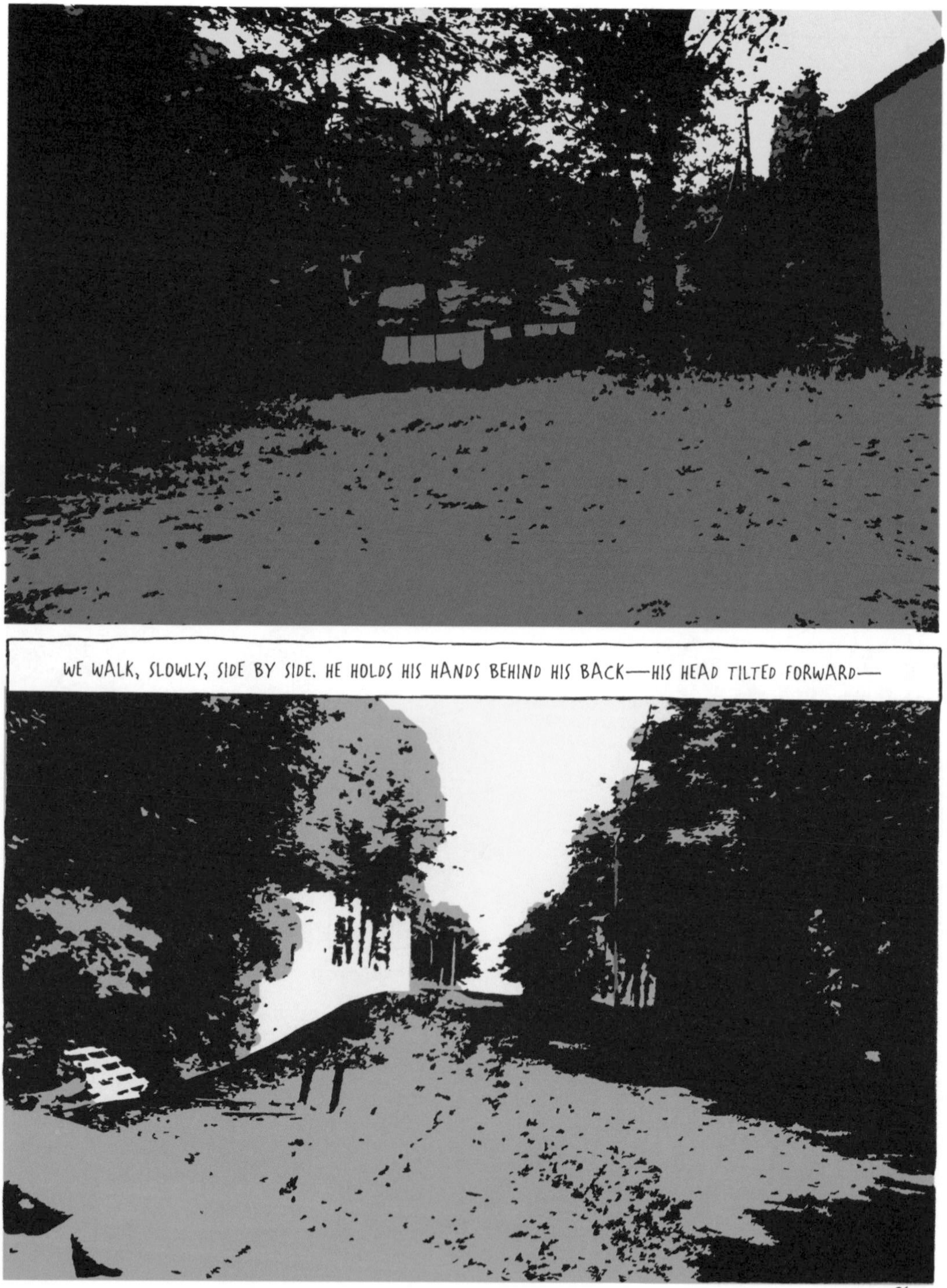
WE WALK, SLOWLY, SIDE BY SIDE. HE HOLDS HIS HANDS BEHIND HIS BACK—HIS HEAD TILTED FORWARD—
96.

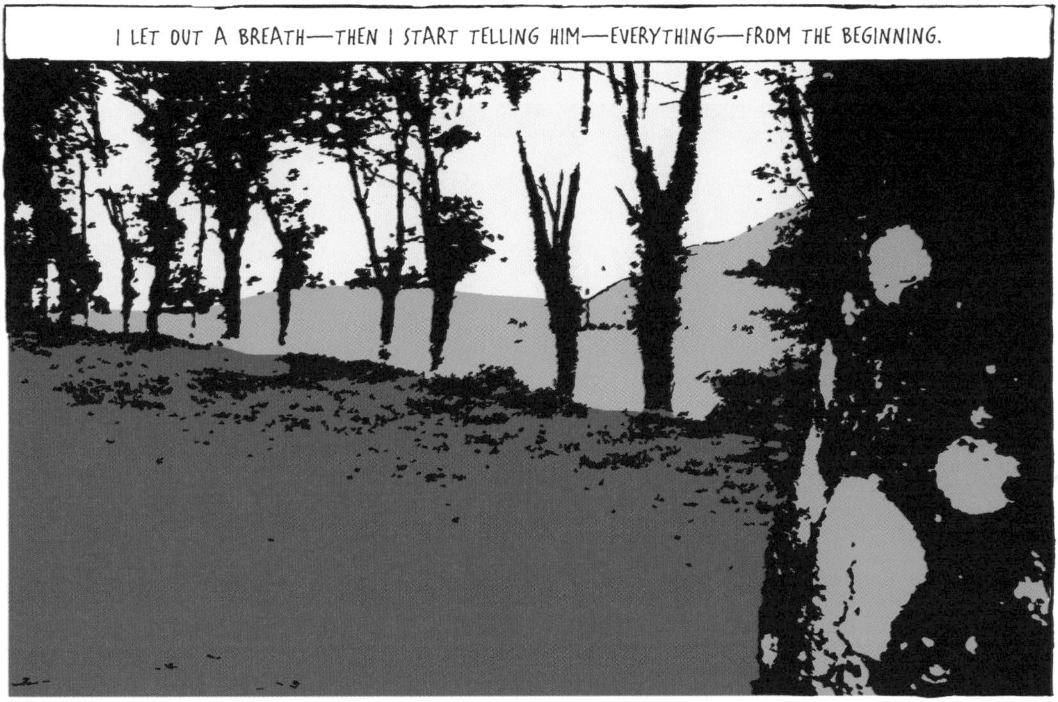
I LET OUT A BREATH—THEN I START TELLING HIM—EVERYTHING—FROM THE BEGINNING.

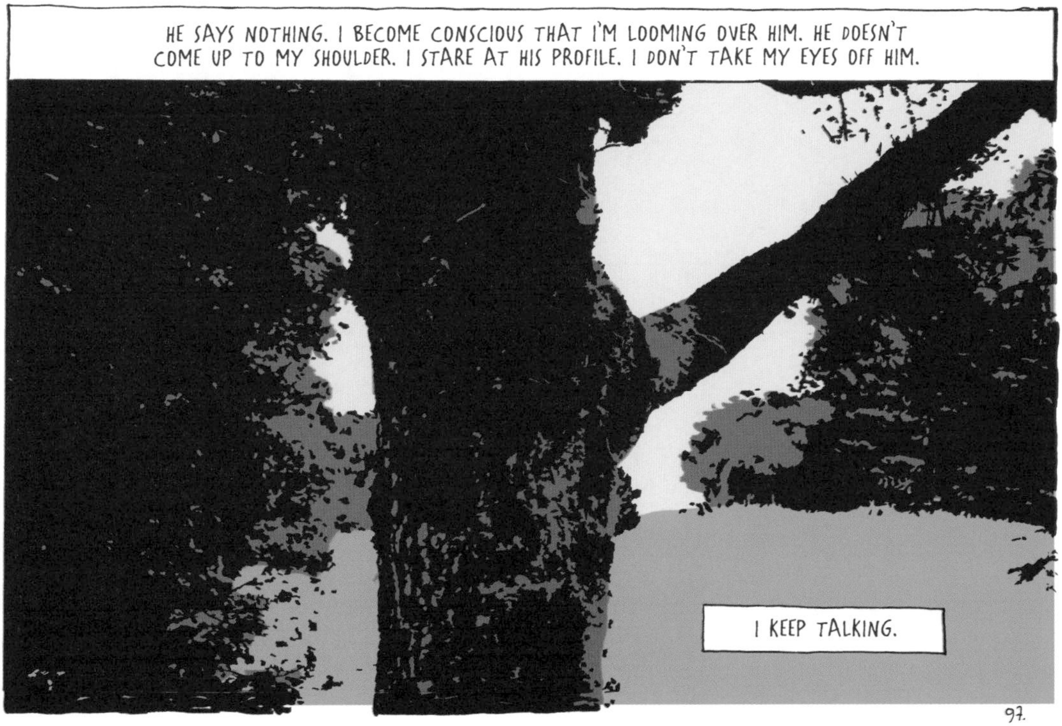
HE SAYS NOTHING. I BECOME CONSCIOUS THAT I'M LOOMING OVER HIM. HE DOESN'T COME UP TO MY SHOULDER. I STARE AT HIS PROFILE. I DON'T TAKE MY EYES OFF HIM.
I KEEP TALKING.
97.

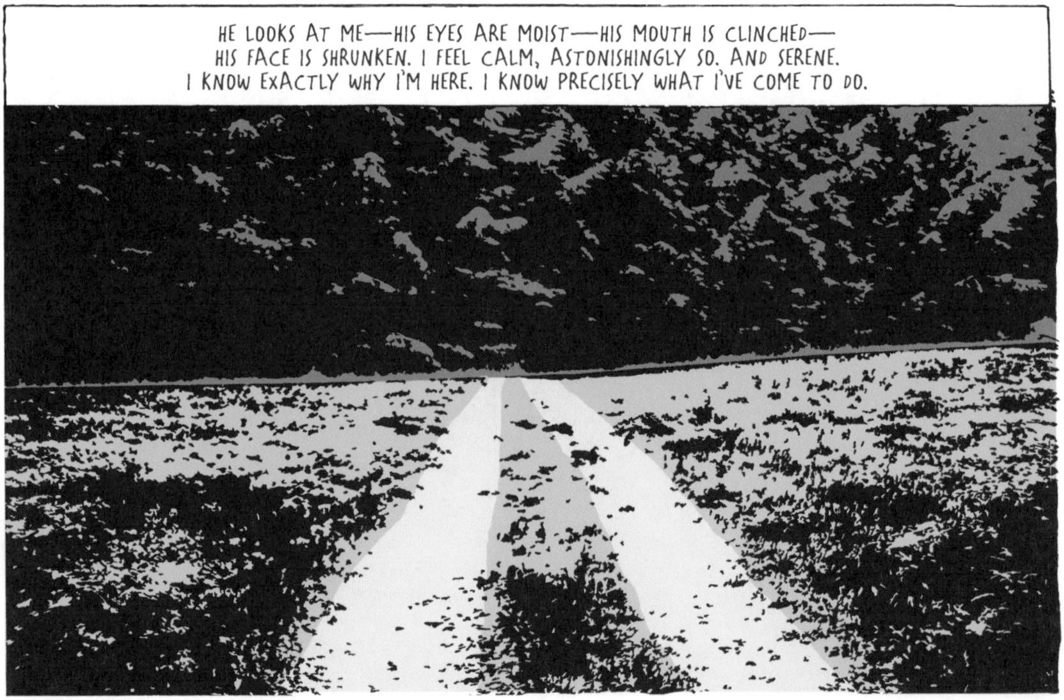
HE LOOKS AT ME—HIS EYES ARE MOIST—HIS MOUTH IS CLINCHED—
HIS FACE IS SHRUNKEN. I FEEL CALM, ASTONISHINGLY SO. AND SERENE.
I KNOW EXACTLY WHY I'M HERE. I KNOW PRECISELY WHAT I'VE COME TO DO.

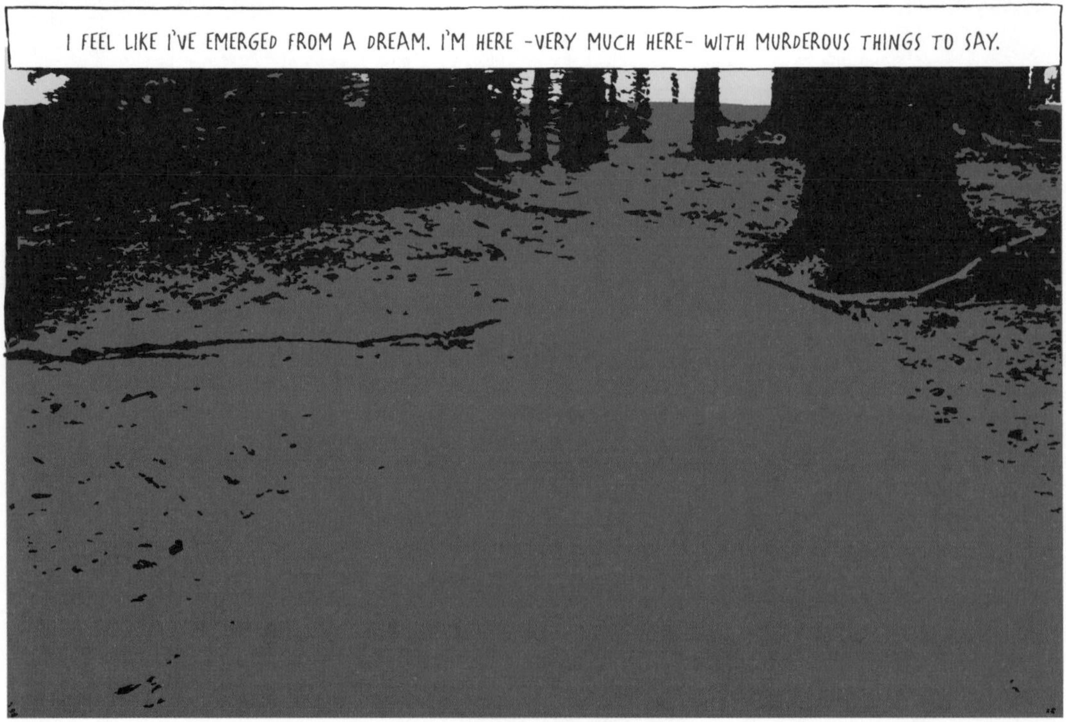
I FEEL LIKE I'VE EMERGED FROM A DREAM. I'M HERE -VERY MUCH HERE- WITH MURDEROUS THINGS TO SAY.

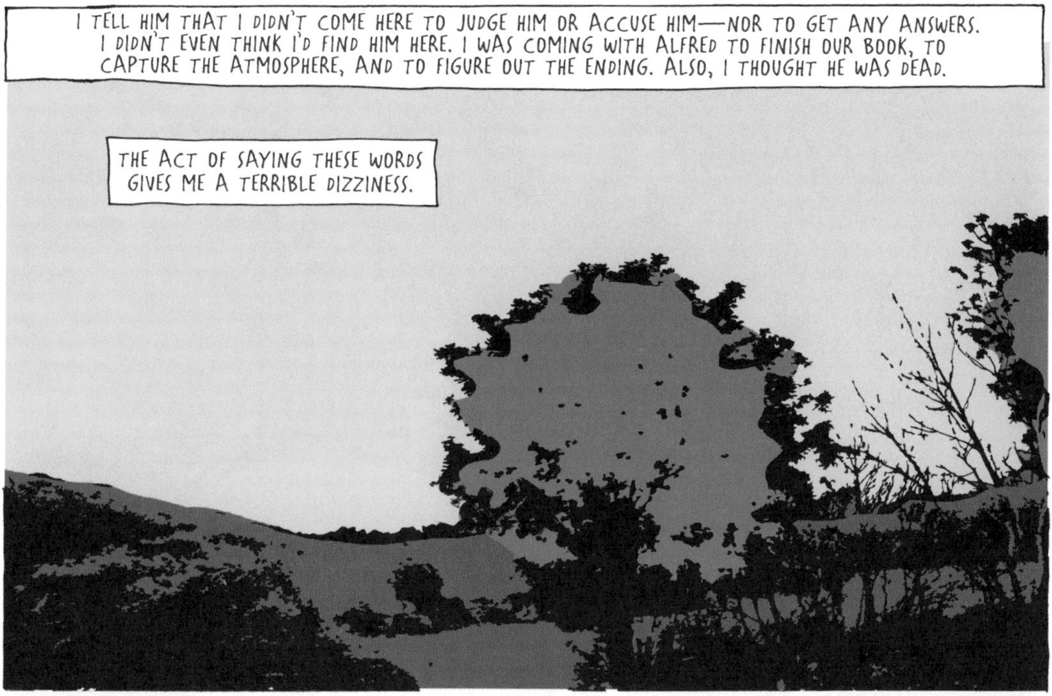
I TELL HIM THAT I DIDN'T COME HERE TO JUDGE HIM OR ACCUSE HIM—NOR TO GET ANY ANSWERS. I DIDN'T EVEN THINK I'D FIND HIM HERE. I WAS COMING WITH ALFRED TO FINISH OUR BOOK, TO CAPTURE THE ATMOSPHERE, AND TO FIGURE OUT THE ENDING. ALSO, I THOUGHT HE WAS DEAD.
THE ACT OF SAYING THESE WORDS GIVES ME A TERRIBLE DIZZINESS.

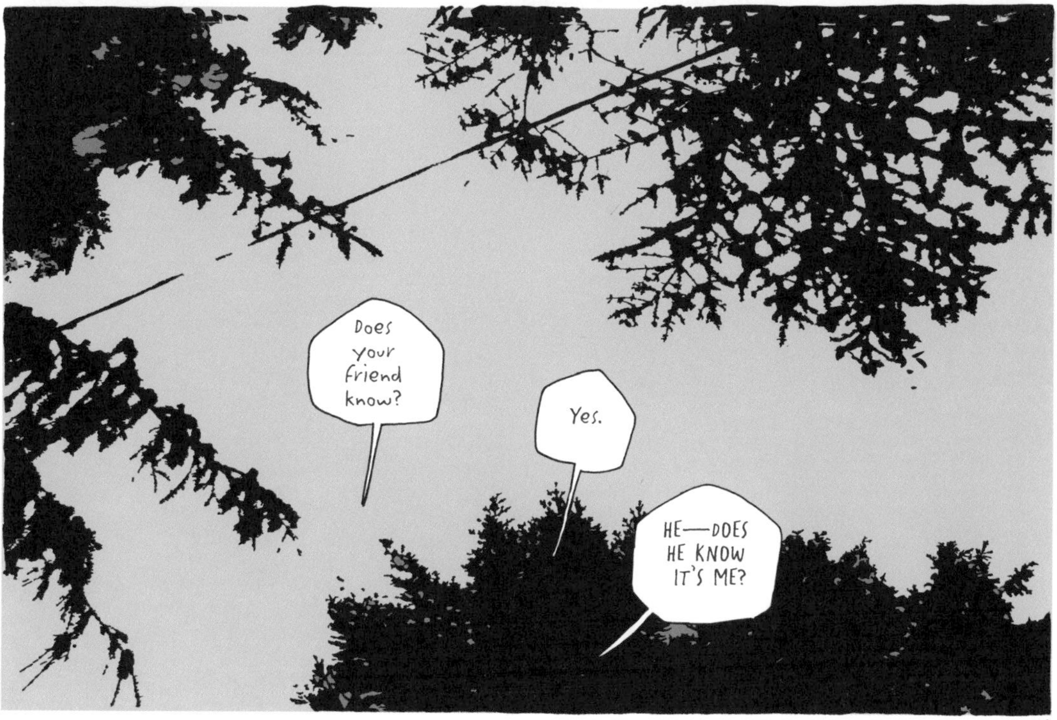
Does your friend know?
Yes.
HE—DOES HE KNOW IT'S ME?

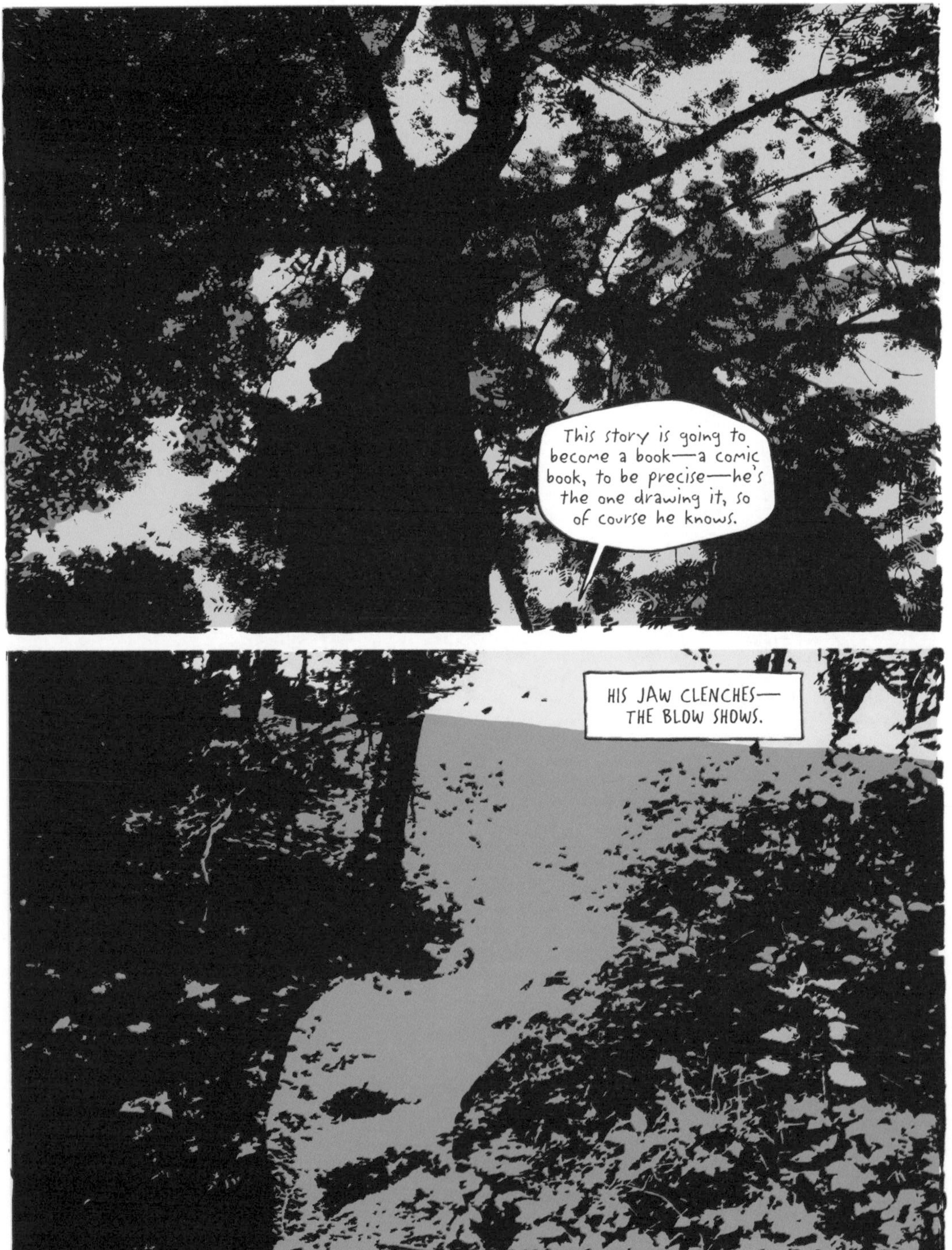
This story is going to become a book—a comic book, to be precise—he's the one drawing it, so of course he knows.
HIS JAW CLENCHES—THE BLOW SHOWS.
100

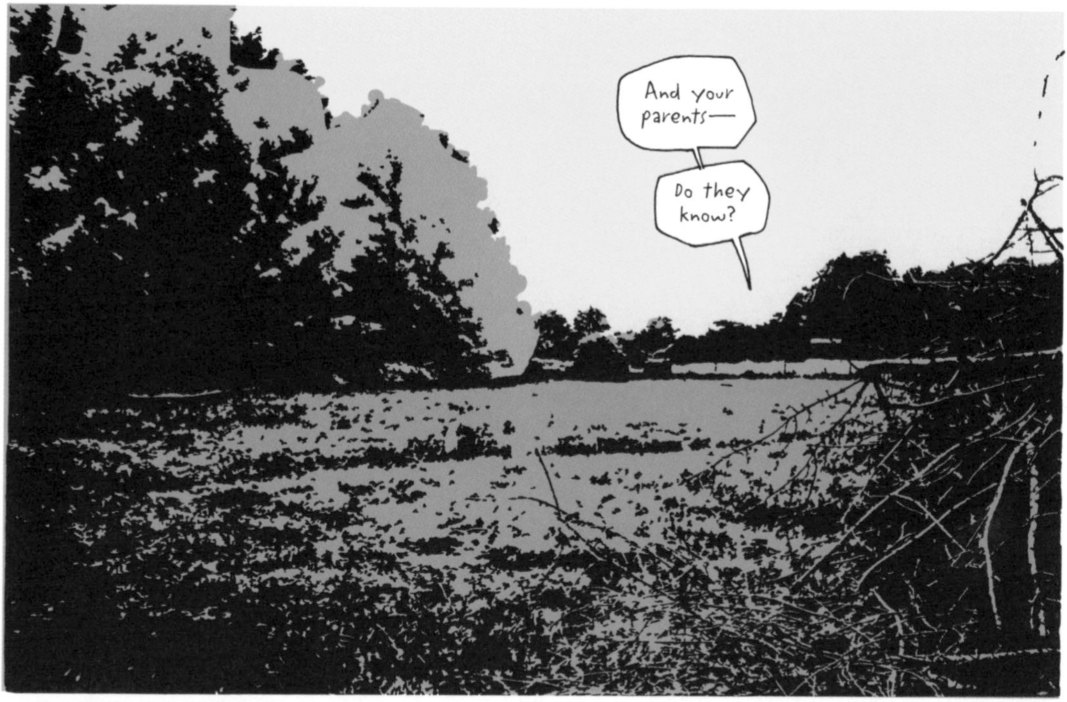
And your parents—
Do they know?

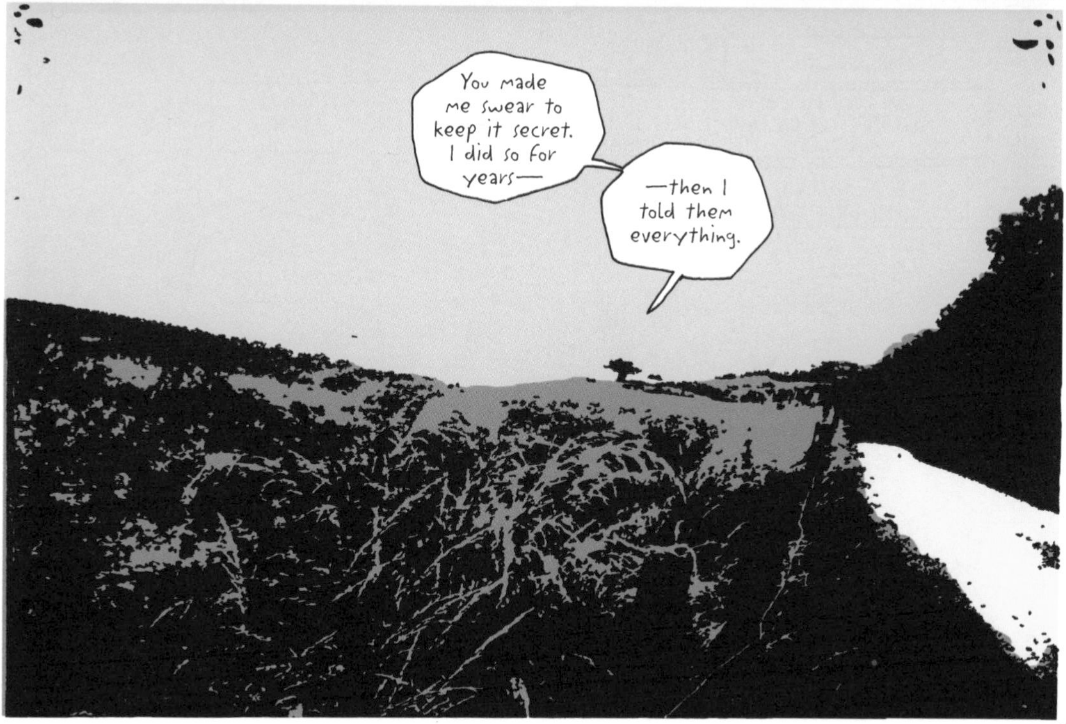
You made me swear to keep it secret. I did so for years—
—then I told them everything.

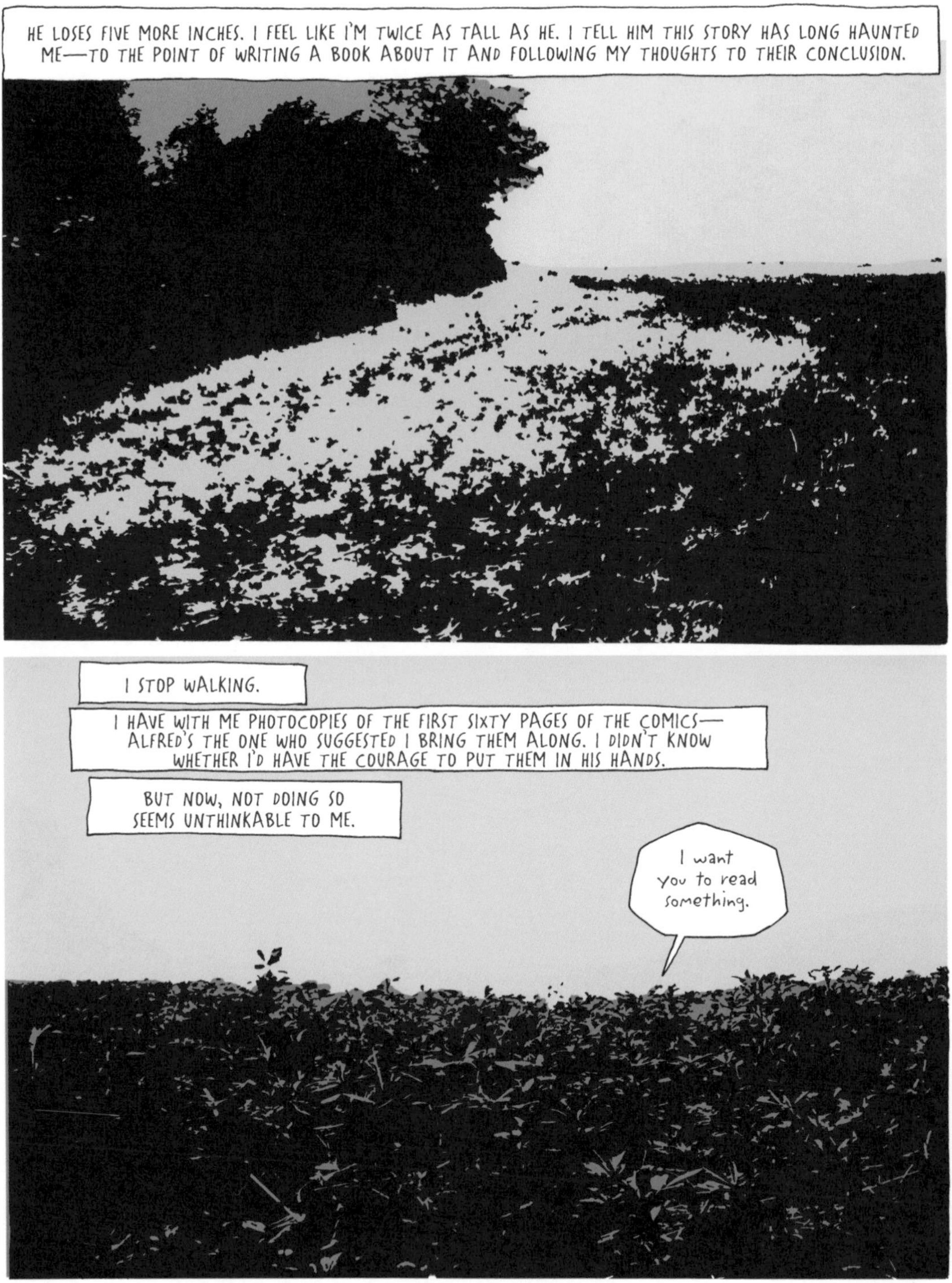
HE LOSES FIVE MORE INCHES. I FEEL LIKE I'M TWICE AS TALL AS HE. I TELL HIM THIS STORY HAS LONG HAUNTED ME—TO THE POINT OF WRITING A BOOK ABOUT IT AND FOLLOWING MY THOUGHTS TO THEIR CONCLUSION.
I STOP WALKING.
I HAVE WITH ME PHOTOCOPIES OF THE FIRST SIXTY PAGES OF THE COMICS—ALFRED'S THE ONE WHO SUGGESTED I BRING THEM ALONG. I DIDN'T KNOW WHETHER I'D HAVE THE COURAGE TO PUT THEM IN HIS HANDS.
BUT NOW, NOT DOING SO SEEMS UNTHINKABLE TO ME.
I want you to read something.

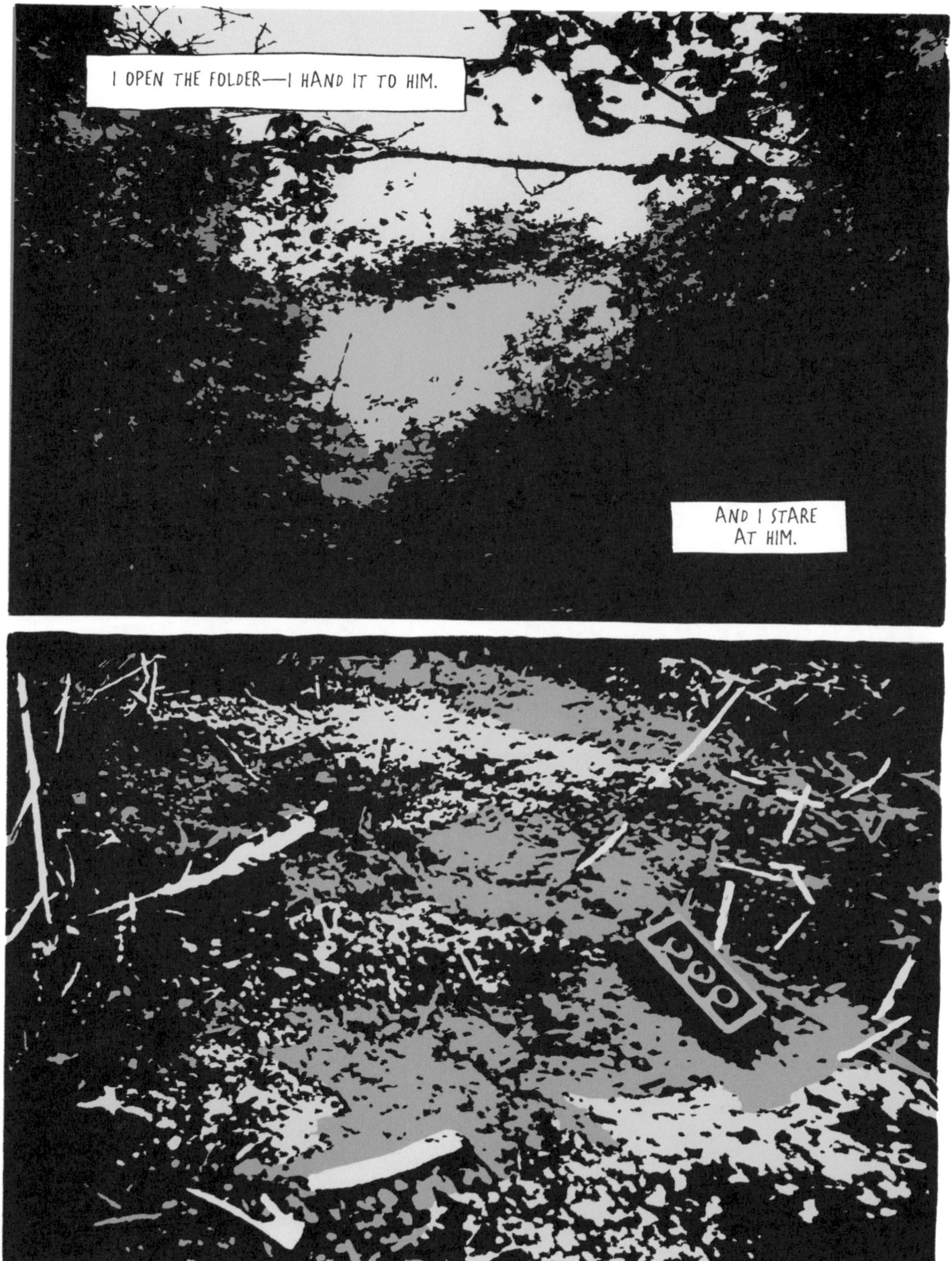
I OPEN THE FOLDER—I HAND IT TO HIM.
AND I STARE AT HIM.

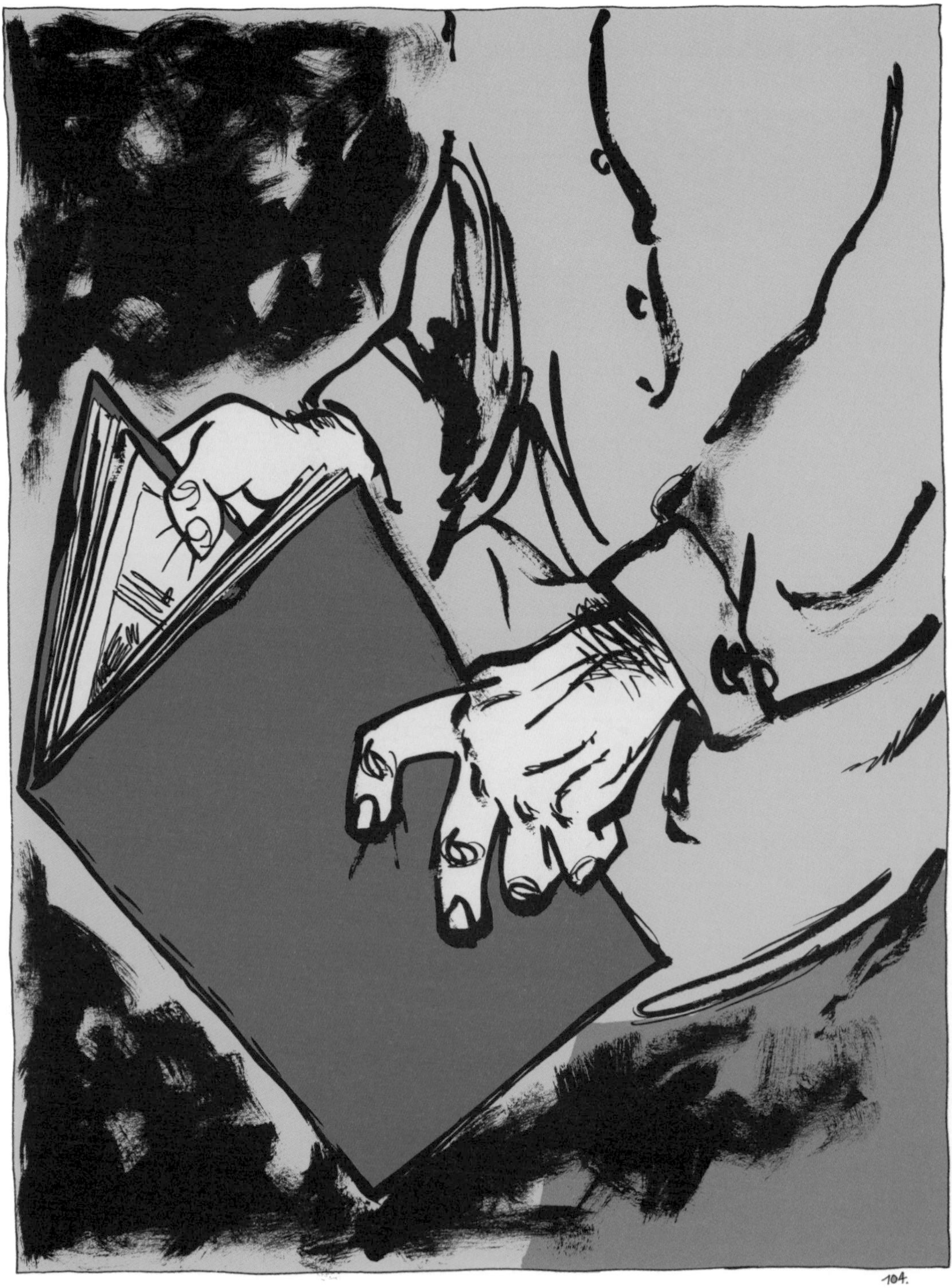

104.

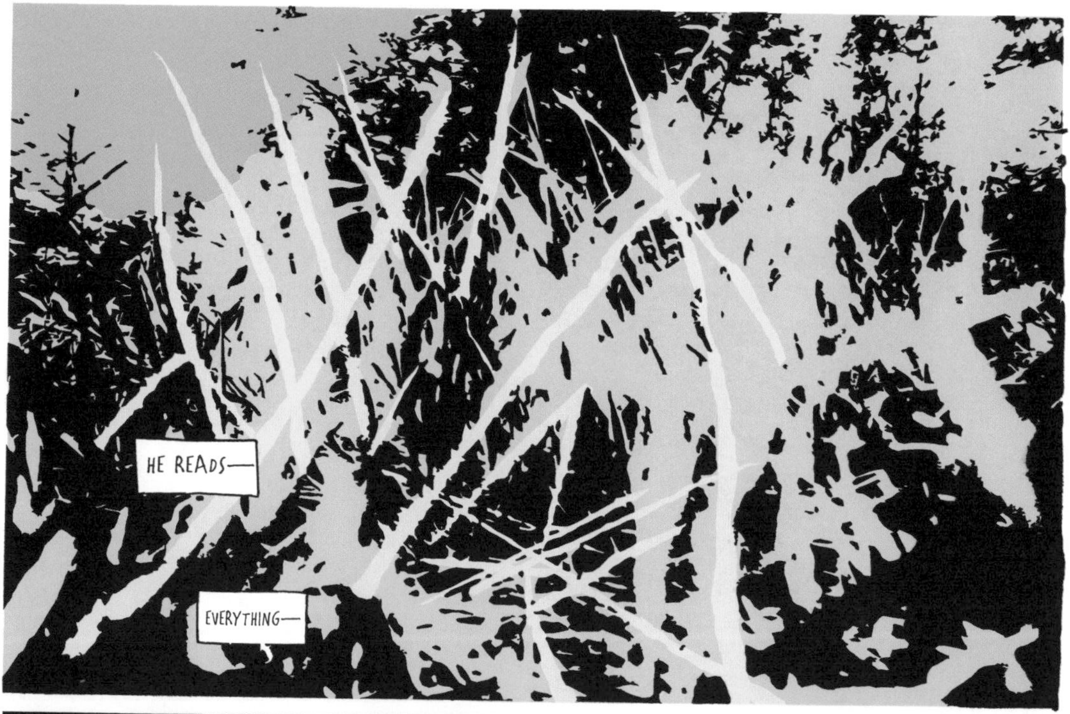
HE READS—
EVERYTHING—

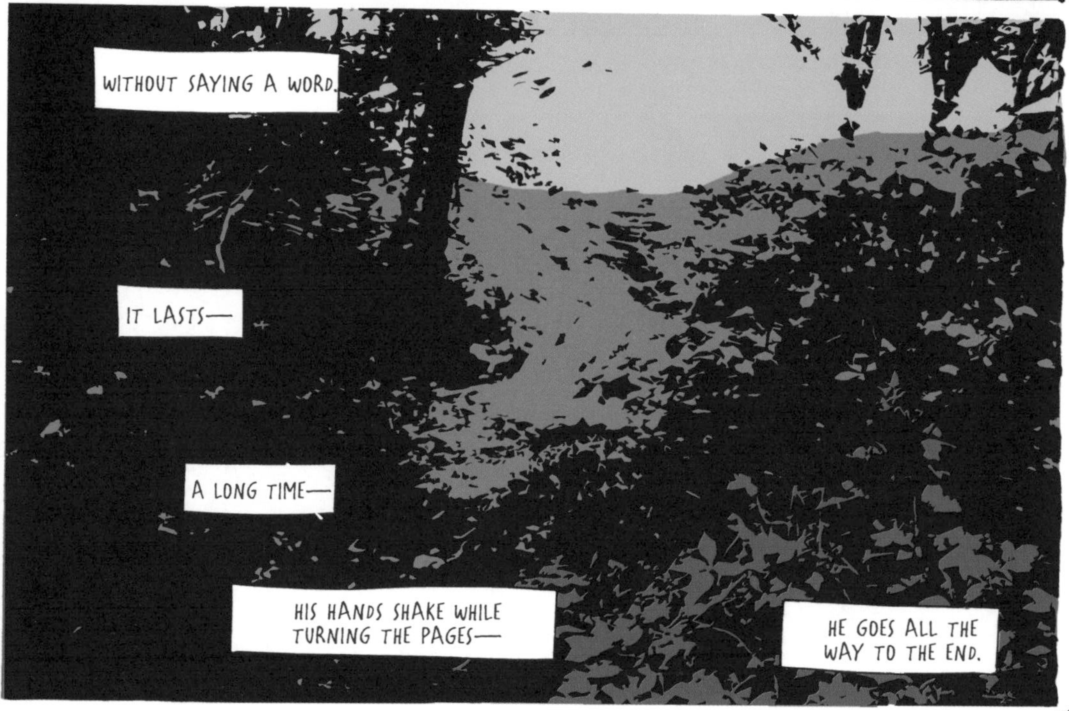
WITHOUT SAYING A WORD.
IT LASTS—
A LONG TIME—
HIS HANDS SHAKE WHILE TURNING THE PAGES—
HE GOES ALL THE WAY TO THE END.

105.

WHEN HE HANDS THE FILE BACK TO ME, HIS FACE LOOKS DEVASTATED—COLLAPSED—HIS EYES ARE RED, HIS MOUTH HANGING—HE'S JUST GOTTEN TWENTY-FIVE YEARS OLDER IN ONE FELL SWOOP—

I GET READY TO WATCH HIM CRY.

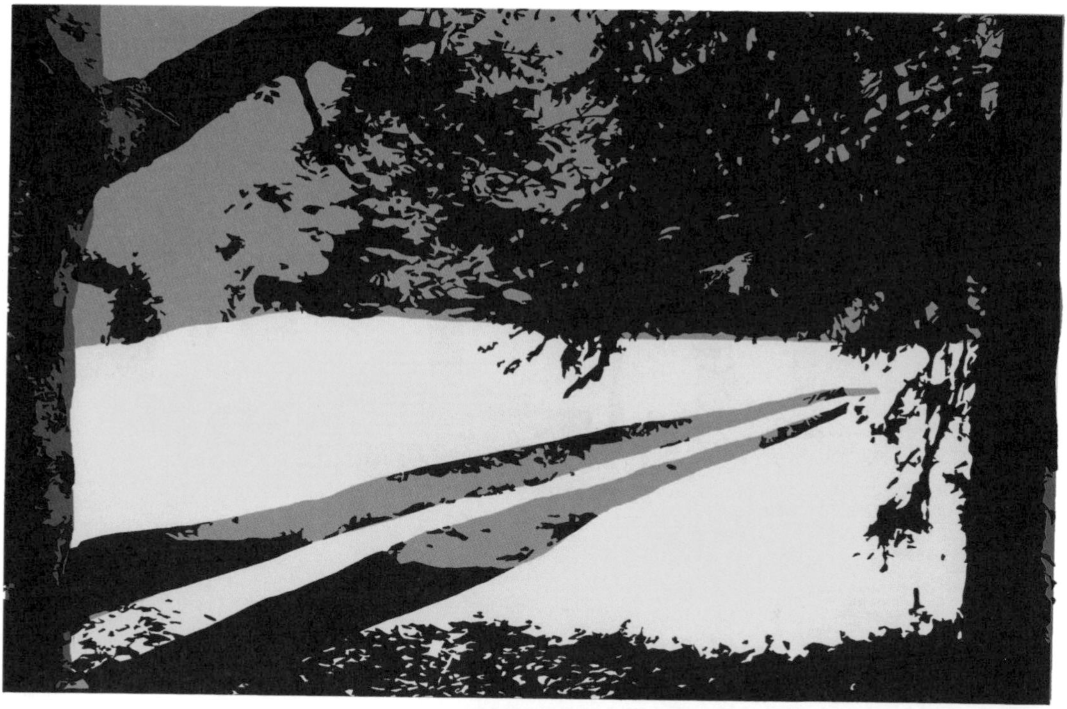

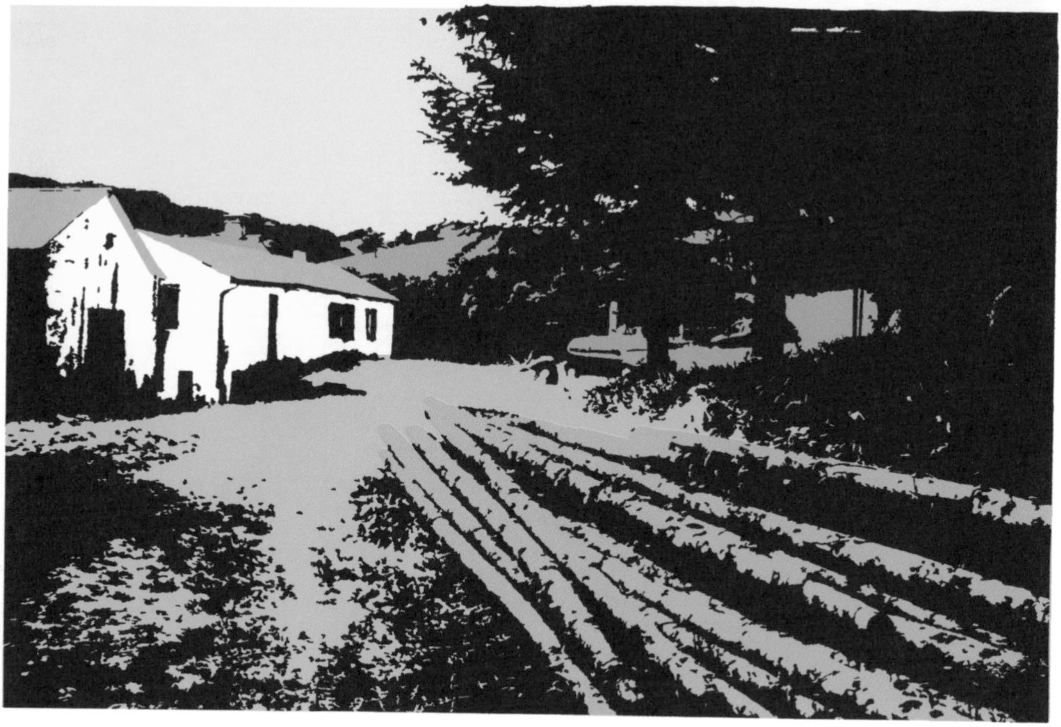

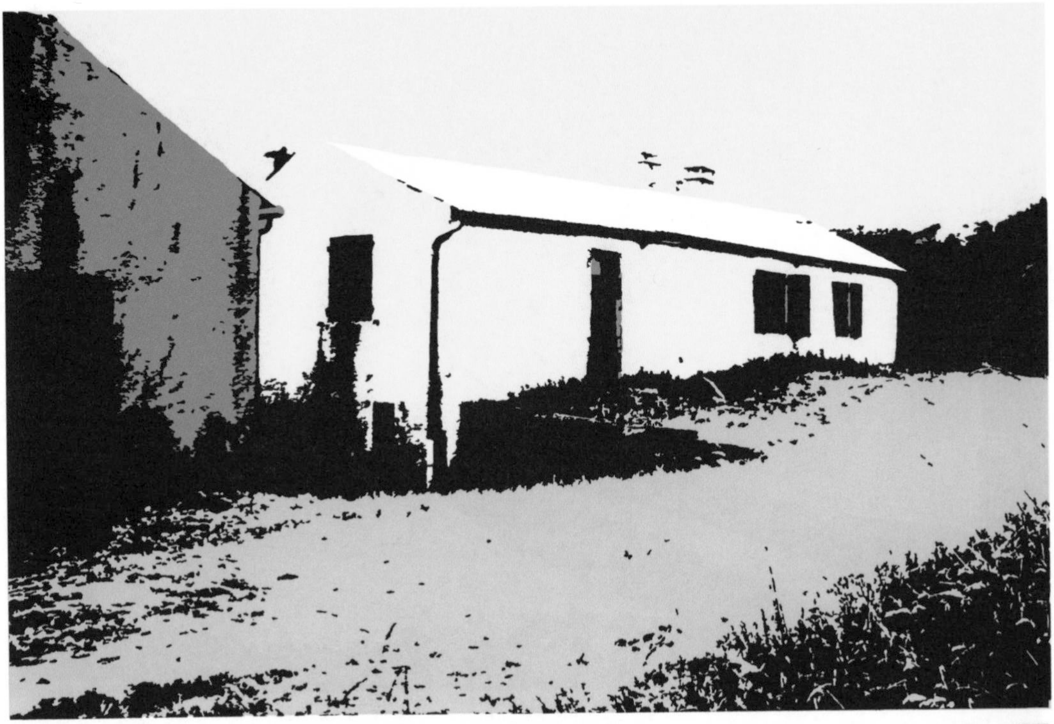

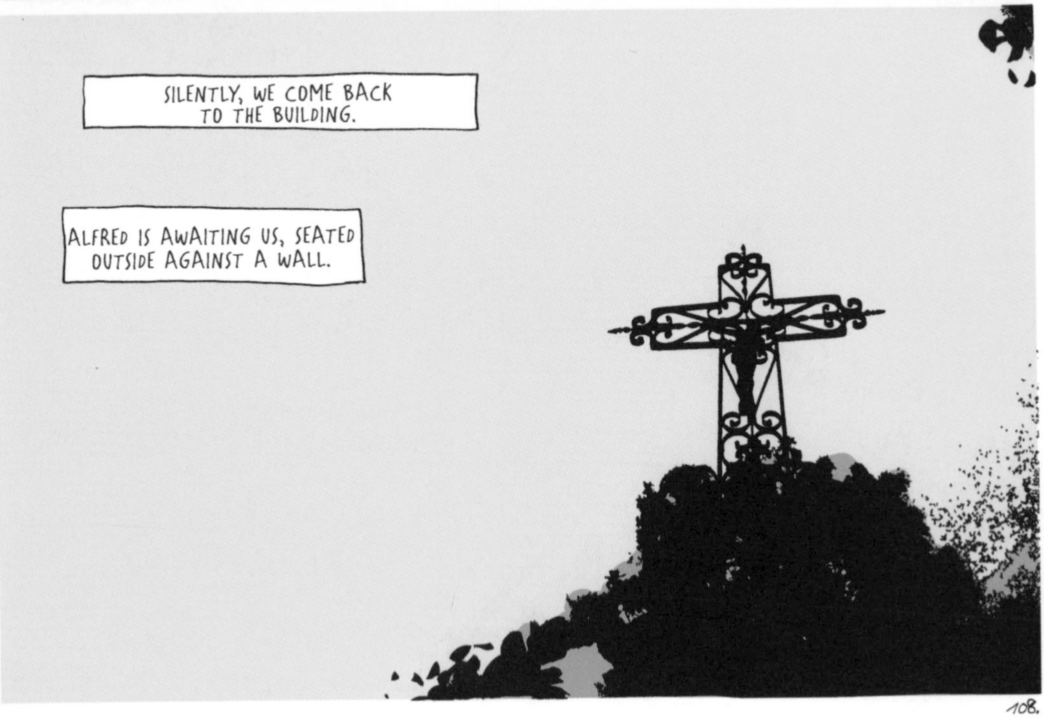
SILENTLY, WE COME BACK TO THE BUILDING.
ALFRED IS AWAITING US, SEATED OUTSIDE AGAINST A WALL.
108.

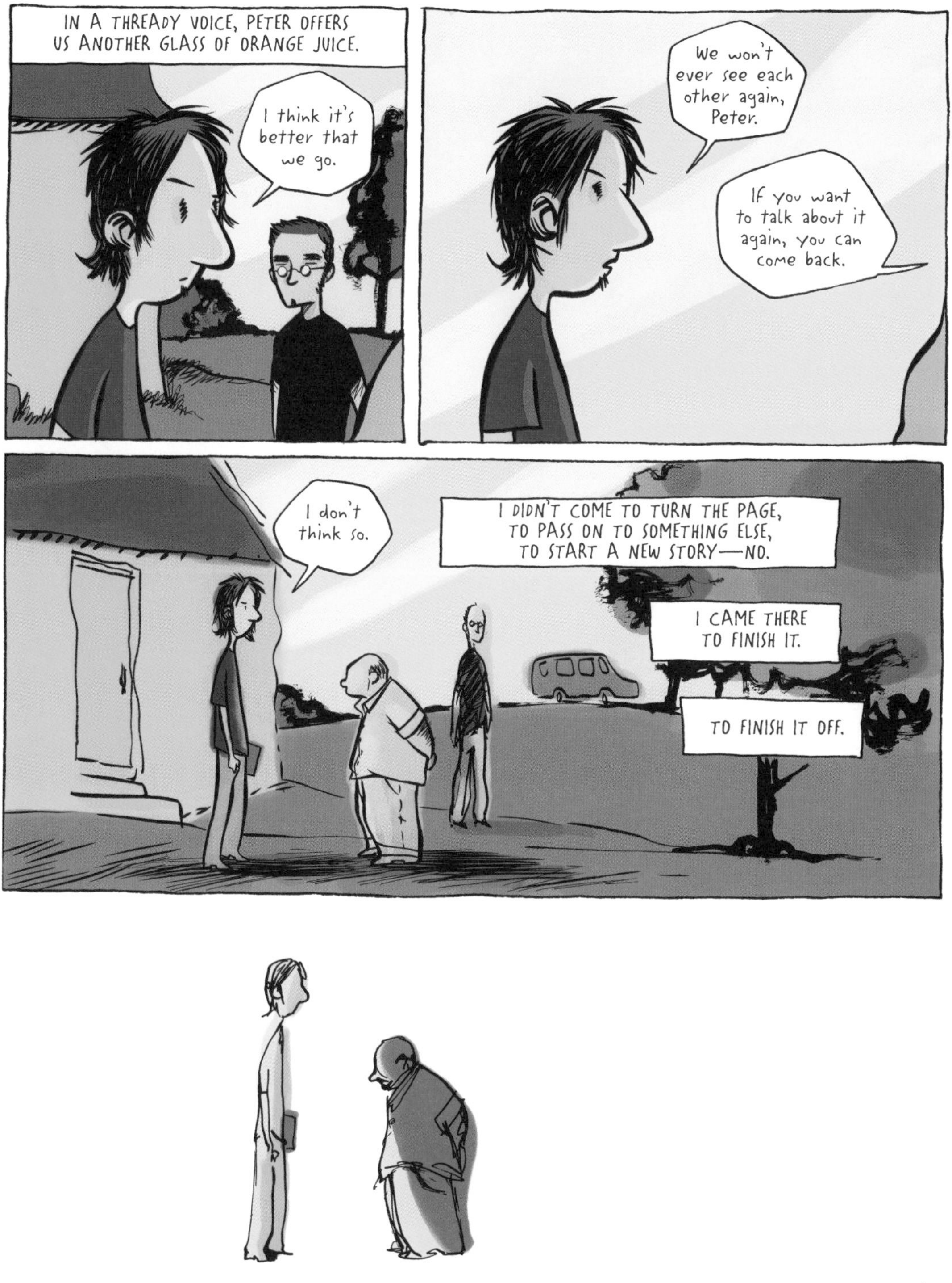

IN A THREADY VOICE, PETER OFFERS US ANOTHER GLASS OF ORANGE JUICE.
I think it's better that we go.
We won't ever see each other again, Peter.
If you want to talk about it again, you can come back.
I don't think so.
I DIDN'T COME TO TURN THE PAGE, TO PASS ON TO SOMETHING ELSE, TO START A NEW STORY—NO.
I CAME THERE TO FINISH IT.
TO FINISH IT OFF.
109.

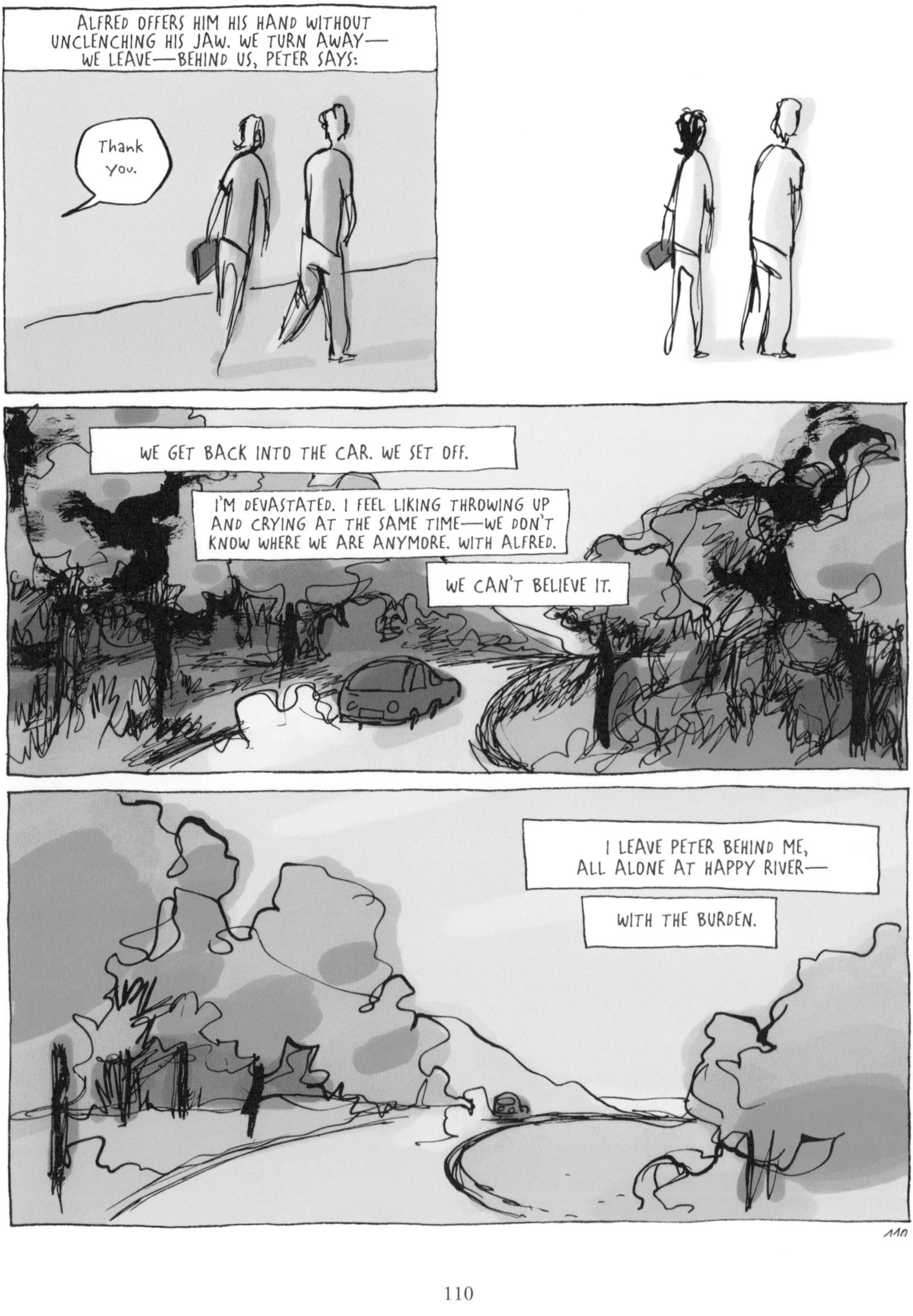
ALFRED OFFERS HIM HIS HAND WITHOUT UNCLENCHING HIS JAW. WE TURN AWAY—WE LEAVE—BEHIND US, PETER SAYS:
Thank you.
WE GET BACK INTO THE CAR. WE SET OFF.
I'M DEVASTATED. I FEEL LIKING THROWING UP AND CRYING AT THE SAME TIME—WE DON'T KNOW WHERE WE ARE ANYMORE. WITH ALFRED.
WE CAN'T BELIEVE IT.
I LEAVE PETER BEHIND ME, ALL ALONE AT HAPPY RIVER—
WITH THE BURDEN.
110

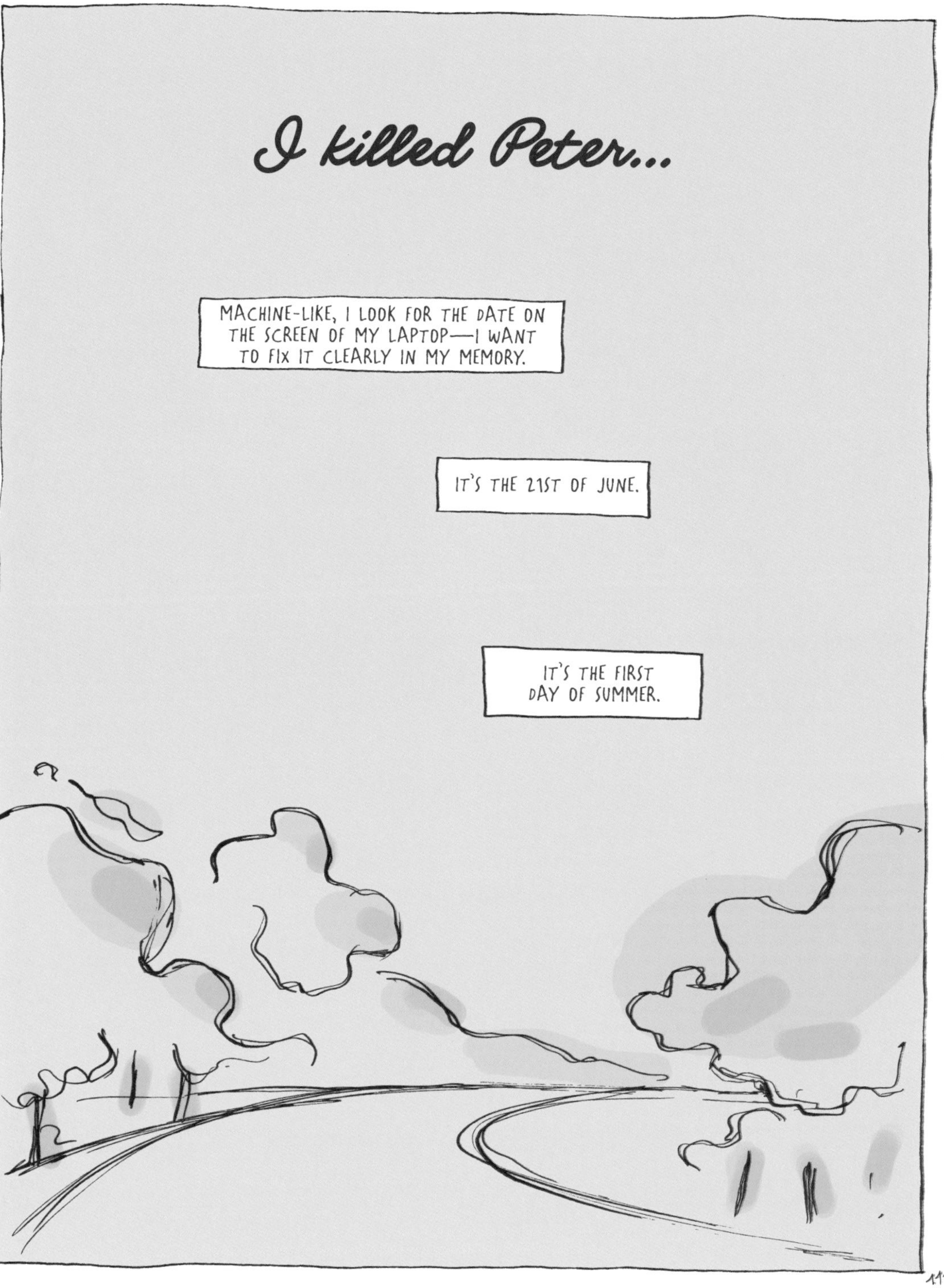
I killed Peter...
MACHINE-LIKE, I LOOK FOR THE DATE ON THE SCREEN OF MY LAPTOP—I WANT TO FIX IT CLEARLY IN MY MEMORY.
IT'S THE 21ST OF JUNE.
IT'S THE FIRST DAY OF SUMMER.

111.

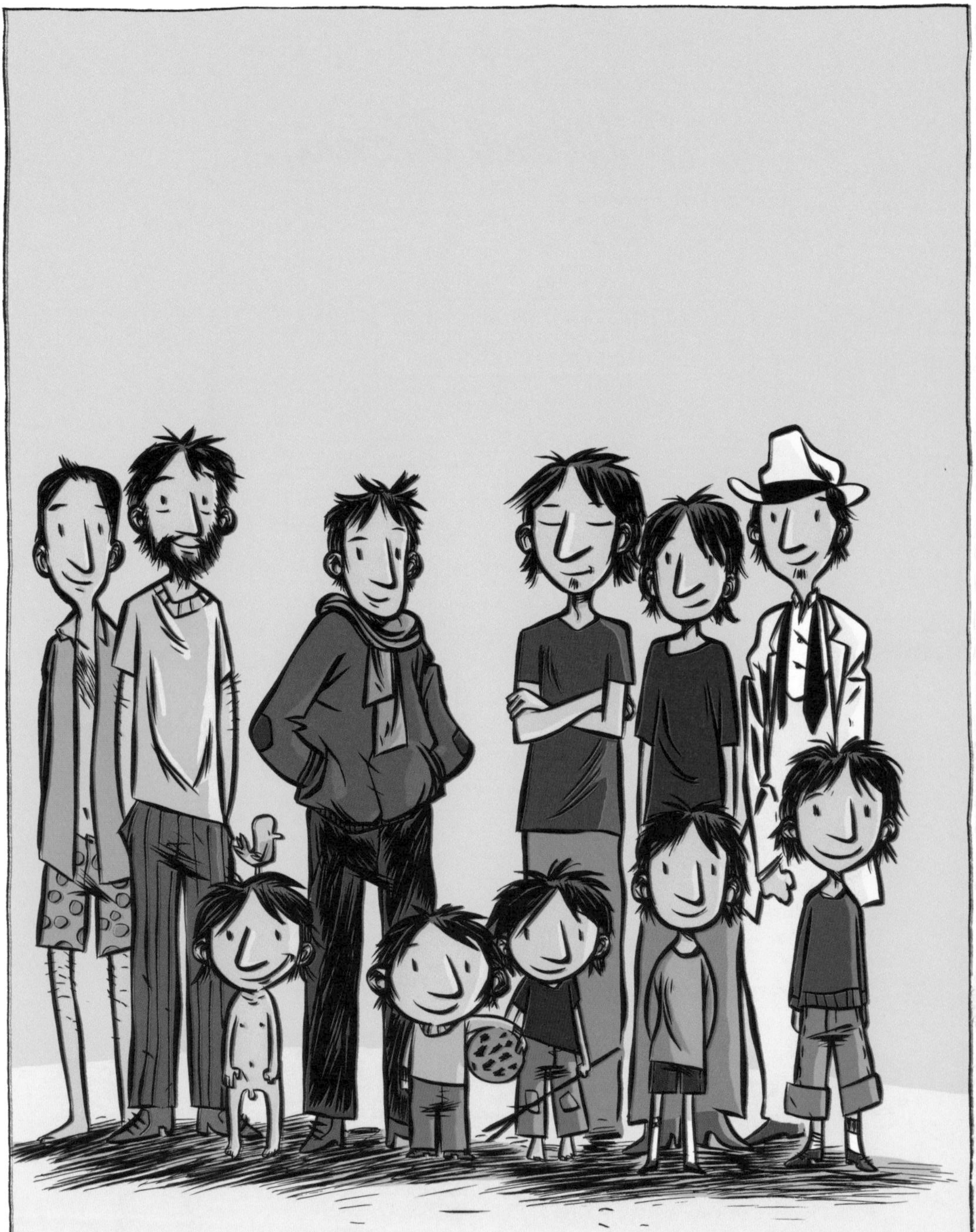

JULY 16, 2006

Olivier Ka - Alfred - Henri Meunier